Concurrent Programming in
Java™
Design Principles and Patterns

Doug Lea

ADDISON-WESLEY
An imprint of Addison Wesley Longman, Inc.

Reading, Massachusetts • Harlow, England • Menlo Park, California
Berkeley, California • Don Mills, Ontario • Sydney
Bonn • Amsterdam • Tokyo • Mexico City

Many of the designations used by manufacturers and sellers to distinguish their products are claimed as trademarks. Where those designations appear in this book and Addison-Wesley was aware of a trademark claim, the designations have been printed in initial caps or all caps.

The author and publishers have taken care in the preparation of this book, but make no expressed or implied warranty of any kind and assume no responsibility for errors or omissions. No liability is assumed for incidental or consequential damages in connection with or arising out of the use of the information or programs contained herein.

The publisher offers discounts on this book when ordered in quantity for special sales. For more information, please contact:

Corporate & Professional Publishing Group
Addison-Wesley Publishing Company
One Jacob Way
Reading, Massachusetts 01867

Library of Congress Cataloging-in-publication Data

Lea, Douglas
    Concurrent Programming in Java: Design Principles and Patterns / Doug Lea.
        p. cm. — (Addison-Wesley Java Series)
    Includes bibliographical references and index.
    ISBN 0-201-69581-2 (pbk.)
        1. Java (Computer program language) 2. Parallel programming (Computer science) I. Title
    II. Series: Java series
QA76.73.J38L4 1996
005.2—dc20

                                                  96-43733
                                                          CIP

Text printed on recycled and acid-free paper.

ISBN 0-201-69581-2
2 3 4 5 6 7 8 9 10–MA–00999897
Second printing, January 1997

Preface

Series Foreword

The Java Series books provide definitive reference documentation for Java programmers and end users. They are written by members of the Java team and published under the auspices of JavaSoft, a Sun Microsystems business. The World Wide Web allows Java documentation to be made available over the Internet, either by downloading or as hypertext. Nevertheless, the worldwide interest in Java technology led us to write and publish these books to supplement all of the documentation at our Web site.

To learn the latest about the Java Platform and Environment, or to download the latest Java release, visit our World Wide Web site at `http://java.sun.com`. For updated information about the Java Series, including sample code, errata, and previews of forthcoming books, visit `http://java.sun.com/Series`.

We would like to thank the Corporate and Professional Publishing Group at Addison-Wesley for their partnership in putting together the Series. Our editor Mike Hendrickson and his team have done a superb job of navigating us through the world of publishing. Within Sun, the support of James Gosling, Ruth Hennigar, Jon Kannegaard, and Bill Joy ensured that this series would have the resources it needed to be successful. In addition to the tremendous effort by individual authors, many members of the JavaSoft team have contributed behind the scenes to bring the highest level of quality and engineering to the books in the Series. A personal note of thanks to my children Christopher and James for putting a positive spin on the many trips to my office during the development of the Series.

Lisa Friendly
Series Editor

Foreword

The Java programming language has taken the world by storm, fueled by growing public exposure to object-oriented programming languages such as C++ and Smalltalk, and launched by the explosion of the Internet. Among other things, Java offers simple and tightly-integrated support for threads, and as a result has given many people their first exposure to concurrent programming.

A *concurrent program* consists of multiple tasks that behave as though they are all in progress at one time. On a computer system with multiple processors, this may literally be true — several tasks may execute at once, each on its own processor. On a system with a single processor, or where there are more tasks than processors, the system can switch between tasks, making it appear that more tasks than there are processors are executing at once.

The tasks of a concurrent program are often implemented using *threads* (short for "threads of control"), sequences of instructions that run independently within the encompassing program. Threads may share access to memory with other threads, and may have means of coordinating their activities with those of other threads, the computer system, or the user to achieve the goals of the program.

Writing concurrent programs requires looking at things in ways that are outside the experience of many programmers. Gaining this new perspective can be difficult. Many threads packages are complex, and perhaps as a result their documentation bogs down in a nuts-and-bolts style. Some approaches are academic and relatively inaccessible. As a result, programming with threads has remained more or less a black art, practiced by the few who manage to figure it all out somehow. Of those, not all learn to use threads elegantly or reliably.

Despite the relative simplicity of Java's threading model, writing concurrent programs in Java can still be strange and confusing. Most treatments of the Java language cover concurrent programming in a single chapter that introduces Java's thread classes but doesn't give the reader the conceptual background to program with threads effectively.

This is the first book dedicated to concurrent programming in Java. Doug Lea extends the object-oriented design paradigm using the now-familiar patterns approach of books like *Design Patterns* (Gamma, Helm, Johnson, Vlissides). He bridges the gap between typical programming experience and reference material by providing the conceptual structure necessary to design efficient, reliable, and elegant concurrent programs.

While covering programming with Java threads in detail, Doug shows the reader how to think about concurrent programming in a way that is equally appropriate when using other approaches to concurrent programming — not just when using Java. In the process he presents a pragmatic cookbook of design patterns for concurrent programming that will be instructive and useful for new threads programmers and experienced programmers alike.

Tim Lindholm
JavaSoft
September, 1996

Acknowledgments

This book began as a small set of Web pages that I put together in spring 1995, while trying to make sense of my own early attempts to use Java concurrency features in experimental development efforts. Then it grew; first on the World Wide Web, where I extended, expanded, and removed patterns to reflect my and other people's increasing experience with Java concurrency; and now into this book, which places patterns within the perspective of concurrent software development principles. The web pages also live on, but they now serve as a supplement to the conceptual presentations best suited to book form.

There have been many changes along the way, in a process that has benefited from commentary, suggestions, and exchanges with many kind and knowledgeable people. They include Taranov Alexander, Il-Hyung Cho, Bruce Eckel, Ed Falis, Randy Farmer, Alain Hsiung, Johannes Johannsen, Istvan Kiss, Jonathan Locke, Mike Mills, Trevor Morris, Andrew Purshottam, Simon Roberts, Joel Rosi-Schwartz, Aamod Sane, Doug Schmidt, Kevin Shank, Sumana Srinivasan, Henry Story, Satish Subramanian, Jeff Swartz, Patrick Thompson, Volker Turau, Cees Vissar, Bruce Wallace, Greg Wilson, and Steve Yen, as well as the many people who submitted anonymous electronic mail commentary.

The members of Ralph Johnson's patterns seminar (especially Brian Foote and Ian Chai) read through early forms of some patterns and suggested many improvements. Official and unofficial reviewers of the book manuscript also made substantial contributions. They include Ken Arnold, Joseph Bowbeer, Patrick Chan, Gary Craig, Desmond D'Souza, Tim Harrison, David Henderson, David Holmes, Tim Lindholm, James Robins, Greg Travis, Mark Wales, and Deborra Zukowski. Very special thanks go to Tom Cargill for his many insights and corrections over the past year, as well as for permission to include a description of his Specific Notification pattern (in Chapter 8).

Rosemary Simpson contributed numerous improvements in the course of creating the index. Ken Arnold patiently helped me deal with FrameMaker. Mike Hendrickson and the editorial crew at Addison-Wesley have been continually supportive.

This book would not have been possible without the generous support of Sun Labs. Thanks especially to Jos Marlowe for providing opportunities to work collaboratively on fun and exciting research and development projects.

Thanks above all to Kathy, Keith, and Colin for tolerating all this.

Doug Lea, September, 1996

Table of Contents

Online Supplement . . . . see http://java.sun.com/Series

CHAPTER 1

Introduction

THE Java programming language (hereafter simply "Java") is one of the relatively few object-oriented (OO) programming languages that incorporate threads and related concurrency constructs without requiring special tools or support systems. Concurrent programming in Java is much easier and more natural than in most other languages.

1.1 Applications of Concurrency

This book discusses different ways of thinking about, designing, and implementing multithreaded code in Java. But before reading about how to do this, you might want to consider why and when to use concurrent designs in the first place.

1.1.1 Advantages

Concurrency opens up design possibilities that are impractical in sequential programs. Threads liberate you from the limitations of code that invokes a method and then blocks, doing nothing while waiting for a reply. Using threads, you can additionally trigger new independent activities that run concurrently, with or without waiting out their completion. Reasons to exploit threads include:

Reactive programming. Some programs are required to do more than one thing at a time, performing each activity as a reactive response to some input. For example, a World Wide Web browser may be simultaneously performing an http GET request to get a Web page, playing an audio clip, displaying the number of bytes received of some image, and engaging in an advisory dialog with the user. While it is possible to program such systems in a single-threaded manner by manually interleaving the different activities, this is complicated, fragile, and error-prone. Reactive programs are easier to design and implement using threads. In fact, the vast majority of design principles and patterns described in this book are geared for use in reactive programs.

Availability. Concurrency allows you to maintain high availability of services. For example, among the more common concurrent design patterns (seen in most internet services and even in many applets) is to have one object serve as a gateway interface to a service, handling each request by constructing a new thread to asynchronously perform the associated actions. The gateway is able to accept another request quickly. This helps avoid bottlenecks by draining the communications network of pending messages. It can also improve the fairness of access: new, quickly-serviceable requests do not have to wait for old time-consuming requests to complete.

Controllability. Activities within threads can be suspended, resumed, and stopped by other objects. This provides simplicity and flexibility not found in sequential programming, where the desire to stop an activity (for a while, or forever) and do something else is often difficult to implement.

Active objects. Software objects often model real objects. Most real objects display independent, autonomous behavior. At least in some cases, the easiest way to program this is to fire up a new thread whenever you create such an object.

Asynchronous messages. When one object sends a message to another, the first object does not always care when the resulting action is performed. Threads allow the first object to continue with its own activity without having to wait for unrelated actions to complete.

Parallelism. On machines with multiple CPUs, concurrent programming can be used to exploit available computing power to improve performance. Even without multiple CPUs, interleaving activities in threads avoids delays associated with time-consuming processing that need not complete before other activities are started.

Required concurrency. Even if you do not explicitly intend to write concurrent programs, many predefined Java support classes and run-time features operate in a concurrent manner. These include the `java.applet` and `java.awt` classes for playing audio clips and displaying images, and the mechanisms that cause every Java `Applet` to run in its own thread.

1.1.2 Limitations

If concurrency is great, then you should use it everywhere. But you shouldn't. The benefits of concurrency must be weighed against its costs in resource consumption, efficiency, and program complexity:

Safety. When multiple threads are not completely independent, each can entail objects sending messages to other objects that may also be involved in other threads. All of these objects must utilize synchronization mechanisms or structural exclusion techniques to ensure that they maintain consistent state. Attempts to use multiple threads involving objects that were designed to work only in sequential settings can lead to random-looking, hard-to-debug inconsistencies. On the other hand, synchronization mechanics can add complexity to programs.

Liveness. Activities within concurrent programs may fail to be *live*. That is, one or more activities can simply stop, for any of a number of reasons; for example because other activities are consuming all CPU cycles, or because two different activities are *deadlocked*, both endlessly waiting for each other to continue.

Nondeterminism. Multithreaded activities can be arbitrarily interleaved. No two executions of the same program need be identical. Activities requiring a lot of computation may finish before those requiring practically no computation. This can make multithreaded programs harder to predict, understand, and debug.

Threads versus method calls. Threads are not very useful for request/reply-style programming. When one object must logically wait for a reply from another in order to continue, the same thread should be used to implement the entire request-execute-reply sequence. Constructing a new thread achieves no benefit when there is no room for concurrency. Conversely, an activity running as a thread cannot use the standard sequential invocation style in which a client sends arguments, waits for them to be processed, and then receives results in a reply. These effects can be obtained in threads, but require special coding.

Objects versus activities. In essentially all object-oriented systems, there are many fewer asynchronously executing concurrent activities than there are objects. Even from an active object approach, it makes sense to create a new thread only when an invocation actually generates a new asynchronous activity, not automatically whenever constructing a new object that may or may not ever engage in asynchronous activities.

Thread construction overhead. Constructing a thread and setting it in motion is typically slower and more memory-intensive than constructing a normal object or invoking a method on it. If an activity is only a matter of a few primitive statements, then it is much faster just to invoke it via a method call than to use threads.

Context-switching overhead. When there are more active threads than there are CPUs, the Java run-time system occasionally switches from running one activity to running another, which also entails *scheduling* — figuring out which thread to run next.

Synchronization overhead. Java methods employing synchronization can be slower than those that do not provide proper concurrency protection. And methods that must postpone and resume actions depending on the current states of objects can be yet more expensive. Between thread and synchronization overhead, concurrent programs can run more slowly than sequential ones unless you have multiple CPUs, and sometimes even if you do.

Threads versus processes. Activities that are intrinsically self-contained and sufficiently heavy may be simpler to encapsulate into standalone programs. Standalone programs can be accessed via system-level (concurrent) execution facilities or remote invocation mechanisms rather than as multithreaded components of a single process. (Although the borderlines can be slippery, a *process* is usually defined as an active entity that maintains its own set of resources, while a *thread* uses the resources of its enclosing process.)

1.2 Overview

Concurrency introduces design and programming opportunities and problems not found in sequential OO programming. This book describes some ways to exploit the opportunities and solve the problems, mainly by reusing constructions and techniques that others have found to be useful solutions to common concurrent OO design problems.

Thread packages that are not integrated into programming languages tend to be pretty hard to use. Fat manuals are often needed just to figure out how to express simple constructions. This is not so in Java. The latter part of this chapter surveys the few Java constructs specifically related to concurrent programming. (It assumes that you are familiar with other aspects of Java programming.) The rest of the book focuses on the roles and uses of these constructs in the design of classes, components, frameworks, and applications.

This book is about design, not about specialized concurrent algorithms or their formal analysis. There are already many good texts (in particular the one by Andrews listed in the Further Readings) presenting algorithms that can be implemented in Java. This book instead collects standard design techniques from non-OO concurrent programming, useful constructions found in other concurrent programming languages, new ideas from the research literature on OO concurrency, and practical considerations from the application of concurrency in actual software development. It presents them in a way that is meant to be used and reused in constructing concurrent Java components, applets, and applications.

Some concepts are introduced by first showing what they would look like using pidgin-Java equivalents of constructs found in the languages and systems that introduced the ideas, and then showing how to obtain the effects in Java proper. This provides different conceptual tools for designing concurrent components. It also makes it easier for you to adapt techniques not covered here that originate from other languages or other approaches to concurrency.

Design patterns are used to help organize the wealth of techniques available for structuring concurrent Java programs. A pattern describes a design form, usually an *object structure* (also known as a *micro-architecture)* consisting of one or more interfaces, classes, and/or objects that obey certain static and dynamic constraints and relationships. Patterns are an ideal vehicle for presenting designs and techniques that need not be implemented in exactly the same way across different contexts, and thus cannot be usefully encapsulated as reusable components. Reusable components and frameworks can play a central role in software development. But much of concurrent OO programming consists of the reuse, adaptation, and extension of recurring design forms and practices rather than of particular classes.

A pattern-based approach also helps bridge the unfortunate gap between theory and practice in concurrent programming. Research on concurrency sometimes relies on models and techniques that are ill-suited for everyday OO software development. At the other extreme, some thread-based programs are the result of reckless hacking. This book tries to take a middle ground, stealing good ideas and best practices from everywhere and codifying them into readily applicable forms.

Most of the terminology and notation used here is adapted from the pioneering book *Design Patterns* by Gamma, Helm, Johnson, and Vlissides (see the Further Readings). Some of the patterns presented here are extensions or applications of common sequential OO design patterns to concurrent programming problems. In particular, most of the patterns presented in *Design Patterns* are used or referenced in this book. These are summarized upon first encounter, although only very briefly in cases of tangential tie-ins. You can ignore these references if you have not yet read *Design Patterns*.

Unlike those in the *Design Patterns* book, the patterns here are embedded within chapters discussing sets of related contexts and software design principles that generate the main forces and constraints resolved in the patterns. This presentation style helps organize an otherwise bewildering array of patterns that range from tiny idiomatic programming constructions to application-level structuring techniques. Still, this book maintains a pattern-based approach, clarifying underlying design forms, contexts, applicability, and consequences. It describes solutions in a constructive, recipe-like fashion. In fact, many patterns include *design steps* in addition to presentations of object structures, and so are a bit more recipe-like than those in the *Design Patterns* book.

Because this book concentrates on Java in particular, most pattern descriptions are less complete and wide-ranging than those in the *Design Patterns* book. For example, there are few discussions of *known uses* that reference larger examples in existing systems. Even though these patterns are seen in existing Java programs, the language is still too new for there to be many significant usage examples. Also, some patterns focus on object-oriented designs that, once established, allow you to exploit concurrency techniques that are covered in readily available sources in more extensive detail than can be accommodated here.

Most techniques and patterns in this book are illustrated by variants of an annoyingly small set of toy running examples. This is not an effort to be boring, but to be clear. Concurrency constructs are often subtle enough to get lost in otherwise meaningful examples. Reuse of small examples makes small but critical differences across patterns more obvious. Also, the presentations include many code sketches and snippets illustrating Java implementation techniques.

Most concurrent Java applications use only a few of the designs presented in this book, as appropriate to the problems at hand. All of these designs can be implemented in Java 1.0. Many of the examples rely on classes in the standard Java packages, including `java.awt` and `java.applet`. But no special concurrency properties of these packages are relied on. No other special tools or extensions are needed.

1.2.1 Chapter Preview

Each chapter alternates between general discussions of concepts and principles and pattern-style presentations of particular design forms. Each chapter concludes with a Further Readings section listing related books and articles, sometimes accompanied by minor points omitted from the text.

The remainder of this chapter presents introductory examples of Java concurrency constructs and a reference summary of their properties. The Further Readings section contains a master list of general-purpose sources on issues related to concurrency and OO development.

Chapter 2 discusses the central notion of *safety* in multithreaded contexts and presents three conservative strategies (based on immutability, synchronization, and containment) that result in safe designs.

Chapter 3 discusses the equally central notion of *liveness* and presents two general-purpose techniques (analyzing instance variables and splitting synchronization) that can avoid or reduce liveness and efficiency problems.

Chapter 4 deals with designs applicable when actions are *state-dependent*, that is, cannot be guaranteed to be successful unless objects are in appropriate states. The chapter describes state-based techniques for preventing and delaying actions, along with those for recovering from undesired effects.

Chapter 5 presents three approaches to *concurrency control,* the layering of synchronization and control over basic functionality. Subclassing, delegation, and meta-level control provide the basis for composing concurrent components in a bottom-up fashion.

Chapter 6 lays out options for creating and invoking threads to perform *services*. It presents a set of design choices, implementation techniques and patterns that can be tailored to particular contexts and applications.

Chapter 7 describes *flow architectures* — application-level patterns for structuring multithreaded activities by standardizing communication patterns among objects serving as producers and consumers.

Chapter 8 surveys three approaches to coordinating the interaction of cooperating, independent objects across multiple threads: *Transaction*, *notification*, and *scheduling* techniques provide tools for attacking the intrinsic complexity of cooperative designs.

The on-line supplement can be accessed on the World Wide Web via links from `http://java.sun.com/Series`. The supplement includes:

- All source code, including full versions of examples that are only briefly sketched in this book and those implemented as applets.

- Example applications. To compensate for lack of variety in examples, the supplement includes several applications that demonstrate issues faced when using patterns to build programs.

- Links to sites containing related information. When possible, references in this book list easily accessible books and articles. The supplement contains links to papers, reports, and web pages available electronically.

- Hyperlinked synopses of patterns described in the book, showing their dependencies and relations. The concepts and discussions in this book are organized sequentially. But the patterns presented in each chapter can be used with others from distant chapters. The hyperlinked synopses make it easier to put patterns into practice once you know why they exist.

- Other extensions, supplements, corrections, contributed examples, and commentary produced after this book went to press, including discussions of the usage of new Java features introduced after the Java 1.0 release.

1.3 Java Concurrency Support

Java contains only a few basic constructs and classes specifically designed to support concurrent programming:

- The class `java.lang.Thread` (along with a few related utility classes), used to initiate and control new activities.

- The keywords `synchronized` and `volatile`, used to control execution of code in objects that may participate in multiple threads.

- The methods `wait`, `notify`, and `notifyAll` defined in `java.lang.Object`, used to coordinate activities across threads.

In the same way that the few constructs supporting sequential programming (mainly just call and return) lead to a wide range of coding practices, idioms, and design strategies, a few concurrency constructs go a long way in opening up new vistas in programming. This section presents examples of these constructs, along with boxed summaries of notation and conventions. It concludes with a reference summary of principal Java concurrency constructs and their properties.

But first, a bit of terminology: Interactions in OO programs revolve around the responsibilities placed upon a *client* object needing an action to be performed, and a *server* object containing the code to perform the action. The terms *client* and *server* are used here in their generic senses, not in the specialized sense of distributed client/server architectures. A client is just any Java object that sends a request to another Java object, and a server is just any object receiving such a request.

Most objects play the roles of both clients and servers. When it doesn't matter whether an object under discussion acts as a client or server or both, it is referred to as a *host*; others that it may in turn interact with are often called *helpers* or *peers*. Also, when discussing the mechanics of Java invocations of the form `obj.msg(arg)`, the recipient (that is, the object bound to variable `obj`) is called the *target* object.

1.3.1 Threads

In the standard sequential form of client-server interaction, the client invokes a method on the server and then waits out the server's computations (as well as those of all the objects in turn accessed by the server) before proceeding. Threads provide another option. The Java `Thread` framework allows an activity to be initiated in a new thread, causing it to proceed asynchronously. Nearly any kind of activity can be performed in a Java `Thread`.

1.3.1.1 *Example*

Here is a class describing objects that print a message to a java.awt.TextArea
when their run method is invoked. (A TextArea is a scrollable text region that
can be used to display textual output in Java applets.)

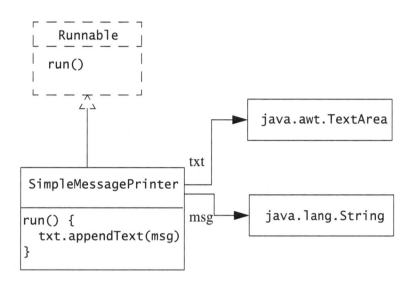

```
public class SimpleMessagePrinter implements Runnable {
  protected String msg_;    // The message to print
  protected TextArea txt_;  // The place to print it

  public SimpleMessagePrinter(String m, TextArea txt) {
    msg_ = m;
    txt_ = txt;
  }

  public void run() {
    txt_.appendText(msg_); // display the message
  }

}
```

Class diagrams. Class and interface diagrams use a minor variant of the simplified OMT notation used in the *Design Patterns* book:

- Solid boxes represent classes. Boxes have two parts:

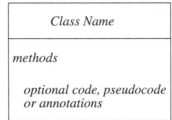

- The *methods* part of a box is omitted when there is no reason to list any of the methods. Even when present, qualifiers, arguments, return types, constructors, inherited methods, and unreferenced methods are often omitted to reduce clutter.

- Dashed boxes represent interfaces.

- Lines with triangles denote subclassing (`extends`).

- Lines with dashed triangles denote interface implementation (`implements`).

- Lines with filled arrowheads denote references (normally implemented via instance variables) from instances of one class to another. They also are omitted when there is no reason to show them.

- Arrows ending in circles denote references from instances of one class to multiple instances (arrays or collections) of the other.

- Lines beginning with diamonds denote unique containment, as explained in Chapter 2.

Object diagrams. Simplified object (instance) diagrams are sometimes used to illustrate relationships among particular objects when class membership and structure can be determined from context. They use ovals of the form:

> **Notes on code examples.** Among the very few unusual coding conventions used here is that non-public instance variables (and sometimes even methods) have names ending in underscores. This is ugly but useful in highlighting concurrency issues that revolve around state representations.
>
> For both clarity and economy of presentation, code is sometimes packed more or less tightly into lines than would otherwise be stylistically desirable. Most documentation commentary for most classes is presented in the text accompanying the code rather than in the code itself.
>
> The majority of classes illustrated in this book are complete, but omit `imports` clauses necessary for compilation. However, import requirements are limited to the standard Java packages and/or to other classes defined in this book, and thus can always be determined from context. The on-line supplement contains downloadable, compilable and/or runnable code, including full versions of classes only sketched out in this book, and versions of classes that add a few niceties that make them more convenient to use. If you'd like to use an example class directly, you can get it from the on-line supplement.

1.3.1.2 *Runnable Objects*

The `SimpleMessagePrinter` class is declared to implement interface `java.lang.Runnable`. This interface lists only the single method `run`, taking no arguments and returning no results:

```
public interface Runnable {
  public void run();
}
```

The Java thread framework requires that the principal methods performed in threads be called `run` and that their classes implement `Runnable`.

In Java, an interface encapsulates a coherent set of services and attributes (broadly, a *role*) without assigning this functionality to any particular object or code. Interfaces are more abstract than classes since they say nothing at all about representations or code. All they do is describe the *signatures* (names, arguments, and result types) of public operations, without even pinning down the classes of the objects that can perform them. The classes that can support `Runnable` typically have nothing in common except that they contain a `run` method and can thus be used within the Java thread framework.

1.3.1.3 *Sequential Version*

Instances of class `SimpleMessagePrinter` can be used in both sequential and multithreaded applets. In a sequential version, you can just call `run` directly from another object as you would in any sequential program. For example:

```
public class SequentialApplet extends Applet {
  protected TextArea txt_;
  protected SimpleMessagePrinter hello_;
  protected SimpleMessagePrinter goodbye_;

  public SequentialApplet() {
    txt_ = new TextArea(4, 40); // 4 rows, 40 columns
    hello_ = new SimpleMessagePrinter("Hello\n", txt_);
    goodbye_ = new SimpleMessagePrinter("Goodbye\n", txt_);
  }

  public void init() {
    add(txt_); // add text area to applet display
  }

  public void start() {
    hello_.run();
    goodbye_.run();
  }

}
```

The `SequentialApplet` class maintains the single-threaded sequential protocol illustrated in the accompanying interaction diagram, which shows the permitted order of events in terms of states and message traffic among the three objects (the applet and the two message printers). The level of detail in the diagram is overkill here, but becomes valuable when describing interactions in concurrent settings.

The protocol shown in the diagram commences with a `start` invocation to the applet and continues up through the `return` from the `start` method. The fact that all of the links connect one-by-one into a single linear chain reflects the sequentiality of execution. (However, the gaps encountered at `appendText` imply that we do not know whether or not the entire invocation is strictly sequential. It might be that `appendText` generates or relies on additional threads.)

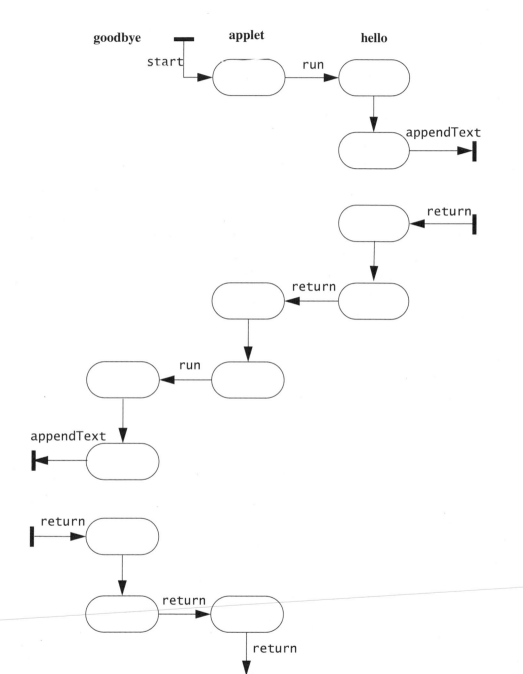

Sequential Version

Interaction diagrams. Interaction diagrams display *protocols* — permitted dynamic relations among objects in the course of a given activity. The diagrams here differ from those used in the *Design Patterns* book in that columns are broken out into discrete steps:

- Each column describes the world from the point of view of the object listed at the top of the column. (Sometimes Threads themselves are included as objects, but usually they are implicit.)

- Nodes (rounded boxes) represent *situations* — states of affairs with respect to one or more objects. The nodes in each column describe situations from the point of view of the indicated object. Nodes may contain expressions that *must* hold in order for the interaction to continue.

- Links (lines with arrows) between nodes indicate the followed-by relation (*not* necessarily the *immediately*-followed-by relation).

- Links with bars as endpoints refer to nodes and objects that lie "outside" the diagram and play no further role in the protocol being displayed.

- When a link is annotated with a message (or throw or return), the originating node represents a situation in which the message has been sent and the destination node represents a situation in which it has been received. Message arguments are omitted when they are not necessary for illustrating the protocol. Unless otherwise indicated, a return or throw corresponds to the most closely associated message from the same sender.

- Dashed links indicate messages that do not require replies (not even void returns). When nailed down to code, they always correspond to built-in Java concurrency support methods (usually Thread.start). Continuations on each side of a dashed link progress independently of the other.

- Nodes nested within other nodes (used first in Chapter 4) represent conditional situations: those that occur only in some states.

- As a convention, time proceeds downward, although nodes at the same levels do not necessarily represent situations that occur at the same times. The lengths and placements of lines and nodes have no temporal significance.

- Even though links do not indicate that one connected node in any sense immediately follows another, ellipses are sometimes used to highlight the fact that necessary steps have been omitted. Other informal elisions and abbreviations are used freely to suppress unnecessary detail.

1.3.1.4 *Multithreaded Version*

The second way to use a `Runnable` is to create a new `Thread` around it using the new `Thread(Runnable x)` constructor and then starting[1] it, which will execute the `Runnable`'s `run` method in a new thread. For example:

```java
public class ThreadedApplet extends SequentialApplet {
  public void start() {
    new Thread(hello_).start();
    new Thread(goodbye_).start();
  }
}
```

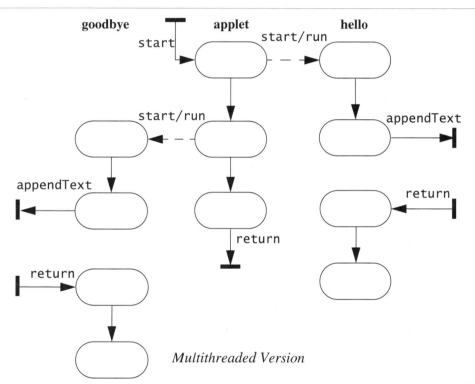

Multithreaded Version

The following trace diagram shows one possible execution sequence for this applet, demonstrating that it is possible for the "Goodbye" thread to execute its `appendText` first.

---

1. The name of the method you *define* in a `Runnable` is `run`, but the name of the method you *call* in a `Thread` is `start`. `Thread.start` causes `Runnable.run` to commence in a new thread. (This sequence is often abbreviated in diagrams as start/run.) Even more confusingly, `Thread.start` is not related to method `Applet.start`, even though they share the same name.

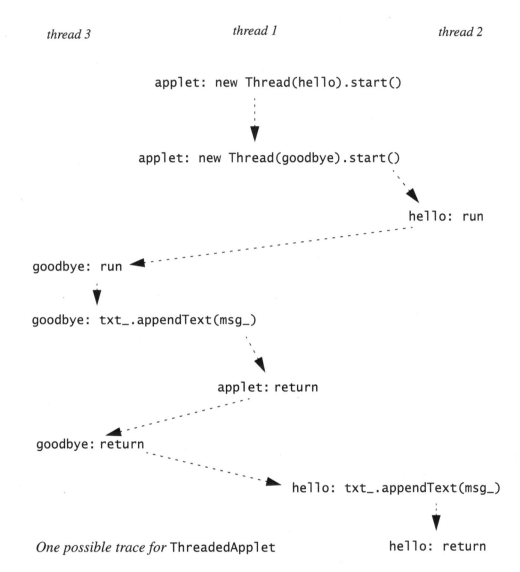

thread 3   *thread 1*   *thread 2*

One possible trace for `ThreadedApplet`

Trace diagrams. An interaction diagram describes the *possible* orderings of
events. A trace diagram illustrates one (sometimes hypothetical) *actual* ordering. Trace diagrams connect lines of code with dotted lines indicating their execution order. When necessary, code is prefixed by the object performing it. For
clarity, diagrams are arranged approximately in columns in which each column
contains the actions performed by a different thread.

1.3.2 Synchronization

When two or more threads all access the same object(s), they can *interfere* with one another. Different forms of interference (see Chapters 2-3) reflect different senses in which a method running in a multithreaded context might not have the same effect as it would in a single-threaded context.

For example, if the `java.awt.TextArea` class were not already coded to be usable in multithreaded programs, the results of `ThreadedApplet` might be `HeGoodlbyelo`, or `GHoeoldlboye`, or any other arbitrary mixture of the characters in the messages.

The main tool for avoiding this kind of interference is the `synchronized` keyword, which can be applied as a qualifier to any Java method as well as to any code block within any method. The main application of synchronization is to ensure that only one thread at a time obtains access to an object. This prevents arbitrary interleaving of the actions in the method bodies.

1.3.2.1 *Example*

If the `java.awt.TextArea` class were not already coded using synchronization, we could (among other possible remedies) create a little helper class that ensured that the `appendText` calls proceed without interference. The use of `synchronized` in the following `append` method helps guarantee that at most one thread executes `TextArea.appendText` at any given time.

The `Appender` class could then be used in minor variants of the `SimpleMessagePrinter` and `SimpleMessageApplet` classes in which all access to the `TextArea` is relayed through a common `Appender`:

```
class Appender {
  private TextArea textArea_;

  Appender(TextArea t) {
    textArea_ = t;
  }

  synchronized void append(String s) {
    textArea_.appendText(s);
  }

}
```

```
public class ThreadedAppletV2 extends Applet { // fragments
  protected TextArea txt_;
  protected Appender appender_;
  protected SimpleMessagePrinterV2 hello_;
  protected SimpleMessagePrinterV2 goodbye_;
  // ...

  public ThreadedAppletV2() {
    txt_ = new TextArea(4, 40);        // as before
    appender_ = new Appender(txt_); // wrap in appender
    hello_ = new SimpleMessagePrinterV2("Hello\n",
                                          appender_);
    goodbye_ = new SimpleMessagePrinterV2("Goodbye\n",
                                            appender_);
  }
}

public class SimpleMessagePrinterV2 implements Runnable {
  protected Appender appender_; // instead of TextArea
  // ...
  public void run() {
    appender_.append(msg_); // use appender to display message
  }
}
```

1.3.3 Waiting and Notification

The synchronized qualifier is used to prevent unintended interactions among threads. The wait, notify, and notifyAll methods are used in constructions in which activities in different threads are intended to affect one another.

Any synchronized method in any object can contain a wait, which suspends the current thread. *All* threads waiting on the target object are resumed upon invocation of method notifyAll. *One* (arbitrarily chosen) thread waiting on the target object is resumed upon invocation of method notify. Waiting and notification methods are sometimes referred to as *monitor* methods, since they are rooted in the programming notion of a monitor that controls threads accessing an object. These constructs are most often used in *guarded* methods (see Chapter 4) that hold up activities in situations where objects are not in the right state to proceed with their intended actions, and later resume them when conditions change.

1.3.3.1 *Example*

Suppose we'd like to ensure that the multithreaded SimpleMessageApplet first prints Hello and then Goodbye. The easiest way to do this is just to use the sequential version. But we can also do it using waiting and notification methods.

The following version of the message printer class adds an instance variable that records whose turn it is to print, and another that records whose turn is next. The `run` method is changed so that each object delays appropriately. After taking its turn, each object informs and wakes up threads waiting in the other. So long as `setNext` is called appropriately to initialize the sequencing, any number of message printer objects can be established, not just two.

Notification in method `turn` is arranged via `notifyAll`. As discussed in more detail in Chapter 4, it is a good idea to use `notifyAll` routinely instead of `notify` unless you've carefully analyzed a design to be sure that `notify` applies, and believe that it should also apply in expected subclasses. Especially when attempting to create reusable classes and classes intended to be subclassed, you normally do not know enough about the context under which an object is operating to be absolutely sure that only one thread should be notified. Since you cannot specify which of the various threads that may be waiting are signaled by a given `notify` operation, you can only use `notify` when it is acceptable to resume any one of the threads that may be waiting and not to resume the others.

For illustration, the `run` method is set up as a loop, so that sets of `AlternatingMessagePrinters` run "forever". They delay on each iteration via the `Thread.sleep` method. When started from the applet, each instance waits on average about five seconds before attempting to print its message until it is somehow stopped.

```
public class AlternatingApplet extends ThreadedApplet {

  public AlternatingApplet() {
    txt_ = new TextArea(4, 40);

    AlternatingMessagePrinter h =
      new AlternatingMessagePrinter("Hello\n", txt_);
    hello_ = h;

    AlternatingMessagePrinter g =
      new AlternatingMessagePrinter("Goodbye\n", txt_);
    goodbye_ = g;

    // initialize links and turn
    h.setNext(g);
    g.setNext(h);
    h.turn();
  }

}
```

```
public class AlternatingMessagePrinter
          extends SimpleMessagePrinter {

  protected AlternatingMessagePrinter next_; // the other object
  protected AlternatingMessagePrinter turn_; // go if turn==this

  public AlternatingMessagePrinter(String m, TextArea txt) {
    super(m, txt);
    turn_ = null; // it's nobody's turn until told otherwise
    next_ = null; // don't know yet who next is
  }

  // called by applet to establish other object
  public synchronized void setNext(AlternatingMessagePrinter p){
    next_ = p;
  }

  // called by another object telling you that it is your turn
  public synchronized void turn() {
    turn_ = this;
    notifyAll(); // signal thread waiting in run
  }

  public synchronized void run() {
    for (;;) {

      while (turn_ != this) {    // wait until turn
        try { wait(); }          // woken up from turn method
        catch (InterruptedException ex) { return; }
      }

      txt_.appendText(msg_);     // take turn

      // alert next
      turn_ = null;
      next_.turn();

      try {                              // do nothing for a while
        long delay = (long)(Math.random() * 10000.0);
        Thread.currentThread().sleep(delay);
      }
      catch (InterruptedException e) { return; }
    }

  }

}
```

In Java, both `sleep` and `wait` can be broken abnormally by an `Interrupte-dException`. In this example, the only response is to return out of the `run` method. Ignoring interruptions, the main protocol is shown in the interaction diagram:

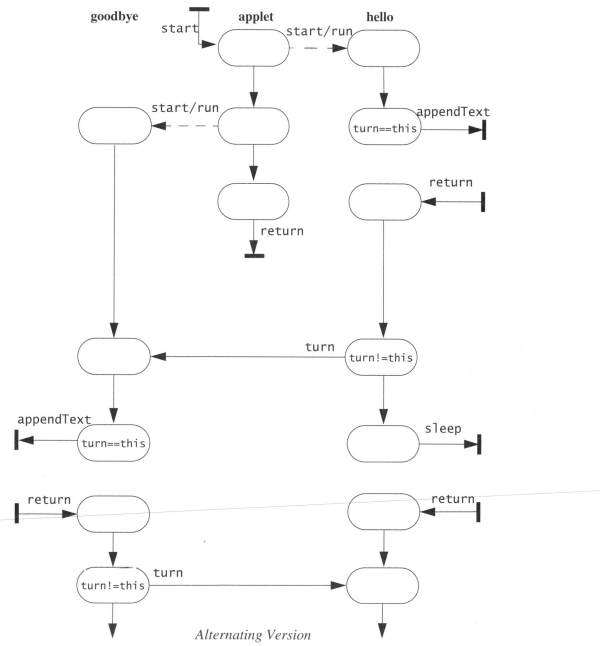

Alternating Version

1.3.4 Summary

Here is a summary of Java concurrency constructs that most directly influence concurrent object design. These constructs and properties are illustrated throughout this book, but are collected here for easy reference. The Java Language Specification should be consulted for more detailed descriptions.

1.3.4.1 *Thread Construction*

- Different `Thread` constructors accept as arguments:
  - A `Runnable` object, in which case a subsequent `Thread.start` invokes `run` of the supplied `Runnable` object. If no `Runnable` is supplied, the default implementation of `Thread.run` returns immediately.
  - A `String` that can serve as an identifier for the `Thread`. This can be useful for tracing and debugging, but plays no other role.
  - The `ThreadGroup` in which the new `Thread` should be placed. If access to the `ThreadGroup` is not allowed, a `SecurityException` is thrown.

- Every Java `Thread` is constructed as a member of a `ThreadGroup`, by default the same group as that of the `Thread` issuing the constructor for it. The main purpose of class `ThreadGroup` is to enforce security policies by dynamically restricting access to `Thread` operations. For example, it is not legal to `stop` a thread that is not in your group. This protects against problems that could occur, for example, if an applet were to try to kill the main Java screen display update loop thread. For similar reasons, `ThreadGroups` may place a ceiling on the maximum priority that any member thread can possess.
  - `ThreadGroups` nest in a tree-like fashion. When an object constructs a `new` `ThreadGroup`, it is nested under its current group.
  - Members of a `ThreadGroup` and its enclosing groups can invoke operations that affect the behavior of all members. These include `ThreadGroup` methods `stop`, `suspend`, and `resume`, which are each equivalent to issuing the corresponding messages to each member individually.

- The initialization method `setDaemon` asserts that the thread represents a task that should be terminated when all other non-daemon threads in the program terminate. It must be called before the thread is started. The `isDaemon` method can be called to check daemon status. It is usually set for background activities that never exit. (The spelling of *daemon* is a relic of systems programming tradition. System-level daemons are continuous reactive processes, for example print queue managers, that are "always" present on a system.)

22

1.3.4.2 *Thread Control Methods*

- `start` causes a thread to call its `run` method as an independent activity. None of the synchronization locks held by the caller thread are automatically retained by the new thread. Unless a special control method (such as `stop`) is called on the thread, it terminates when the `run` method returns.

- `isAlive` returns `true` if a thread has been started but has not terminated. (It will return `true` if the thread is merely suspended in some way.)

- `stop` irrevocably terminates a thread. This is the most common way of terminating threads. Stopping a thread does *not* in any sense kill the `Thread` object, it just stops the activity. However, stopped methods cannot be restarted. When terminated and no longer referenced, `Thread` objects may be garbage collected.

  - An alternative form, `stop(Throwable)`, stops the thread by throwing the listed exception. The no-argument version is equivalent to `stop(new java.lang.ThreadDeath())`.

  - A more extreme variant, `destroy`, stops and kills a thread without giving it or the Java run-time system any chance to intervene. It is not recommended for routine use.

- `suspend` temporarily halts a thread in a way that will continue normally after a (non-suspended) thread calls `resume` on that thread.

- `sleep` causes the thread to suspend for a given time (specified in milliseconds) and then automatically resume. The thread might not continue immediately after the given time if there are other active threads.

- `join` suspends the *caller* until the target thread completes (that is, it returns when `isAlive` is `false`). A version with a (millisecond) time argument returns control even if the thread has not completed within the specified time limit.

- `interrupt` causes a `sleep`, `wait`, or `join` to abort with an `InterruptedException`, which can be caught and dealt with in an application-specific way. (While exceptions stemming from interruptions are discussed, the `interrupt` method itself is not used in this book since it is not fully implemented in Java 1.0. However, the online supplement to this book contains examples of this and other features introduced subsequent to version 1.0.)

23

1.3.4.3 *Priorities and Scheduling*

- Unless you have better-than-average hardware, all the active threads in a Java application share the same CPU, which means that each *runnable* thread has to take turns executing for a while. A thread is runnable if it has been started but has not terminated, is not suspended, is not blocked waiting for a lock, and is not engaged in a `wait`.

- When they are not running, runnable threads are held in priority-based scheduling queues managed by the Java run-time system:

  ◆ By default, each new thread has the same priority as that of the thread that created it.

  ◆ Priorities can be changed by calling `Thread.setPriority` with a priority argument between `Thread.MIN_PRIORITY` and `Thread.MAX_PRIORITY`.

- If there are multiple runnable threads at any given time, the Java run-time system generally picks one with the highest priority in accord with the following rules. However, the specification does not strictly demand that Java implementations conform to these priority rules.

  ◆ If there are more than one thread with the highest priority, it picks any arbitrary one of them (Java does not strictly require *fairness*).

  ◆ A running lower-priority thread is *preempted* (artificially suspended) if a higher-priority thread needs to be run, but threads with equal priority are not *necessarily* preempted in favor of each other.

- The `Thread.yield` method relinquishes control, which may enable one or more other threads to be run.

1.3.4.4 *Synchronization*

- Java guarantees that most primitive operations are *atomic* and will always work safely in multithreaded contexts without explicit synchronization. These operations include accesses and assignments to all built-in scalar types (including reference types) *except* `long` and `double`. Without synchronization, concurrent assignments to `long` and `double` variables are allowed to be interleaved in ways that could result in the reading of inconsistent values.

- The specification allows compilers to perform optimizations that cache values of variables in ways that may cause assignments in other threads to be ignored unless the variables are marked as `volatile` or access is `synchronized`. This is normally a concern only in classes with native methods or busy-wait loops (see Chapter 3).

- In addition to methods, individual code blocks within any Java method can be synchronized via `synchronized(anyObject) { anyCode(); }`. In Java, block synchronization is considered to be a more basic construct than method synchronization. A `synchronized` method is equivalent to one that is not marked as synchronized but has all of its code contained within a `synchronized(this)` block.

- Class-level `static` methods and blocks within `static` methods may be declared as `synchronized`. A non-`static` method can also lock `static` data via a code block enclosed within `synchronized(getClass())`.

- Synchronization is implemented by exclusively accessing the underlying and otherwise inaccessible internal *lock* (sometimes called a *mutex*) that is associated with each Java `Object` (including `Class` objects for `statics`). Each lock acts as a counter. If the count value is not zero on entry to a synchronized method or block because another thread holds the lock, the current thread is delayed (*blocked*) until the count is zero. On entry, the count value is incremented. The count is decremented on exit from each `synchronized` method or block, even if it is terminated via an exception.

- Any method or code block marked as `synchronized` is executed in its entirety (unless explicitly suspended via `wait`) before the object is allowed to perform any other `synchronized` method called from any other thread.

- Code in one `synchronized` method may make a self-call to another method in the same object without blocking. Similarly for calls on other objects for which the current thread has obtained and not yet released a lock. Only those calls stemming from other threads are blocked. Synchronization is retained when calling an unsynchronized method from a synchronized one.

- If a method is *not* marked as `synchronized`, then it may execute immediately whenever invoked, even while another synchronized method is executing. Thus, declaring a method as `synchronized` is *not* sufficient to ensure exclusive access: any other unsynchronized methods may run concurrently with it.

- The `synchronized` qualifier for methods can be overridden in subclasses. A subclass overriding a superclass method must explicitly declare it as `synchronized` if so desired. Otherwise, it is treated as unsynchronized. (In other words, the qualifier is *not* automatically inherited.)

- Methods declared in Java `interfaces` cannot be qualified as `synchronized`. Listing a method in an `interface` does not provide any information or constraints about whether implementations employ synchronization.

1.3.4.5   *Waiting and Notification*

- The methods `wait`, `notify`, and `notifyAll` may be invoked only when the synchronization lock is held on their targets. This is normally ensured by using them only within methods or code blocks synchronized on their targets. Compliance cannot usually be verified at compile time. Failure to comply results in an `IllegalMonitorStateException` at run time.

- A `wait` invocation results in the following actions:

  - The current thread is suspended.

  - The Java run-time system places the thread in an internal and otherwise inaccessible *wait queue* associated with the target object.

  - The synchronization lock for the target object is released, but all other locks held by the thread are retained. (In contrast, `suspended` threads retain *all* their locks.)

- A `notify` invocation results in the following actions:

  - If one exists, an arbitrarily chosen thread, say *T*, is removed by the Java run-time system from the internal wait queue associated with the target object.

  - *T* must re-obtain the synchronization lock for the target object, which will *always* cause it to block at least until the thread calling `notify` releases the lock. It will continue to block if some other thread obtains the lock first.

  - *T* is then resumed at the point of its `wait`.

- A `notifyAll` invocation works in the same way as `notify` except that the steps occur for all threads waiting in the wait queue for the target object.

- Two alternative versions of the `wait` method take arguments specifying the maximum time to wait in the wait queue. If a timed wait has not resumed before its time bound, `notify` is invoked automatically.

- If an `interrupt` occurs during a `wait`, the same `notify` mechanics apply except that control returns to the `catch` clause associated with the `wait` invocation.

1.4 Further Readings

Most applications and systems are concurrent in many senses. For example, a multithreaded Java program may be running concurrently with several other programs on a multitasking workstation. This book is not concerned with operating-system multitasking or other forms of concurrency that fall outside issues traditionally associated with *concurrent programming:* the use of constructs that allow multiple activities to execute within a single program running on a general-purpose computer — not necessarily or even typically a parallel computer. While other aspects of concurrency are mentioned here and there, complete coverage falls outside the scope of this book. Some starting points for learning more about them are listed below.

Also, even though effective concurrent programming often requires a bit more rigor than is typical of everyday sequential programming, this book does not focus on theory or formalisms underlying concurrent and/or object-oriented programming. However, especially if you do a lot of concurrent programming or push hard on some of the more subtle constructions described in this book, you'll eventually want to find out more about these things by reading some of the listed sources.

Java. Other books in the Addison-Wesley Java series describe Java programming techniques and the use of standard Java packages. The Java Language Specification should be consulted for the definitive, guaranteed semantics of Java, including those surrounding the properties of concurrency constructs summarized in this chapter. See:

Arnold, Ken, and James Gosling. *The Java Programming Language*, Addison-Wesley, 1996.

Chan, Patrick, and Rosanna Lee. *The Java Class Libraries: An Annotated Reference,* Addison-Wesley, 1996.

Gosling, James, Frank Yellin, and The Java Team. *The Java Application Programming Interface,* Addison-Wesley, 1996.

Gosling, James, Bill Joy, and Guy Steele. *The Java Language Specification*, Addison-Wesley, 1996.

Concurrent programming. Concurrent and OO programming have about equally long histories, going back to the 1960s. Hardly any of the designs presented in this book are very new (which is why many are organized around patterns — recurring problems and solutions). On the other hand, many of the details of how to approach and implement them in Java are a bit novel. In some cases, particulars of the Java programming language lead to substantial differences between Java versions of design patterns and versions in other languages. For example, some constructions described here as patterns requiring particular combinations of Java mechanics are single built-in constructs in other languages, and vice versa. Keep this in mind when reading other sources on concurrent programming. Accounts of concurrency so often focus on isolated smart procedures operating on isolated dumb data that it is sometimes hard to see how the same ideas apply to object-oriented designs in general or Java in particular.

The standard general-purpose reference-quality text on most aspects of (non-object-oriented) concurrent programming is:

Andrews, Gregory. *Concurrent Programming: Principles and Practice*, Benjamin Cummings, 1991.

It presents several algorithms (for example, deadlock detection) mentioned but not described in this book. Other useful texts on concurrency include:

Ben-Ari, M. *Principles of Concurrent and Distributed Programming*, Prentice Hall, 1990.

Burns, Alan, and Geoff Davis. *Concurrent Programming*, Addison-Wesley, 1993.

Bustard, David, John Elder, and Jim Welsh. *Concurrent Program Structures*, Prentice Hall, 1988.

Pioneering works that introduced concepts, problems and constructs that form the basis of most approaches to concurrent programming include:

Dahl, Ole-Johan, Edsger Dijkstra, and C. A. R. Hoare (eds.). *Structured Programming*, Academic Press, 1972.

Hoare, C. A. R. *Communicating Sequential Processes*, Prentice Hall, 1985.

Milner, Robin. *Communication and Concurrency*, Prentice Hall, 1989.

Concurrent OO programming languages. Java is by no means the first OO language to support concurrency. In fact, the first concurrent OO language, *Simula*, was also the first OO language (circa 1966). Simula contained constructs that were more primitive than those found in Java. For example, concurrency was based around *coroutines* (thread-like constructs requiring that programmers explicitly hand off control from one task to another). But Java is closer to Simula than it is to many other OO languages. Java concurrency constructs (as well as several other features) also resemble those in Modula-3, Mesa, and Euclid. More information about these and other concurrent OO languages can be found in:

Birtwistle, Graham, Ole-Johan Dahl, Bjorn Myhrtag, and Kristen Nygaard. *Simula Begin*, Auerbach Press, 1973.

Filman, Robert, and Daniel Friedman, *Coordinated Computing*. McGraw-Hill, 1984.

Gehani, Narain, and Andrew McGettrick (eds.). *Concurrent Programming,* Addison-Wesley, 1988.

Holt, R. C. *Concurrent Euclid, the Unix System, and Tunis*, Addison-Wesley, 1983.

Nelson, Greg (ed.). *Systems Programming with Modula-3*, Prentice Hall, 1991.

Threads. Most books, articles, and manuals on using threads concentrate on the details of implementations available on particular operating systems or thread packages. For example:

Kleiman, Steven, Devang Shah, and Bart Smaalders. *Programming with Threads,* Prentice Hall, 1995.

Lewis, Bil, and Daniel Berg. *Threads Primer*, Prentice Hall, 1996.

Northrup, Charles. *Programming with Unix Threads*, Wiley, 1996.

Most texts on operating systems and systems programming describe the construction of underlying support mechanisms for language-level thread and synchronization constructs. See, for example:

Hanson, David. *C Interfaces and Implementations*, Addison-Wesley, 1996.

Silberschatz, Avi and Peter Galvin. *Operating Systems Concepts*, Addison-Wesley, 1994.

Tanenbaum, Andrew. *Modern Operating Systems*, Prentice Hall, 1992.

Parallelism. Parallel programming is concerned with techniques that improve efficiency by exploiting multiple CPUs, normally CPUs connected according to particular parallel machine architectures (for example, a hypercube). Parallel software design focuses more on parallelizing not-obviously-parallel problems, while concurrent software design focuses more on coping with intrinsic concurrency. This book occasionally addresses designs that make most sense in multi-CPU environments. But it does not explicitly deal with algorithms devised solely for use on particular configurations of parallel processors, or consider how to map out the placement of different processes on different processors. These issues are discussed in such sources as:

Foster, Ian. *Designing and Building Parallel Programs*, Addison Wesley, 1995.

Wilson, Gregory. *Practical Parallel Programming*, MIT Press, 1995.

Zomaya, Albert (ed.). *Parallel and Distributed Computing Handbook*. McGraw Hill, 1996.

Distribution. Distributed programming is concerned with communication among different self-standing programs and processes, usually residing on different machines. Distribution and concurrency have much in common. Many Java programs display some of each, and frameworks such as Java Remote Method Invocation (RMI) can make the differences between them seem even smaller. However, this book addresses only single-process Java concurrency. It includes designs that can make the use of distribution tools and packages possible, but not those explicitly using or supporting them. In particular, even though concurrency is often associated with network programming, this book does not describe designs based around Java network support classes such as `Socket` or other special-purpose networking packages.

In some ways, the kinds of concurrency seen in distributed programming are simpler to deal with than those seen in concurrent programming. For example each node in a distributed system is already an active process, so you do not always need to start new threads when sending asynchronous messages. On the other hand, distribution introduces new issues of its own — naming, routing, message encoding and transport, security, persistence, crash recovery, fault tolerance, migration, lack of centralized control, and reliance on special infrastructure support. These have little to do with single-process concurrency, and require more extensive treatment than the fleeting discussions scattered throughout this book. General-purpose texts on distribution include:

Coularis, George, Jean Dollimore, and Tim Kindberg. *Distributed Systems: Concepts and Design,* Addison-Wesley, 1994.

Lynch, Nancy. *Distributed Algorithms*, Morgan Kaufman, 1996.

Mullender, Sape (ed.), *Distributed Systems*, Addison-Wesley, 1993.

Raynal, Michel. *Distributed Algorithms and Protocols,* Wiley, 1988.

Distributed languages and tools. Distributed OO programming languages, tools and systems pioneered several structuring techniques and constructs now common in both sequential and concurrent OO programming. The use of interfaces in OO development was popularized by OMG CORBA-IDL, a mostly implementation-independent language for specifying functionality in distributed object systems. Most OMG and CORBA documents are available electronically — see the on-line supplement for pointers. The distributed programming language Emerald was among the first to employ interfaces; see:

Raj, Rajendra, Ewan Tempero, Henry Levy, Andrew Black, Norman Hutchinson, and Erik Jul. "Emerald: A General purpose programming language", *Software — Practice and Experience,* 1991.

The interaction diagrams used in this book are based in part on a CORBA-IDL based specification framework described in:

Lea, Doug, and Jos Marlowe. *PSL: Protocols and Pragmatics for Open Systems*, Technical Report 95-36, Sun MicroSystems Laboratories, 1995.

Real-time programming. Real-time programming is concerned with the measurement and control of external phenomena and devices, as seen for example in aircraft navigation systems and factory process control. Nearly all real-time systems are concurrent. Many are also parallel and/or distributed. Some of the most central techniques employed in general-purposes concurrent programming are based on those first used in real-time systems.

These days, the main distinction of real-time methods lies in their focus on *hard-real-time* problems in which, for the sake of safety and/or correctness, certain activities must be performed within certain time constraints. In part because

Java does not supply primitives that provide such guarantees, this book does not cover deadline scheduling and related real-time concerns. Sources on real-time design that take an OO perspective include:

Gomaa, Hassan. *Software Design Methods for Concurrent and Real-Time Systems,* Addison-Wesley, 1993.

Jarvinen, Hannu-Matti, Reino Kurki-Suonio, Markku Sakkinnen and Kari Systa. "Object-Oriented Specification of Reactive Systems", *Proceedings, 1990 International Conference on Software Engineering,* IEEE, 1990.

Levi, Shem-Tov and Ashok Agrawala. *Real-Time System Design,* McGraw-Hill, 1990.

Selic, Bran, Garth Gullekson, and Paul Ward. *Real-Time Object-Oriented Modeling,* Wiley, 1995.

Special issue on Object-Oriented Real-Time Systems, *ACM OOPS Messenger,* January, 1996.

Database systems. Database systems are of course concerned with the storage, management, and retrieval of persistent data. Most database systems are both distributed and multithreaded. As with real-time systems, many general-purpose concurrency techniques have roots in database systems. However, the particular senses of "concurrency control" and "transactions" seen in accounts of database systems are more narrow and specialized, yet in some cases more extensively studied than those seen in the context of concurrent programming. See:

Bacon, Jean. *Concurrent Systems,* Addison-Wesley, 1993.

Cattell, R. G. G. *Object Data Management*, Addison-Wesley, 1991.

Cellary, Wojciech, E. Gelenbe, and Tadeusz Morzy, *Concurrency Control in Distributed Database Systems,* North-Holland, 1988.

Khoshafian, Setrag. *Object-Oriented Databases,* Wiley, 1993.

Lynch, Nancy, Michael Merritt, William Weihl, and Alan Fekete. *Atomic Transactions*, Morgan Kaufmann, 1994.

Concurrent systems. Several specialized fields of software development rely heavily on concurrency. For example, essentially all simulation systems, telecommunications systems, and multimedia systems are highly multithreaded. While basic concurrency techniques form much of the basis for the design of such systems, this book stops short of describing large-scale software architectures or specialized programming techniques associated with particular concurrent applications. See, for example:

Fishwick, Paul. *Simulation Model Design and Execution,* Prentice Hall, 1995.

Gibbs. Simon and Dennis Tsichritzis. *Multimedia Programming*, Addison-Wesley, 1994.

Watkins, Kevin. *Discrete Event Simulation in C,* McGraw-Hill, 1993.

Concurrent software design. Accounts of high-level object-oriented software analysis and design that cover at least some concurrency issues include:

Atkinson, Colin. *Object-Oriented Reuse, Concurrency and Distribution,* Addison-Wesley, 1991.

Booch, Grady. *Object Oriented Analysis and Design*, Benjamin Cummings, 1994.

Buhr, R. J. A., and R. S. Casselman, *Use Case Maps for Object-Oriented Systems*, Prentice Hall, 1995.

de Champeaux, Dennis, Doug Lea, and Penelope Faure, *Object Oriented System Development,* Addison-Wesley, 1993.

Reenskaug, Trygve. *Working with Objects,* Prentice Hall, 1995.

Rumbaugh, James, Michael Blaha, William Premerlani, Frederick Eddy, and William Lorensen. *Object-Oriented Modeling and Design*, Prentice Hall, 1991. (This book introduced OMT notation.)

Accounts of non-object-oriented approaches to concurrent software specification and design include:

Chandy, K. Mani, and Jayedev Misra. *Parallel Program Design*, Addison-Wesley, 1989.

Francez, Nissim, and Ira Forman. *Interacting Processes*, ACM Press, 1996.

Harel, David. "StateCharts: A Visual Formalism for Complex Systems", *Science of Computer Programming,* Volume 8, 1987.

Jensen, Kurt, and Grzegorz Rozenberg (eds.). *High-level Petri Nets: Theory and Application*, Springer-Verlag, 1991.

Lamport, Leslie. *The Temporal Logic of Actions*, SRC Research Report 79, Digital Equipment Corp, 1991.

Manna, Zohar, and Amir Pneuli. *The Temporal Logic of Reactive and Concurrent Systems*, Springer-Verlag, 1991.

Patterns. There are many useful design patterns besides those that are special to concurrent Java programming, and surely many others relating to concurrency that are not included in this book. Other books presenting patterns and pattern-related aspects of software design include:

Buschmann, Frank, Regine Meunier, Hans Rohnert, Peter Sommerlad, and Michael Stal. *Pattern-Oriented Software Architecture: A System of Patterns,* Wiley, 1996.

Coplien, James. *Advanced C++: Programming Styles and Idioms*, Addison-Wesley, 1992.

Gamma, Erich, Richard Helm, Ralph Johnson, and John Vlissides. *Design Patterns,* Addison-Wesley, 1994.

Shaw, Mary, and David Garlan. *Software Architecture*, Prentice Hall, 1996.

(Various editors) *Pattern Languages of Program Design,* Addison-Wesley. This series incorporates patterns presented at the annual Pattern Languages of Programming (*PLoP*) conference.

Software engineering. Technical issues form only one aspect of concurrent software development, which also entails testing, organization, management, human factors, maintenance, tools, and engineering discipline. For an introduction to basic engineering methods that can be applied to both everyday programming and larger efforts, see:

Humphrey, Watts. *A Discipline for Software Engineering*, Addison-Wesley, 1995.

Research in concurrent OO languages and systems. The kinds of concurrency constructs found or easily emulated in Java are representative of those in most other concurrent OO languages. Some languages differ in that they contain constructs that *implicitly* create threads when executed. For example, some languages and tools support *oneway* qualifiers for requests and/or *early reply* constructs for results. Additionally, there have been several attempts to create completely different kinds of experimental concurrent OO languages, most notably *Actor* languages in which each object is a process-like entity. See:

Agha, Gul. *ACTORS: A Model of Concurrent Computation in Distributed Systems*, MIT Press, 1986.

Research papers on other systems and languages can be found in proceedings of OO conferences (*ECOOP, OOPSLA, COOTS*). Also, the following collections contain chapters surveying most current approaches and issues:

Agha, Gul, Peter Wegner, and Aki Yonezawa (eds.). *Research Directions in Concurrent Object-Oriented Programming,* MIT Press, 1993.

Guerraoui, Rachid, Oscar Nierstrasz, and Michel Riveill (eds.). *Object-Based Distributed Processing,* LNCS 791, Springer-Verlag, 1993.

Nierstrasz, Oscar, and Dennis Tsichritzis (eds.). *Object-Oriented Software Composition*, Prentice Hall, 1995.

Verification. Most critical properties of concurrent software cannot be checked automatically in the same way as, for example, type safety. It can be very difficult to test concurrent programs for correctness, safety and liveness failures. Formalisms and formal methods have been introduced to help developers rigorously specify and analyze properties of concurrent programs. The best-studied methods are not geared for use with object-oriented programs, and are not fully enough developed to be applied readily to several problems of practical interest. They tend to be most useful for analyzing relatively small sections of programs that it is vitally important to prove problem-free. See, for example:

Apt, Krzysztof and Ernst-Rudiger Olderog. *Verification of Sequential and Concurrent Programs,* Springer-Verlag, 1991.

Theory. Given the diversity of forms of concurrency seen in software, it's not surprising that there have been a large number of approaches to the basic theory of concurrency. Until recently, few of these applied in any obviously useful way to concurrent object-oriented programming. However, work on process calculi (in particular the π-calculus), event structures, linear logic, Petri nets, and temporal logic has potential relevance to the understanding of concurrent OO systems. Most of this work is still scattered throughout the technical literature; see, for example, proceedings of conferences such as *CONCUR*. For overviews of basic approaches to the theory of concurrency, see:

van Leeuwen, Jan (ed.). *Handbook of Theoretical Computer Science, Volume B,* MIT Press, 1990.

CHAPTER 2

Safety

OBJECTS within multithreaded Java programs may interact. Unless explicitly designed and programmed otherwise, interacting objects involved in multiple threads can interfere with each other. There are two aspects of interference prevention and two corresponding properties that concurrent software should possess:

Safety. The property that nothing bad ever happens.

Liveness. The property that anything ever happens at all.

Safety failures lead to unintended behavior at run time — things just start going wrong. Liveness failures lead to no behavior — things just stop running.

You have to balance the relative effects of different kinds of failure in your own programs. But it is a standard engineering (not just software engineering) practice to place primary design emphasis on safety. The more your code actually matters, the better it is to ensure that a program does nothing at all rather than something that leads to random, even dangerous behavior.

On the other hand, the majority of time spent in tuning concurrent designs in practice usually surrounds liveness and liveness-related efficiency issues. And there are sometimes good, conscientious reasons for selectively sacrificing safety for liveness. However, these reasons tend to emerge only at larger scales of concern than those addressed here. For example, in distributed financial systems, using a stock quote that is possibly wildly incorrect is sometimes better than not using one at all.

Sadly enough, some of the easiest things you can do to improve liveness properties can destroy safety properties, and vice versa. Getting them both right is sometimes a challenge. This chapter introduces design methods that get the safety part right. The next chapter balances these against liveness concerns.

2.1 Safe Objects

Safe concurrent programming practices are generalizations of safe sequential programming practices. In fact, safety in concurrent designs is very similar to the notion of *type* safety. A type-checked program might not be correct, but at least it doesn't do dangerous things like misinterpret the bits representing a `float` as if they were an object reference. Similarly, a safe concurrent design might not have the intended effect, but at least it never encounters errors due to corruption of representations by contending threads.

One practical difference between type safety and multithreaded safety is that most type-safety matters can be checked automatically by compilers. A program that fails to pass compile-time checks cannot even be run. Most multithreaded safety matters cannot be checked automatically, and so must rely on programmer discipline. Methods for *proving* designs to be safe fall outside the scope of this book (see the Further Readings). The techniques for dealing with safety described here rely on careful engineering practices (including several with roots in formalisms) rather than formal methods themselves.

The main goal in safety preservation is ensuring that all objects in a system maintain *consistent* states: states in which all instance variables, and all instance variables of other objects on which they depend, possess legal, meaningful values. As discussed in subsequent chapters, it sometimes takes hard work to nail down exactly what "legal" and "meaningful" mean in a particular class. This chapter focuses on classes in which consistency is easy to determine.

Safe objects may occasionally enter transiently inconsistent states, but never attempt to perform actions when they are in inconsistent states. If every object is designed to perform actions only when it is logically able to do so, and if all the mechanics are properly implemented, then you can be sure that an application using these objects will not encounter any errors due to object inconsistency.

The remainder of this chapter describes three conservative strategies that intrinsically result in safe designs by relying exclusively on a single ingredient of safe concurrent programs:

Immutability. Avoiding state changes.

Synchronization. Dynamically ensuring exclusive access.

Containment. Structurally ensuring exclusive access.

Each of these has a principal variant (stateless methods, partial synchronization, and managed ownership, respectively) that applies when only some of the conditions for using the simplest versions are met. Chapter 4 describes additional strategies applying to classes with actions that should not occur at all when objects are in particular states.

2.2 Immutable Objects

The only approach to concurrent object design that always completely bypasses the need to synchronize the activities of objects is *not* to change the objects.

Programs are much simpler to understand if existing objects are never changed, but instead new ones are continually created during the course of any computation. Unfortunately, such programs are almost totally unable to handle interaction via user interfaces, cooperating threads, and so on.

However, selective use of immutability is a very useful tool in concurrent OO programming. Immutable constructions are potentially applicable in situations including:

- When objects serve as instances of simple abstract data types representing values; for example, colors (`java.awt.Color`), numbers (`java.lang.Integer`) and strings (`java.lang.String`).

- When different classes, supporting different usages, can be arranged for the immutable versus updatable versions of some concept. For example, `java.lang.String` is immutable, while `java.lang.StringBuffer` is updatable.

- When creating different variants, versions, or states of an object by creating new objects through partial copying is relatively rare and/or cheap, and is thus outweighed by the benefits of never needing to synchronize state changes.

- When you'd like to have multiple objects represent the same values and/or perform the same functionality without knowing or caring about exactly which object you have at any given time.

As a reminder of this property, immutable instance variables are annotated as `fixed` in code examples in the remainder of this book. Fixed variables are always initialized upon construction (which makes them more general than Java `final` variables), but never assigned to otherwise. (This is an analog of one of the senses of `const` in C++.)

In addition to classes serving as traditional closed data abstractions, many simple helper classes used in concurrent settings are intrinsically immutable. For example:

```
class Relay { // a within-package helper for some Server class
  private Server server_; // fixed

  Relay(Server s) {
    server_ = s;
  }

  void doIt() {
    server_.doIt();
  }

}
```

2.2.1 Stateless Methods

Some services provided by otherwise mutable objects are purely *stateless*, that is, have no bearing on a mutable object's state. Stateless methods can be used as if they were methods on immutable objects. They can be, but are not necessarily, static; for example:

```
class NumericalOps {
  static int plus(int a, int b) { return a + b; }
}

public class Sorter { // fragments
  private CollatingRule rule_; // fixed

  public Sorter() {
    rule_ = new DefaultCollatingRule();
  }

  public String[] sort(String[] array) {
    String[] copy = new String[array.length];
    // place sorted elements in copy
    return copy;
  }
  // ...
}
```

2.2.1.1 *Copying*

As implied in the sort example, stateless methods often make local copies of arguments and results instead of holding them in objects that may be accessed by other threads and thus subject to interference. This trade-off of copying versus synchronization works so long as arguments, variables, and results local to a method are used only for strictly local purposes. Java does not possess any kind of pass-by-copy mechanism for non-scalar variables or require locality, so you need to enforce this usage by convention.

For example, the `Sorter.sort` method must explicitly construct a local copy of the array and pass back a reference to it as the return value. It must be sure not to pass this reference to any other object that may access it in any way that could ever interfere. Like immutable classes, copy-based strategies tend to work best for arguments and results that serve conceptually as data values, as opposed to interesting objects in their own right.

2.3 Fully Synchronized Objects

When visible objects may change state, synchronization is necessary to ensure that these changes occur only in consistent ways. At the bottommost levels of execution, safety preservation requires the avoidance of two kinds of conflicts that could otherwise occur when manipulating storage locations representing variables:

Read/Write conflicts. Access by clients (or even by the object itself) of illegal *transient* state values — intermediate values of instance variables that appear only momentarily in the course of an update method, and would be wrong or nonsensical to report out.

Write/Write conflicts. Inconsistent assignment to variables by concurrently executing update methods. This includes, especially, cases in which multiple threads both read and write. For example if two threads both execute ++i for some location i that starts out with a value of 0, the value of i after execution could be either 2 (if the threads turned out to proceed sequentially) or 1 (if they were interleaved so that both threads first read the value 0 and then wrote the value 1).

Another way of phrasing conflicts is through the notion of *transient states*. Without explicit prevention or control, concurrent objects are always ready to receive new messages, even when they are in the midst of performing other methods. This means that other objects may access values of instance variables that momentarily take illegal or nonsensical values while the host object is in the course of performing some method. This issue is of less concern in most sequential settings. If each method runs to completion before the next one executes, other objects never see inconsistent values that occur in the middle of actions. (Analogous issues do however arise in sequential programs when exceptions may cause termination while objects are in inconsistent states or when callback sequences occur in the midst of processing.)

In Java, safety is a per-object (or per-class) design issue. In the absence of any additional control, each object must protect itself from any interference that could occur when participating in multiple threads.

The only primitive Java construct for dynamically ensuring safety is the `synchronized` keyword, which allows you to guarantee that an object is in full control of its own operations. A class in which *every* method is declared as `synchronized` (and in which there are no `public` instance variables or other evasions of encapsulation) guarantees *locally* sequential behavior, which is often just as easy to think about as the *globally* sequential behavior seen in non-concurrent programming.

Fully synchronized objects can be doing only one thing at any one time. After construction, they can only be in one of the *execution states Active, Ready,* or *Waiting.* (Ultimately, when they are no longer referenced by any other objects, they may become *Dead* and be reclaimed by the Java garbage collector).

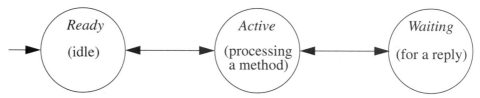

In Java, state *Ready* is equated with lack of possession by any thread of the synchronization lock on the object.

Each method in a fully synchronized object is *atomic* from the point of view of clients: no transient states are ever visible. Even simple methods that return values of instance variables are processed only in *stable* states; that is, when the object is *Ready*. Full synchronization achieves this by arranging that every method invocation take the form:

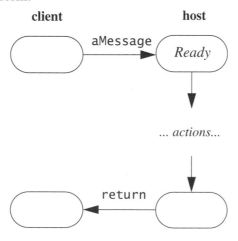

For example, consider a fully synchronized ExpandableArray class; a simplified variant of java.util.Vector:

```
public class ExpandableArray {
  private Object[] data_; // the elements
  private int size_; // the number of slots used in the array

  public ExpandableArray(int cap) {
    data_ = new Object[cap];
    size_ = 0;
  }

  public synchronized int size() {
    return size_;
  }

  public synchronized Object at(int i) // subscripted access
    throws NoSuchElementException {
    if (i < 0 || i >= size_ )
      throw new NoSuchElementException();
    else
      return data_[i];
  }

  public synchronized void append(Object x) { // add at end
    if (size_ >= data_.length) { // need a bigger array
      Object[] olddata = data_;
      data_ = new Object[3 * (size_ + 1) / 2];
      for (int i = 0; i < size_; ++i)
        data_[i] = olddata[i];
    }
    data_[size_++] = x;
  }

  public synchronized void removeLast()
    throws NoSuchElementException {
    if (size_ == 0)
      throw new NoSuchElementException();
    else
      data_[--size_] = null;
  }

}
```

Without synchronization, an instance of this class would not be usable in concurrent settings. For example, it could encounter a read/write conflict if processing the accessor at while in the midst of a removeLast operation. And it could encounter a write/write conflict if concurrently performing two append operations, in which case the state of the data array would be very difficult to predict.

Note that constructors cannot be marked as synchronized in Java. This is rarely an issue. Synchronization in constructors is needed only when partially constructed objects could be involved in multiple threads. This might be possible if, for example, a constructor passed this to an object that generated another thread. When necessary, block synchronization can be used to protect such code.

2.3.1 Statics

In addition to using synchronized methods, instances of classes with updatable static variables require one further bit of protection. The use of per-instance synchronized methods does not automatically preclude two instances of the same class from running methods that mutually interfere with each other's use of static variables. To help protect static data, Java supports per-class locks.

Methods accessing statics can be controlled using block synchronization based on the Class object of the current instance (available from any Object via getClass). Additionally, static methods may themselves be declared as synchronized, which locks the Class object. For example, suppose a class maintains a count of those instances that are using a certain file. Access to the count may be controlled via methods such as:

```
class FileUsers { // fragments
  private static int using__ = 0; // never access directly

  protected void beginUsing() {
    synchronized(getClass()) {
      ++using__;
    }
  }

  protected void endUsing() {
    synchronized(getClass()) {
      --using__;
    }
  }

  static synchronized int numberUsing() {
    return using__;
  }
}
```

The Java run-time system internally obtains and releases the synchronization locks for Class objects during class loading and initialization. Unless you are writing a special ClassLoader, these internal mechanics do not interfere with the use of ordinary methods and blocks synchronized on Class objects.

2.3.2 Partial Synchronization

When an object possesses both mutable and immutable instance variables, you do not always need to synchronize the entire bodies of all methods. This allows other waiting `synchronized` methods to execute during unsynchronized sections. Partial synchronization can be implemented using `synchronized(this)` code blocks within only one *critical section* of an otherwise unsynchronized method. Alternatively, an unsynchronized method may internally invoke a synchronized helper method that performs the critical section.

Synchronization can be split across a method only when the different parts of the method are not in any way dependent, so it would be acceptable for other methods to "see" and use the object before full method completion. The most easily exploited opportunities for splitting synchronization are methods that proceed by first dealing with mutable aspects of state, and then releasing synchronization to deal with immutable aspects, or vice versa.

2.3.2.1 *Example*

Consider a `LinkedCell` class in which each cell contains a reference to a successor cell, and for which we require that successor cell references be fixed upon construction. This is common requirement for cells serving as Lisp-style lists. Methods and sections of methods solely involving the successor need not be synchronized.

```
public class LinkedCell {
  protected double value_;
  protected LinkedCell next_; // fixed

  public LinkedCell (double v, LinkedCell t) {
    value_ = v;
    next_ = t;
  }

  public synchronized double value() {
    return value_;
  }

  public synchronized void setValue(double v) {
    value_ = v;
  }

  public LinkedCell next() {  // no synch needed
    return next_;
  }
```

```
public double sum() { // add up all element values
  double v = value(); // get value via synchronized accessor
  if (next() != null)
    v += next().sum();
  return v;
}

public boolean includes(double x) { // search for x
  synchronized(this) { // synch to access value
    if (value_ == x)
      return true;
  }
  if (next() == null)
    return false;
  else
    return next().includes(x);
}
}
```

In Java, an object remains locked when a synchronized method makes a self-call to an unsynchronized one. So it would *not* avoid full synchronization to write sum as:

```
synchronized double ineffectivelyUnsynchedSum() { // bad idea
  double v = value_;
  return v + nextSum(); // synch still held on call
}
double nextSum() {
  return (next() == null)? 0: next().sum();
}
```

Notice that sum, includes, and all similar methods would need to be overridden if you wrote a subclass introducing a setNext method that allowed assignment to the next pointer.

2.4 Contained Objects

Synchronization achieves exclusion by *dynamically* ensuring that only one thread at a time accesses an object. An alternative approach is to guarantee exclusive access *structurally* by avoiding *shared variables*. The need for synchronization can be avoided by defining classes in which only one thread at a time could conceivably ever access an object.

Short of arranging that only one thread exist in an entire program, the simplest and most effective means of structuring composite classes to obtain exclusion is to "piggyback" synchronization and/or method visibility control by logically embedding objects within others. In this way, dynamic synchronization of the outer object suffices to protect accessible operations in the inner object(s).

Containment extends the encapsulation techniques implicitly used when building fully synchronized objects holding instances of primitive "direct" Java types like `double`. But here they are applied to classes holding *references* to arbitrary objects.

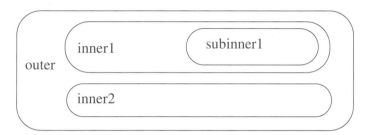

The resulting classes are highly constrained composites in which the outer object may be thought of as *owning* the inner ones. Conversely, the inner objects may be thought of as being "physically" contained in the outer one. Containment leads to strictly nested object structures in which unique references form bridges to isolated islands of functionality. (An *island* is the *communication-closed* set of all objects ultimately reachable from a unique reference, and all of its unique references, and so on.)

- The outer object constructs new instances of each inner object upon its own construction, assigning references to non-public instance variables. Fresh construction guarantees that references to the inner objects are not shared by any other object.

- The outer object never *leaks* inner references to any other object: it never passes the references as arguments or return values of any method. This ensures that the inner objects are only accessible via methods on the outer object.

- In the most conservative variant, *fixed containment*, the outer object never reassigns reference variables pointing to the inner objects. This avoids the need for synchronization surrounding instance variable updates in the outer object. (Fixed containment implements the main sense of *aggregation* discussed in the *Design Patterns* book.)

- The outer object is fully synchronized or is in turn uniquely embedded within another fully synchronized object. This guarantees that all accesses to the inner objects (and all objects recursively constructed within them) are ultimately synchronized.

Containment is often needed for reasons of functionality that are only indirectly related to synchronization. For example, the ExpandableArray class strictly contains its data_ array so that other objects cannot use it in ways that might interfere with internal requirements.

For another example, consider an Interval class that represents a time interval using a pair of Date objects. The java.util.Date class might not itself provide desired synchronization for its methods. However, by embedding unique instances within the fully synchronized Interval class, the Date class can be used without any further concern for synchronization.

As a reminder, references to uniquely embedded instance variables are annotated as unique in code examples and by diamonds in class diagrams. In cases where the references are never reassigned, they are also qualified as fixed.

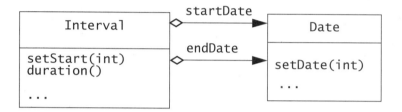

```
public class Interval { // fragments
  private Date startDate_; // fixed, unique
  private Date endDate_;   // fixed, unique

  public Interval() {
    startDate_ = new Date();
    endDate_ = new Date();
  }

  public synchronized void setStart(int date) {
    startDate_.setDate(date);
  }

  public synchronized int duration() {
    return endDate_.getDay() - startDate_.getDay();
  }
}
```

Nearly all interesting classes in object-oriented designs are structured as composites, performing some or all actions via operations on *acquaintance* objects known to hosts via non-public references. Composites using strict containment represent only a small subset of this design space. Containment is a very conservative composite design strategy. It can limit opportunities to employ common peer-to-peer object interactions, notification schemes, and collaborative design patterns. A further disadvantage is that it introduces additional context dependence for classes of embedded objects. Designing a class to operate correctly only when instances are embedded in others limits its range of usability.

These restrictions can sometimes be relaxed without having to resort to full synchronization. However, completely unconstrained composite designs can require the heavier concurrency control techniques presented in later chapters.

2.4.1 Managed Ownership

The simplest strategy for structurally maintaining exclusion is *fixed* containment, whereby each outer object constructs a new instance of the inner object type in its own constructor and assigns it to an instance variable for subsequent internal use, never leaking the reference to any other object or reassigning it. Fixed containment applies only in situations where it is possible for the outer object itself to create the inner object, where the outer object manages only one inner object, and where it is never necessary to reveal the reference to other objects. Further safeguards extend the range of applicability of structural exclusion techniques even when these conditions fail to hold.

The notion of *exclusive resources* helps organize the design space. Exclusive resources are always owned by only one object, but ownership may change hands over time. Exclusive resources may be seen as analogs of physical objects, at least in the sense that:

- If you have one, then you can do something (with it) that you couldn't do otherwise.

- If you have one, then no one else has it.

- If you give one to someone else, then you no longer have it.

- If you destroy one, then no one will ever have it.

A more concrete way of characterizing this policy is that at most one accessible reference to any exclusive resource may exist in a program at any given time. Each reference is unique, although not necessarily fixed.

In some contexts and senses, constructions involving exclusive resources have been termed *tokens, batons, linear objects, capabilities,* and, sometimes, just *resources.* Many concurrent and distributed algorithms hinge on the idea that only one object at a time possesses a token. For a hardware-based example, token ring networks maintain a single token that is continually circulated among the nodes. Each node may send messages only when it has the token.

Exclusive resource policies may apply whenever you want to establish any kind of one-at-a-time ownership protocol. They can serve as an extension of sorts to the *Singleton* pattern described in the *Design Patterns* book. Singletons can be used to ensure that there is only one resource. Exclusion mechanics ensure that there is only one *user* of a resource at any given time.

There are two principal steps in establishing resource management policies:

1. Choosing operations.

2. Choosing conventions surrounding their use and enforcement.

2.4.1.1   *Operations*

Transfer operations may include any subset or variant of the following, for Resource objects r and s, and Owner objects x and y that may hold them in instance variable ref.

Keep in mind that Resources are ultimately manipulated via references to Java Objects that in turn may use yet other objects as Resources. But here they are viewed specially for purposes of laying out options. For example, in the terminology of some other patterns, Owner maps to *Host* and Resource to *Helper*. In others, Owner maps to *Adapter* and Resource to *Adaptee*. And so on.

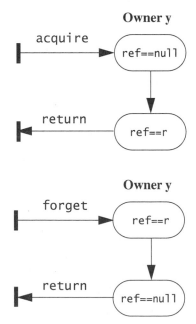

Acquiring. Owner y establishes initial possession of r. This is usually just the result of constructing or otherwise initializing r.

Forgetting. Owner y causes Resource r not to be possessed by any Owner. This is sometimes associated with special cleanup operations on r.

Giving. Owner x sends a message to Owner y containing a reference to Resource r as an argument, after which x no longer has possession of r but y does. Another common name for this operation is put.

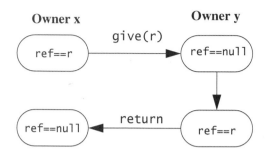

Taking. The converse of giving. Owner y requests a Resource from Owner x, which then sends r as the return value, relinquishing possession.

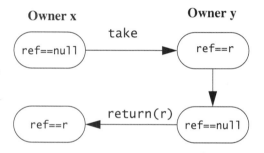

Exchanging. Owner x trades its Resource r for Owner y's Resource s.

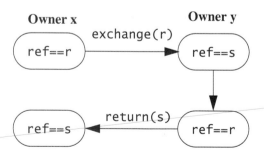

Duplicating. Owner y makes a functionally equivalent but different Resource from r, for example via r.clone, returning new Resource s.

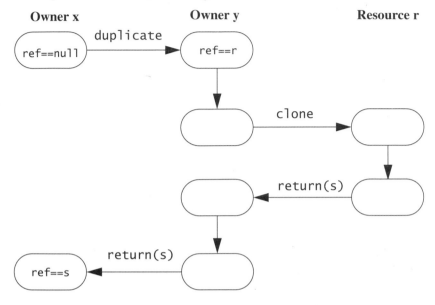

2.4.1.2 *Conventions*

The fundamental implementation problem surrounding exclusive resources is that references to objects just don't act much like physical objects when it comes to the notion of possession. To implement exclusive possession in an absolutely fool-proof fashion, you'd have to selectively override the semantics of assignment, that is, statements of the form p = q where p and q are variables referencing resources. If this were real life rather than a programming language, the transfer would cause q to lose possession after completion of the operation. But the assignment statement results in both p and q still being bound.

   You cannot selectively yet completely disable reference assignment and replace it with a transfer operation in Java. Thus, any solution must entail a certain amount of programmer convention. Variant solutions make it more or less difficult for programmers to evade conventions, but no scheme can ensure that they are flawlessly adhered to. This state of affairs is analogous to real-life problems in dealing with intellectual property rights and other forms of permission that do not intrinsically entail physical transfer operations. This has led to a vast array of solutions, ranging from informal conventions to arbitrarily heavy legal apparatus.

   Between variations in possible operations and choices for expressing and securing their implementations, there is no universally applicable design form.

However, it is pretty easy to establish your own policies on the basis of these considerations. Options include:

- Usage conventions among the `Owner` classes that operate upon `Resources`.

- Methods in and usage conventions for the `Resource` classes themselves.

- Methods in and usage conventions for special resource control or holder classes that may help track more than one `Resource` at a time.

In all cases, the goal is to make it as difficult as possible for objects (and their programmers) to obtain references to `Resources` that they ought not to have. Measures can be applied to deal with any or all of the four ways that some potential `Owner` object x can obtain a reference to object r:

- Object x was created knowing the reference to r because r was passed as a constructor argument or used as an initializer.

- Object x created r itself via `new`.

- Some other object passed the reference to r as a message argument or return value to x.

- Object x obtained the reference from a public variable held by some other object.

2.4.1.3 *Rings*

Transfer protocols can be used to ensure that a *group* of cooperating objects together strictly contain a resource. The most straightforward way to implement this is to arrange a set of peer objects in a ring in which each node communicates only with a single neighbor.

For example, consider a set of `PrintService` objects arranged as nodes in a ring, passing around rights to use a `Printer`. If a node is asked to print but does not currently have access, it tries to take it from its neighbor. This request cascades down to a node that has a printer. Defining the relevant methods as synchronized ensures that nodes do not give up the printer until they are finished with it. The accompanying object diagram illustrates a snapshot of one possible configuration.

This design results in the desired effects only if all nodes obey the transfer protocol, the connections are set up appropriately, and at least one node has a printer. A sample start-up method shows one way to establish the required structure.

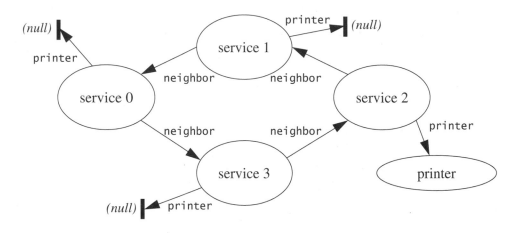

```
public class Printer {
  public void printDocument(byte[] doc) { /* ... */ }
  // ...
}

public class PrintService {
  protected PrintService neighbor_ = null; // node to take from
  protected Printer printer_ = null; // unique

  public synchronized void print(byte[] doc) {
    if (printer_ == null) // get printer from neighbor
      printer_ = neighbor_.takePrinter();

    printer_.printDocument(doc);
  }

  synchronized Printer takePrinter() { // called from others
    if (printer_ != null) {
      Printer p = printer_; // implement take protocol
      printer_ = null;
      return p;
    }
    else
      return neighbor_.takePrinter(); // propagate
  }
}
```

```
// initialization methods called only during start-up
synchronized void setNeighbor(PrintService n) {
  neighbor_ = n;
}

synchronized void givePrinter(Printer p) {
  printer_ = p;
}

// Sample code to initialize a ring of new services
public static void startUpServices(int nServices, Printer p)
 throws IllegalArgumentAxception {

  if (nServices <= 0 || p == null)
    throw new IllegalArgumentException();

  PrintService first = new PrintService();
  PrintService pred = first;

  for (int i = 1; i < nServices; ++i) {
    PrintService s = new PrintService();
    s.setNeighbor(pred);
    pred = s;
  }

  first.setNeighbor(pred);
  first.givePrinter(p);
}

}
```

2.4.1.4 *Resource Variables*

It is difficult to see the transfer conventions embedded in the PrintService class. One way to make these protocols more concrete is to encapsulate them in classes such as the following ResourceVariable class. Instances of this class are in essence one-slot buffers that can be used instead of instance variables in other classes.

This minimal version defines only the exchange method, which turns out to suffice to implement most of the others. For example, a take can be implemented by exchange(null). Instances of this class could be used, for example, in a reworked version of PrintService in which each instance maintains a ResourceVariable holding the Printer rather than a direct reference.

```
public class ResourceVariable {
  protected Object ref_;

  public ResourceVariable(Object res) {
    ref_ = res;
  }

  public synchronized Object resource() {
    return ref_;
  }

  public synchronized Object exchange(Object r) {
    Object old = ref_;
    ref_ = r;
    return old;
  }
}
```

As discussed in Chapter 7, this design can also be generalized to accommodate resource *pools* that manage groups of resources in a collection.

2.4.1.5 *Finalization*

Series of ownership transfers often take the form of *sessions* in which:

- Owner a acquires Resource r and uses it.

- Owner a gives r to Owner b, which uses it.

- ...

- Owner y gives r to Owner z, which uses it and then forgets it.

Session traces start with an acquire, contain any number of uses, and end with a forget. For example, this may apply to a program in which r is a file, acquiring corresponds to opening it, and the uses are reads.

Session-based designs introduce the complicating factor of tracking and controlling the ultimate need for depletion and reclamation of forgotten resources. For example, in the case of files, the final forget should cause the file to be closed. But because of the garbage collection facilities in Java, you do not have to explicitly arrange to do this in the Owner methods themselves.

Java provides an extension to basic garbage-collection facilities, *finalization*, that can be used to arrange depletion-related cleanup activities of any kind, as long as they can be triggered by the fact that the resource is not being referenced by any other live object. (This is the same condition that allows the collector to reclaim memory.) Any code that needs to be performed at garbage-collection time may be defined by overriding Object.finalize in the Resource class itself.

This code is executed prior to reclamation of the memory occupied by the object. For example, a `finalize` method might take the form:

```
class PrinterV2 {
  protected RemoteSpoolerConnection spooler_;
  // ...

  protected void finalize() throws Throwable {
    super.finalize()
    spooler_.removePrintQueue(myMachineID);
  }

}
```

Careful use of references is the strategy of choice for most resource control problems in Java. Simple conventions normally suffice. Any object that maintains an instance variable referencing another object should set it to `null` when the object is no longer needed. As a nice byproduct of this practice, nullness of instance variables often serves as an easy way to test logical state.

2.5 Further Readings

Multithreaded safety is only one aspect of system safety. For a broader perspective, see:

Leveson, Nancy. *Safeware: System Safety and Computers*, Addison-Wesley, 1995.

The Hermes programming language pioneered several language constructs and techniques for structuring concurrent and distributed programs, including reference transfer as a primitive. See:

Strom, Robert, David Bacon, Arthur Goldberg, Andy Lowry, Daniel Yellin, and Shaula Yemini. *Hermes: A Language for Distributed Computing*, Prentice Hall, 1991.

The Spring OO operating system interface definition language embedded similar reference-passing policies as argument qualifiers for methods. See:

A Spring Collection, SunSoft Press, 1994.

Techniques based on unique references have also played roles in other OO design and analysis methods. See, for example:

Hogg, John. "Islands: Aliasing protection in object-oriented languages". *OOPSLA 91 Proceedings*, ACM, 1991.

Hogg, John, Doug Lea, R. C. Holt, Alan Wills, and Dennis de Champeaux. "The Geneva Convention on the Treatment of Object Aliasing", *OOPS Messenger*, April 1992.

CHAPTER 3

Liveness

DESIGNS based on combinations of immutable objects, fully synchronized objects, and strictly contained composites constitute the simplest, safest, and most understandable approaches to concurrent OO software development. Unfortunately, these are not always the *best* possible design strategies. Any use of synchronization can lead to liveness problems. This chapter introduces ways to avoid and solve them.

3.1 Liveness Failures

Liveness problems are just as serious as safety problems, yet can be harder to identify and avoid at design time. Most liveness issues stem from "action at a distance" — the interactions of multiple threads operating across multiple objects. There are four interrelated senses in which one or more threads in a concurrent Java program can fail to be live:

Contention. A thread fails to run even though it is in a runnable state because another thread, or even a completely separate program running on the same computer, has taken over CPU resources. (Failure to run because of contention is frequently called *starvation* or *indefinite postponement*, although the terms are sometimes used in relation to other liveness problems as well.)

Dormancy. A non-runnable thread fails to become runnable. In Java, this occurs when a `suspend` is never balanced by a `resume`, and when a `wait` is never balanced by a `notify` or `notifyAll`. (Similar problems, due to the same underlying mechanics, may occur with `join`.)

Deadlock. Two or more threads block each other in a vicious cycle while trying to access synchronization locks needed to continue their activities.

Premature termination. A thread is killed via `stop` or otherwise terminated before it should be.

Liveness properties are more context-dependent than safety properties. It is usually possible to design components to be safe across *all* possible contexts. For example, a synchronized method that refuses to commence until it possesses the synchronization lock will do so no matter how it is used. But it can be much more challenging to design components to be live across different contexts. Two components that are each live when used in other contexts may fail to be live when used together in certain ways.

Liveness problems can also be viewed as extreme cases of *efficiency* (run-time performance) concerns. An activity that is not running at all is surely not very efficient! In practice, the two tend to go hand in hand: eliminating liveness problems usually improves other aspects of performance as well. In particular, calls to `synchronized` methods are slower than those to unsynchronized methods in current Java run-time implementations. Eliminating the need for synchronization in frequently called methods can be a useful hand-optimization even in the absence of other liveness concerns. Also, overly conservative or coarse-grained synchronization policies can cause threads to block and unblock needlessly, reducing performance.

3.1.1 Deadlock

Liveness problems can take many different forms, and will be encountered in many contexts throughout the remainder of this book. Among the most central and subtle liveness failures is deadlock. Without care, just about any design using synchronization on multiple cooperating objects can contain the possibility of deadlock. To illustrate, consider a `Document` class in which each `Document` communicates with others for purposes of printing a complete composite document:

```
class Document { // oversimplified fragments
  Document otherPart_; // for simplicity, only one other part

  synchronized void print() { // print this part
    System.out.println("first line");
    // ... lots more printing ...
    System.out.println("last line");
  }

  synchronized void printAll() { // print all parts
    // (In a more useful version, printing order would be
    //    based on content.)
    otherPart_.print();
    print();
  }
}
```

Suppose that there are two threads, one involving Document `letter` and the other Document `enclosure`, where each refers to the other as its `otherPart`, and that both threads start executing `printAll`.

If none of these methods were `synchronized`, then you'd probably get unusable garbage as output. Statements in the two `print` methods could be randomly interleaved. This cannot happen with synchronization, but you could instead encounter deadlock if an actual execution trace were, for example:

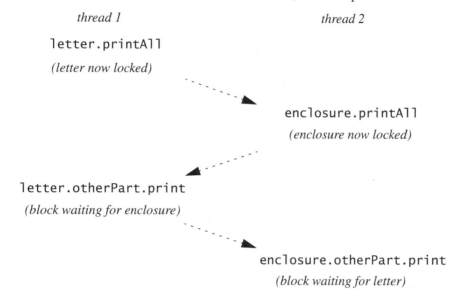

thread 1

`letter.printAll`

(letter now locked)

thread 2

`enclosure.printAll`

(enclosure now locked)

`letter.otherPart.print`

(block waiting for enclosure)

`enclosure.otherPart.print`

(block waiting for letter)

At this point each thread blocks forever, waiting for the lock already held by the other thread.

Although the `Document` class is safe in the sense that the printing methods never generate garbage output, the fact that they may produce no output at all is unsettling at best, in part because the problem is so well hidden. Concurrent designs permit execution scenarios that you probably wouldn't think of if you were thinking in terms of purely sequential programming. These sometimes include scenarios that result in deadlock.

In general, deadlock may be possible in any design containing a cycle of references among objects; for example, from `letter` to `enclosure` and back. Of course, it is the invocation sequence, not the references themselves that causes deadlock. But most references exist in OO programs to make communication possible via method calls. Cycles of references are common and normally problem-free in sequential OO designs, but usually require special care in concurrent OO designs.

3.1.2 Balancing Forces

Liveness and efficiency concerns can be so great in practice as to cause developers to recklessly ignore safety problems by leaving out synchronization and hoping for the best. Better approaches exist. In fact, there are two complementary approaches to class design that tend to balance safety and liveness concerns:

Top-down (safety first). Initially design methods and classes assuming full synchronization (when applicable), and then remove unnecessary synchronization as needed to obtain liveness and efficiency. From a top-down view, removing unnecessary synchronization can be thought of as an optimization similar to any other performance enhancement, that should be attempted only after safety and correctness have been ascertained.

Bottom-up (liveness first). Initially design methods and classes without concern for synchronization policies, and then add them via composites, subclassing, and related layering techniques. This provides opportunities to impose multiple special-purpose synchronization policies on top of base mechanisms, and to ensure that compatible policies are used among cooperating sets of objects.

There are very good reasons for taking either approach, or some of each. Beyond matters of preference, design contexts often dictate which of these tactics to take. For example, nearly all guarded methods (see Chapter 4) must be synchronized anyway, often leading to a top-down approach. Conversely, several special-purpose synchronization policies (see Chapter 5) intrinsically take a layered form, leading to a bottom-up approach.

From either direction, the goal is to assure liveness across the largest possible set of contexts without sacrificing safety. Since the main source of liveness problems is synchronization, live solutions typically avoid as much synchronization as possible, and limit synchronization to the smallest units of granularity necessary to preserve correct functionality. But the extreme solution of using no synchronization at all limits applicability to a single context — purely sequential applications.

3.1.2.1 *Reusability*

A reusable component is one that can be used and/or extended in many different contexts. Every component in a system is directly employed by one or more other components and ultimately by system users. Components are reusable if they can be employed by many others, even those the original author did not have in mind.

Liveness considerations in concurrent software development introduce context dependencies that can make the construction of reusable components harder than in strictly sequential settings.

One reaction to this issue is to restrict concurrency to *closed* systems. A closed design is one in which you have full knowledge and control of the entire execution context of all objects and classes. Often, the very first solution to a concurrency problem that you think of is a closed design that works only in a very narrow range of contexts. When these designs represent entire self-contained systems, then you do not have to worry much: you may be able to know enough about the context in which each object is used not to bother thinking through the consequences of other potential interactions. This works only until you try to reuse or compose the code in some other program.

There *are* sequential and concurrent design problems that are so tricky to solve, or in which efficiency pressures and the like are so great that the best you can do is come up with a fully closed, one-shot design. But you can usually do much better by establishing *policies* that hold across all components in a given framework or package.

Common policies form the basis for constructing the building blocks for entire suites of applications or *open systems* (residing for example on the World Wide Web), in which just about any object can be used just about anywhere so long as it obeys common policies. The attractions of design for open systems are just too great to ignore. Closed systems by nature are sooner or later just thrown away; often sooner. Without opportunities for extension or evolution, they cannot adapt to the ever-changing situations they find themselves in.

Common policies for dealing with *distributed* liveness failures (as opposed to those that occur in single concurrent programs) are familiar to anyone who has used the Internet. Distributed systems can fail to be live for all sorts of unpreventable reasons: machines crash, name-servers fail, communication lines become saturated, and so on. In concurrent programs, liveness problems are more often strictly preventable via use of special design policies that preclude, for example, deadlock among all components that obey a given policy.

3.1.2.2 *Criteria*

"Openness" and "reusability" are relative terms. There is no universal policy governing all possible components and applications for the World Wide Web or most other open systems. Implementation constraints surrounding any component can further limit its fitness for particular uses.

Different design patterns and their implementations rank better or worse on reusability criteria such as the ones listed below. Metrics for such attributes are notoriously hard to come by, and are usually an issue only in their negative senses, for example when trying to use a class that turns out to require fifty others that you don't want and can't use.

Lack of coupling. Usefulness as a standalone entity, without requiring other special classes or capabilities.

Tunability. Ability to dynamically alter policies and implementations.

Utility. Providing services that other components actually need, and delivering these services in the way they are needed.

Interoperability. Separating abstract functionality from implementation details, allowing functionality to be implemented in more than one way.

Extensibility. Structuring via interfaces and classes that allow others to define variants and extensions.

Regularity. Reliance on simple policies governing couplings and communication.

Locality. Lack of uncontrolled interaction with other visible objects. For example, use of private instance variables, security measures, and final classes that ensure that variables and objects are used only for particular purposes. This isolates aspects of a design that must be implemented in closed system mode while still allowing wider reuse of the resulting functionality.

Robustness. Safely performing even under various kinds of abuse.

Documentation. Making clear those policies, constraints, and applicability limitations that cannot be expressed directly in Java code itself, but must be made known through documentation.

Many of the design patterns and techniques discussed in the remainder of this book present specific policy-based solutions that balance conflicts surrounding safety, liveness, and reusability. The remainder of this chapter introduces two techniques that may be applicable just about anywhere, analyzing instance variable usage and splitting synchronization. Each can lead to the removal or reduction of synchronization that is not strictly necessary for correct functionality, and can thus avoid synchronization-induced liveness and efficiency problems across a wide range of contexts.

3.2 Instance Variable Analysis

At the bottommost levels of execution, synchronization exists to protect storage locations serving as variables. Opportunities for loosening synchronization can sometimes be found by examining constraints on instance variables and the methods using them to determine whether this protection is actually required.

3.2.1 Accessors

Some liveness problems can be solved just by defining as unsynchronized one or more *accessors* to mutable variables. An accessor is a method that reveals the value of an instance variable or a related *derived attribute* — a stateless expression on an instance variable.

Accessors need not be marked as `synchronized` whenever there is no possibility of a read/write conflict for the instance variables being reported on. Except for immutable variables, you need to track usage patterns and constraints in order to determine the need for synchronization. Necessary conditions for leaving accessors unsynchronized include:

- The variable can never take on illegal transient values in the midst of other methods, and so always holds a meaningful, reportable value. This might apply, for example, to the variables holding the temperature and velocity in a `Particle` class. It generally rules out variables holding values that are constrained with respect to any other variables that can be updated separately.

- The variable must be atomically assignable. In Java, this *excludes* variables of type `double` and `long`. The Java language specification allows access and storage of these values (but not those of other scalar types) to be non-atomic. An accessor reading a `double` that is being assigned by two threads could return a value that is not equal to either of the two written values.

3.2.2 Updates

A method that assigns a value to an instance variable should normally be synchronized to ensure that consistent values can be read via accessor methods, as well as to prevent write/write conflicts among multiple updates. Synchronization is not needed on an update method if, in *addition* to the conditions for defining accessors as unsynchronized, the following hold:

- Values of the variable remain legal and meaningful across all possible interleavings of all possible methods that could read and write them. For example, this is sometimes true of variables representing the states of external phenomena (such as the current temperature) in objects that constantly update them with current best estimates.

- No special synchronized actions need to be performed when the variable changes to particular values. This generally excludes variables used in guarded methods (see Chapter 4).

3.2.3   Removing Synchronization

When applying instance variable analyses, it is still a good idea to restrict access to *methods* rather than simply making the variables themselves `public`, which hampers extensibility through subclassing. Access or updates to an instance variable that needs no synchronization in a base class might need synchronization in a subclass. For example, a variable that happens to be unassigned (as opposed to one that is intrinsically designed to be fixed) in superclass methods might be updated in subclass methods. If access is controlled through a method, subclass authors have a chance to cope by overriding the method as `synchronized`. Even so, subclass authors need to know that doing so may reintroduce the liveness or efficiency problems that unsynchronized access was intended to solve.

Removal of synchronization from a class originally designed to be fully synchronized requires a great deal of care. The use of Java synchronization constructs is not a strictly local method-by-method or variable-by-variable matter, but must instead be planned out on a per-class basis, or even for several classes at a time.

When you restrict classes to those in which all methods are synchronized, you don't have to worry about potential interactions between synchronized and unsynchronized code. But when classes contain mixtures of synchronized and unsynchronized code, `synchronized` does *not* mean *atomic*. If one method, say `methodA`, relies on exclusive control but does not have it because there is a another unsynchronized method, say `methodB`, then nothing can be guaranteed about `methodA` in those cases where actions in `methodB` co-occur. When co-occurrences are rare and unforeseen, errors arise that can be almost impossible to diagnose.

Seen from the opposite perspective, failing to list one method as `synchronized` can limit the other kinds of methods you allow yourself or others to write in the class or its subclasses. Classes that mix synchronized and unsynchronized code should contain annotations or comments that describe the execution context the each method relies on (in particular, requiring full exclusive access).

It is just wrong to instead rely on the assumption that two threads are unlikely to interfere because, for example, the first updates a variable immediately upon starting while the second must do a lot of computation before it can use the variable. The problem with this line of thought is that scheduling is largely nondeterministic. Estimates of computation are not always reliable indicators of relative rates of progress. Setting up any such *race condition* among threads almost always eventually leads to safety violations. This observation leads to some ground rules for portable concurrent program design:

- Never make assumptions about relative rates of progress among threads.

- Assume that execution of any thread can be preempted at any point.

3.2.3.1 *Volatile Variables*

When mixing synchronized and unsynchronized accesses to variables, you may need to explicitly disable otherwise legal Java optimizations. Unless a variable is marked as `volatile`, the Java compiler and run-time system are allowed to assume that two references to the same, unassigned instance variable in the same method are associated with the same value. This optimization is sensible and desirable for classes with code that is always executed in a single-threaded manner. It also applies in fully synchronized classes, but sometimes not for classes with combinations of synchronized and unsynchronized update methods. The principal cases in which variables should be marked as `volatile` are:

- Instance variables that are used in `native` methods, in which case marking as `volatile` is the best you can do.

- Instance variables accessed in *busy-wait* loops (see Chapter 4), in which case the declarations force reloading of values that could have been changed by other threads between iterations of the loop.

3.2.3.2 *Unsynchronized Accessors*

In practice, synchronization for accessors can be lifted reasonably often, but each case requires individual analysis. To illustrate, consider again the `ExpandableArray` class from Chapter 2:

```
public class ExpandableArray { // repeated from Chapter 2
  private Object[] data_; // the elements
  private int size_; // the number of slots used in the array

  public ExpandableArray(int cap) {
    data_ = new Object[cap];
    size_ = 0;
  }

  public synchronized int size() { // synch?
    return size_;
  }

  public synchronized Object at(int i) // subscripted access
   throws NoSuchElementException {
    if (i < 0 || i >= size_ )
      throw new NoSuchElementException();
    else
      return data_[i];
  }
```

```
public synchronized void append(Object x) { // add at end
  if (size_ >= data_.length) { // need a bigger array
    Object[] olddata = data_;
    data_ = new Object[3 * (size_ + 1) / 2];
    for (int i = 0; i < size_; ++i)
      data_[i] = olddata[i];
  }
  data_[size_++] = x;
}

public synchronized void removeLast()
  throws NoSuchElementException {
  if (size_ == 0)
    throw new NoSuchElementException();
  else
    data_[--size_] = null;
  }
}
```

The size accessor for the size_ variable need not be synchronized. So long as the size method always returns an *accurate* value — a legal value that reflects the current state of the object — there is no compelling reason to require that it return a *stable* value — one that holds while the object is in execution state *Ready* (not engaged in any action).

Here, all the other methods guarantee that the size_ variable always holds the number of elements that have been fully appended but not fully removed. (Note that ascertaining this fact requires examination of all methods in the class.) This would not be true if, for example, the size_ variable were temporarily set to a negative number in append as a special internal flag indicating that the array was being expanded.

Declaring the size accessor as unsynchronized thus limits internal usage to code that keeps the variable consistent. This decision should be recorded as a policy constraint in class documentation so that subclass authors either obey the constraint or override the accessor method.

If the size method is not synchronized, then it may sometimes report a transient value that is about to be incremented in append or decremented in removeLast. But this cannot matter to clients. While clients might conceptually desire a size accessor that returns a stable value, there is not anything they could do with it that they could not also do with an unsynchronized accessor obeying these weaker semantics. For example, consider a loop traversing ExpandableArray x:

```
for (int i = x.size() - 1; i >= 0; --i)
  System.out.println(x.at(i));
```

Regardless of synchronization, this loop cannot be guaranteed to work as naively intended unless the object performing the loop has some special assurance that no other object or thread has access to the array. The loop could fail (throwing `NoSuchElementException` in `at`) if another object in another thread removed an element in the course of traversal, and could fail to print all elements if one was appended during traversal.

The only conceivable differences between use of a stable versus unsynchronized accessor here are statistical. Since execution of an unsynchronized accessor may overlap with update operations, there could in some applications be a slightly higher probability of an exception or incomplete traversal. But again, this cannot change the way clients use the class.

In contrast, there is little room to question the decision to synchronize the indexed accessor `at`. If method `at` were to execute in some interleaved fashion with `removeLast`, it might, for example, fail to raise an exception when it should. Weakening semantics to allow such behavior would cause the class to be useless.

3.2.3.3 *Regrouping*

Instance variable analysis must be based on the intended semantics of a class, not just the types of its instance variables. For example, in some applications an `int`-based `Point` class needs no special synchronization: you can rest on the atomicity guarantees of elementary `int` operations to preclude low-level conflicts when accessing and updating x-values and y-values.

But consider a `Dot` class that maintains a movable (x,y) location in which it is important to ensure that the pairs always represent a location to which the `Dot` has actually been moved. Observers of `Dots` should not be allowed to access the individually represented x and y values independently. Two statements reading x and y might be interleaved with a `moveTo` call from another thread, causing the observer to have the x-value from one location but the y-value from another. One solution to this is to regroup the underlying instance variables.

The presence or absence of synchronization on individual methods does not always itself address this kind of problem. However, when you encounter such value dependencies among underlying instance variables, you can split out the representation of these variables into a separate, special-purpose abstract data type class with instances that at all times hold consistent sets of values. If instances of this class are immutable, accessor methods need not be synchronized.

To set this up, given some class `Host`:

- Define an immutable class, say `Value`, holding the variables of interest, read-only accessors, and a constructor that initializes all fields.

- In the `Host` class, define:

- An instance variable, say `val`, referencing a `Value`.

- A method, say `updateValue(Value v)`, that atomically attaches a new instance of `Value` to `val`.

- A method, say `Value value()`, that reports the current value.

- To ensure full consistency in all other internal and external usages, access the variables maintained in the `Value` by first assigning to a local, as in `Value current = value()`, and then accessing fields from it. This ensures that all reads access fields of the same value set.

For example, a `Dot` class can rely on an immutable `Point` class to maintain its location value:

```
public class Point { // immutable version
  private int x_,  y_; // fixed

  public Point(int x, int y) {
    x_ = x;
    y_ = y;
  }

  public int x() {
    return x_;
  }

  public int y() {
    return y_;
  }
}

public class Dot {
  protected Point loc_;

  public Dot(int x, int y) {
    loc_ = new Point(x, y);
  }

  public Point location() {
    return loc_;
  }

  // all location assignments go through updateLoc
  protected synchronized void updateLoc(Point newLoc) {
    loc_ = newLoc;
  }
```

```
  public synchronized void moveTo(int x, int y) {
    updateLoc(new Point(x, y));
  }

  public synchronized void shiftX(int deltaX) {
    Point currentLoc = location();
    updateLoc(new Point(currentLoc.x() + deltaX,
                        currentLoc.y()));
  }
}
```

3.2.3.4 *Limitations*

As illustrated by the following example, instance variable analysis by itself is not always the path to solving liveness problems. Suppose you have cells of the form:

```
public class Cell {
  private int value_;

  public synchronized int  getValue() {
    return value_;
  }

  public synchronized void setValue(int v) {
    value_ = v;
  }

  public synchronized void swapContents(Cell other) {
    int newValue = other.getValue(); // (*)
    other.setValue(getValue());
    setValue(newValue);
  }

}
```

This class contains a potential liveness problem: it is possible to construct a set of `Cell`s running in different threads so that two of them, say x and y, will deadlock. For example, if both try to execute line (*) at about the same time, then x will have exclusive control of itself while trying to get control of y (to execute its `setValue` method), and y will be in the opposite situation. Neither can make any progress; both will stall forever.

One (somewhat questionable) approach to eliminating this problem is just to use raw unsynchronized access and assignment to the `value` field in `swapContents`. This stems from the reasoning that in the case of two contending `swapContents` calls, any of the possible outcomes of unsynchronized access and assignment are permissible. That is, for `Cells` x and y, all of the following are valid, both after and in the midst of the `swapContents` method:

- x holds y's previous value and y holds x's previous value.

- Both x and y hold x's previous value.

- Both x and y hold y's previous value.

- x and/or y hold values that are set (and/or read) by threads performing `set-Value` in the midst of those performing `swapContents`.

The conditions under which this would be acceptable seem limited, because of the impact of the decision on the normal `getValue` and `setValue` methods. Users of these methods no longer have any assurance about their atomicity with respect to other conceptually atomic operations. While decisions such as this are indeed sometimes acceptable, more widely applicable solutions to this kind of problem exist (see Chapter 8).

3.3 Splitting Synchronization

When the representations and/or behavior of one class can be partitioned into independent, non-interacting (or just non-conflicting) subsets, it is almost always worth refactoring the class to use distinct finer-granularity helper objects whose actions are delegated by the host.

This rule of thumb holds in object-oriented design generally. But it carries much more force in concurrent OO programming. A set of `synchronized` operations might deadlock or present other liveness or lock-based performance problems if they were all waiting for the single synchronization lock associated with a single object. But they might be deadlock-free and/or run more efficiently if they are waiting on multiple distinct locks. As a general rule, the more finely you can subdivide the intrinsic synchronization of a given class, the better will be its liveness properties across a wider range of contexts.

3.3.1 Splitting Classes

Consider a simplified `Shape` class that maintains both location and dimension information, along with time-consuming methods `adjustLocation` and `adjust-Dimensions` that independently alter them:

```
public class Shape {
  protected double x_ =  0.0;
  protected double y_ = 0.0;
  protected double width_ = 0.0;
  protected double height_ = 0.0;

  public synchronized double x() {
    return x_;
  }

  public synchronized double y() {
    return y_;
  }

  public synchronized double width() {
    return width_;
  }

  public synchronized double height() {
    return height_;
  }
}
  public synchronized void adjustLocation() {
    x_ = longCalculation1();
    y_ = longCalculation2();
  }

  public synchronized void adjustDimensions() {
    width_ = longCalculation3();
    height_ = longCalculation4();
  }

  protected double longCalculation1() { /* ... */ }
  // ...

}
```

Under the (possibly false in practice) assumptions that `adjustLocation`
never deals with dimension information and `adjustDimensions` never deals with
location, better performance could be obtained by revising this class so that callers
of `adjustLocation` do not have to wait for those calling `adjustDimensions` and
vice versa.

3.3.1.1 *Design Steps*

Splitting classes to reduce granularity is a straightforward exercise in class refactoring:

- Partition some functionality of a `Host` class into a standalone class, say `Helper`.

- In the `Host` class, declare a fixed unique instance variable referencing a helper that is initialized to a new `Helper` in the constructor. (In other words, strictly contain each helper in its host.)

- In the `Host` class, forward all appropriate methods to the `Helper` using unsynchronized methods. This works because the methods are stateless with respect to the `Host` class.

The most extreme result of these steps is a *Pass-Through Host* design in which *all* messages are relayed via unsynchronized methods:

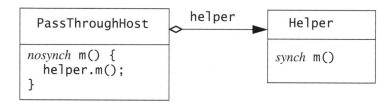

While similar in appearance, this unsynched-host/synched-helper strategy is the opposite of the synched-host/unsynched-helper strategy used in containment designs (see Chapter 2). The conditions for and consequences of using the two forms are complementary:

- Containment hosts that synchronize and/or hide unsynchronized helpers can employ coarse-grained measures providing a single synchronized entry point to a body of unsynchronized code.

- Pass-through hosts enable more efficient usage of fine-grained synchronization measures. They minimize overhead and susceptibility to liveness problems when accessing independently synchronized operations.

For example, here is a pass-through version of the `Shape` class:

```
public class PassThroughShape {
  protected AdjustableLoc loc_ = new AdjustableLoc(0, 0);
  protected AdjustableDim dim_ = new AdjustableDim(0, 0)
  public double x() {
    return loc_.x();
  }

  public double y() {
    return loc_.y();
  }

  public double width() {
    return dim_.width();
  }

  public double height() {
    return dim_.height();
  }

  public void adjustLocation() {
    loc_.adjust();
  }

  public void adjustDimensions() {
    dim_.adjust();
  }
}

public class AdjustableLoc {
  protected double x_,  y_;
  public AdjustableLoc(double x, double y) {
    x_ = x;
    y_ = y;
  }

  public synchronized double x() {
    return x_;
  }

  public synchronized double y() {
    return y_;
  }

  public synchronized void adjust() {
    x_ = longCalculation1();
    y_ = longCalculation2();
  }
}

public class AdjustableDim { /* similar */ }
```

3.3.2 Splitting Locks

Even if you do not want to or cannot split a class, you can still split the synchronization locks associated with each subset of functionality. This technique is equivalent to one in which you first split a class into helpers, and then fold all representations and methods of the helpers *except* their synchronization locks back into the host class. However, there is no need to proceed in exactly this way.

Stripped of all but its synchronization lock, any class is reduced to just `java.lang.Object`. This fact accounts for the idiomatic Java practice of using `Object`s as synchronization aids.

To recover the underlying design whenever you see `Object`s used for synchronization locks in Java code, you might ask yourself what kind of helper object a particular lock is a stand-in for. In the case of lock-splitting, each `Object` controls access to a subset of methods. Each method in each subset is block-synchronized on a common lock object.

3.3.2.1 *Design Steps*

- For each independent subset of functionality, declare an object, say `lock`, initialized in the constructor for the `Host` class and never reassigned:

  ◆ The lock object can be of any subclass of class `Object`. If it will not be used for any other purpose, it might as well be of class `Object` itself.

  ◆ If a subset is uniquely associated with some existing object uniquely referenced from an instance variable, you may use that object as the lock.

  ◆ One of these locks can be associated with the `Host` object (`this`) itself.

- Declare all methods corresponding to each subset as unsynchronized, but surround all code with `synchronized(lock) { ... }`.

For example, here is a split version of the `Shape` class:

```
public class LockSplitShape {
  protected double x_ = 0.0;
  protected double y_ = 0.0;
  protected double width_ = 0.0;
  protected double height_ = 0.0;

  protected Object locationLock_ = new Object();
  protected Object dimensionLock_ = new Object();
```

```
  public double x() {
    synchronized(locationLock_) {
      return x_;
    }
  }

  public double y() {
    synchronized(locationLock_) {
      return y_;
    }
  }

  public void adjustLocation() {
    synchronized(locationLock_) {
      x_ = longCalculation1();
      y_ = longCalculation2();
    }
  }

  // and so on

}
```

3.3.2.2 *Linked Data Structures*

Lock-splitting techniques can minimize access contention to objects serving as entry points into linked data structures, by finding a middle ground between the extreme strategies of fully synchronizing the entry classes (which can limit concurrency unnecessarily) and fully synchronizing all the linked node objects being controlled (which can be inefficient and can even lead to liveness problems).

As with all lock-splitting techniques, the main goal is to associate different locks with different methods. But in the case of linked structures, this often leads to further adjustments in the data structures and algorithms themselves. There are no universally applicable recipes for splitting synchronization in classes controlling access to linked structures, but the following class illustrates some common tactics.

The TwoLockQueue class listed below can serve as a generic unbounded first-in/first-out queue. It maintains only two locks for the entire list, separating out synchronization for put and take. The first lock (implicitly using this as the lock via synchronized methods) is associated with accesses to the head of the list, which always exists in this implementation. After each take the previous first node becomes the header. The second lock protects insertions at the end of the list.

While both safe and efficient, this implementation has weaker semantics than most. Because they are separately synchronized, a take may claim there are no elements (return null) at times when a put has just started to add one.

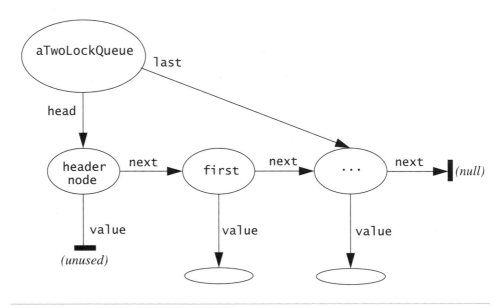

```java
public class TwoLockQueue {
  private TLQNode head_;     // pointer to dummy header node
  private TLQNode last_;     // pointer to last node
  private Object lastLock_;  // protect access to last

  public TwoLockQueue() {
    head_ = last_ = new TLQNode(null, null);
    lastLock_ = new Object();
  }

  public void put(Object x) {
    TLQNode node = new TLQNode(x, null);
    synchronized (lastLock_) {  // insert at end of list
      last_.next = node;
      last_ = node;
    }
  }

  public synchronized Object take() { // returns null if empty
    Object x = null; // return value
    TLQNode first = head_.next; // first real node is after head
    if (first != null) {
      x = first.value;
      head_ = first; // old first becomes new head
    }
    return x;
  }
}
```

```
final class TLQNode { // local node class for queue
  Object value;
  TLQNode next;

  TLQNode(Object x, TLQNode n) {
    value = x;
    next = n;
  }
}
```

3.4 Further Readings

A more formal approach to development is always to start out using design methods that, when flawlessly adhered to, ensure correctness by construction with respect to safety. Transformations can then be applied that improve liveness while provably preserving safety. Top-down class design methods using fully synchronized objects are the Java versions of the most common and usable design strategies along these lines. Accounts of more formal versions that apply in OO contexts are only starting to emerge. See, for example:

Jones. Cliff. "Accommodating Interference in the Formal Design of Concurrent Object-Based Programs", *Formal Methods in System Design*, March 1996.

The TwoLockQueue class is a Java adaptation of an algorithm described in:

Michael, Maged and Michael Scott, "Simple, fast, and practical non-blocking and blocking concurrent queue algorithms", *Proceedings, 15th ACM Symposium on Principles of Distributed Computing, ACM*, 1996.

CHAPTER 4

State-Dependent Action

ACTIONS performed by mutable objects generally have two kinds of triggering conditions:

External. The object receives a message from another object requesting that the action be performed.

Internal. The object is in an appropriate state to perform the action.

As a non-programming example, suppose you are asked to write down a telephone message. In order to do this, you need to have a pencil (or other writing implement).

Safety concerns for classes with state-dependent actions revolve around the considerations necessary to *complete* a design so that you take into account all possible combinations of messages and states, as in:

	have pencil	*do not have pencil*
phone ring	answer phone	answer phone
take message	write message	?

As hinted in the table, designs with state-dependent actions usually need to take account of situations in which the object is not in a state that permits any "normal" action. Or, said differently, actions may have state-based *preconditions* that need not always hold when clients invoke methods on the host object. Conversely, actions may have *postconditions* that are unattainable when the host object is not in a proper state, and/or when the actions of other objects it relies on fail to achieve their own postconditions due to their own state-based requirements.

In an ideal design, all methods would have no state-based preconditions and would always fulfill their postconditions. When sensible, classes and methods should be written in this fashion, thus avoiding all of the issues discussed in this chapter. But many methods are intrinsically state-dependent and just cannot be programmed to achieve postconditions in all states.

4.1 Policies

What should you do if you are asked to write down a phone number and do not have a pencil?

One possibility is simple *unconditional action*: try to proceed anyway, for example by moving your fingers as if you had a pencil whether you have one or not. This is not a very promising strategy unless neither you nor anyone else cares if you fail. In software, unconditional action corresponds to the use of *passive* preconditions — preconditions serving only as disclaimers. If the object is not in the proper state upon reception of the message, then nothing can be guaranteed about the results of the request. (Consider, for example, a request to step on a gas pedal in a car, or to open a valve in a power plant.)

When a host object neither checks its preconditions nor deals with failure, it can be used only when all possible clients know about and can cope with the conditions and byproducts surrounding method invocation. Clients must somehow know enough not to ask the object to perform actions when it is not in the right state, and/or must be prepared to deal with unannounced failure. Clients must be provided with enough information and control to carry this out. Unless you have magically smart tools that can check this automatically (which you don't), it is unlikely that such objects and classes will be very widely reusable across different contexts.

More defensible policies include:

Inaction. Ignoring the request after ascertaining that it cannot be performed.

Balking. Returning failure indications to clients if the requested action cannot be performed.

Guarded suspension. Suspending execution until preconditions become true; for example, waiting until someone hands you a pencil. This may also entail *planning* — determining and initiating a subaction to make preconditions true and suspending the main action until they are true (for example, asking someone to hand you a pencil).

Provisional action. Pretending to perform an action, but not committing to its effects until success is assured.

Rollback/Recovery. Trying to proceed, but upon failure, undoing the byproducts of partially completed actions. (Rollback usually refers to reverting back to the initial state. Recovery usually refers to attaining any comparable state.)

Retry. Repeatedly attempting failed actions after recovering from previous attempts.

Inaction, balking, guarded suspension (usually just called *guarding*), and planned subactions are often categorized as *check-and-act* or *pessimistic* (also called *conservative*) policies. Provisional action, rollback, recovery, and retry are *try-and-see* or *optimistic* policies. Various mixtures are also possible. For example, you could try to proceed but request that someone hand you a pencil if you fail. You could then do something else until someone does, ultimately ignoring the request if you wait too long. In the extreme, you might consult planning experts and invest considerable effort in devising an optimal set of actions.

As a rule of thumb, check-and-act policies lead to simpler and more reliable designs in most concurrent settings. The converse often holds in distributed settings where precondition checks cannot be relied on to preclude remote failure. But none of these policies are at all perfect or even always apply, which is why there are so many of them. Choices ranging from the dumbest to the smartest options can be defended on the basis of a number of situation-dependent considerations.

Decisions about these matters usually need to be made relatively early in the design of an application. Different policies introduce different context dependencies that can restrict ranges of applicability. Choices among policies impact method signatures, internal state representations, class relations, and client-visible protocols. It can be productive to step through these considerations to determine the range of reasonable policies that may apply to a given design problem.

Internal computability of preconditions. Can the host object detect state-based preconditions? This may not be possible when success relies on the actions of other independent objects that the host has no control over or is not even aware of. For example, a write to a file may fail if another concurrently executing program exhausts all disk space. Most file systems are constructed in a way that makes it impossible to guarantee that a write will succeed before actually trying it (although it is often feasible to *estimate* whether it will succeed). It is also possible to have preconditions that are not even logically computable, as well as situations in which an object knows that it cannot assess preconditions because it has detected that it is in an inconsistent state.

External computability of preconditions. Can clients and/or other objects know if the host object is in a state allowing action? Further, is there any way that clients can be sure that an object that has been checked to be in an appropriate state remains so when a subsequent message is issued? This is by no means automatically ensured in concurrent settings, where the host object may otherwise change state between the check and the request.

Cost of computing preconditions. Can preconditions be assessed easily? Determining the preconditions for an action can be computationally more expensive than just trying it and then coping with failures. This must also be balanced against the probability of failure and the cost of recovery.

Acceptability of request. Does the request make sense? Preconditions may include requirements that arguments to requests obey certain properties. For example, if the number you are asked to write down is not a conceivably legal phone number, you might refuse to comply on those grounds alone. Information about the origin of the request may also be considered: are you sure you want to be talking on the phone to this person?

Byproducts of assessing preconditions. Can preconditions be assessed without generating unwanted byproducts? If precondition checks are not stateless, they are at best difficult to cope with. If merely trying to assess an object's current state could change its state, then this would have to be dealt with first as a separate subproblem. On the other hand, there are times when information about a received message itself might alter state (for example, if a message carries an argument indicating its urgency) in a way that may be helpful in deciding what to do about this and/or other requests. The fact that a message has been received is sometimes a meaningful aspect of an object's state.

Reachability of preconditions. Is there some set of operations on the host object that can cause the preconditions to become true? For example, if a non-rewindable File object is asked to perform a read operation when it is at end of file, then there is no possibility that the action can ever succeed. Responsibility for reaching preconditions can be placed on either the host or the client. For example, can or should a File rewind itself in order to service a read request? Or should clients be required to request rewinds before reads?

Resource contention. Does the action require exclusive access to a software object or computing resource? For example, if there is only one pencil, do you have to wait your turn to use it? Will you ever get a turn?

Acceptability of indefinite suspension. Can the activity that invoked the method be allowed to suspend while waiting for preconditions to become true? Some methods are easier to use and control if they have *now-or-never* semantics. For example, if a client of a stream invokes a read operation when there is no input available, it normally does not want to wait until some other object in some other thread writes to the stream. The client would like to treat this as an error condition rather than waiting for input that may never arrive.

Productivity of suspension. Even though a state may be independently reachable, you may know that it could never be reached in the context in which the host object is operating. In particular, in purely sequential settings in which states never change asynchronously, it would be pointless to idly wait for them to change. Even in concurrent settings, this issue can be highly context-dependent. For example, when attempting to open a file, it hardly ever makes sense to wait for it to exist if it doesn't already exist. But every now and again, you might indeed want to wait out another thread that has not yet reached the point of creating a particular file.

Acceptability of failure. Can the action be allowed to fail? If so, would clients ever care about failure and thus need to be informed about it? Some kinds of clients intrinsically don't care about and don't even want to know about failure. For example, applets handling button-push events usually don't care if the actions corresponding to a button push fail since they play no role in these actions other than dispatching them.

Computability of failure. Can the host (or client) detect action failures? For example, it is easy for you to observe that trying to write down a message without a pencil does not have the intended effect, but perhaps impossible for a robot without a vision system.

Availability of multiple actions. Is there more than one way to satisfy the request? If there are several possible algorithms that may be applied, you can run them all (perhaps concurrently), hoping that at least one of them will not fail.

Acceptability of false alarms. Can the object rely on estimates of failure? For example, time-outs giving up on replies over a network may result from slow connections, not outright failures.

Recoverability. Can internal byproducts of failure be undone or uncommitted? If not, the host and/or other objects may enter inconsistent states, after which nothing can be guaranteed about the further behavior of the object or others that depend on it. If actions involve messages to other objects or ultimately affect external devices or systems, then these byproducts may not only be irrevocable, but may also have serious consequences for users.

Client recovery. Do clients need to take any special action upon failure? If so, are there provisions for doing so? Do objects other than clients need to know about and deal with failure as well?

Retryability. Can failed actions be retried internally or externally? If so, are retries more economical or desirable than suspension until success can be assured? Can you be sure that the retries will eventually succeed?

The remainder of this chapter deals with the design and implementation of methods and classes using the principal forms of these policies — guarded suspension, balking, and optimistic control. Chapter 5 describes some ways to establish different policies over the same base functionality.

4.2   Representing State

To cope with state-dependent actions, objects must be equipped with explicit representations of state in sufficient detail to prevent actions from occurring when they are not wanted, and/or taking evasive action when they fail.

State representation plays a more prominent role in pessimistic strategies. Most techniques center around the need to be able to assess state on *entry* to a method. It is possible, and sometimes even necessary, to structure methods so that checked state dependent actions occur in the middle of other processing. But it is simpler and more extensible to structure each method to check state on entry and conditionally perform a single dependent action.

To carry this out, all possible aspects of state that could ever need checking must be represented so they are available upon method entry. This is normally accomplished by relying upon instance variables that are needed anyway to perform the associated actions. However, concurrent objects tend to require more detailed state-tracking via instance variables than do sequential objects.

4.2.1   Interfaces

Interfaces provide scaffolding for defining abstract state and implementing the required representations. As a long-running example, here is an annotated interface describing counters. For the moment, we'll ignore questions of whether or how any of these methods can fail, so no exceptions are listed.

```
public interface BoundedCounter {
  public static final long MIN = 0;  // minimum allowed value
  public static final long MAX = 10; // maximum allowed value

  public long value(); // invariant: MIN <= value() <= MAX
                       // initial condition: value() == MIN

  public void inc();   // increment only when value() < MAX

  public void dec();   // decrement only when value() > MIN
}
```

Interfaces are useful vehicles for informally or semiformally specifying the desired behavioral *contract* of sets of operations and the policies governing their use. Because interfaces cannot reference code or instance variables, they force you to describe invariant properties and functionality in ways that help avoid the need for others to have to read implementation source code just to discover intent.

The idea here is that implementations of `BoundedCounter` are all obligated to maintain a `value` between `MIN` and `MAX`.[1] There is nothing in the Java declarations that specifically requires or enforces this, so these matters are left as annotations.

Invariants (sometimes called *monitor invariants*) such as the ones listed for `value` are surprisingly useful in guiding placement and use of concurrency constructs within implementation classes. Many concurrency control measures revolve around the semantic and structural relations inherent in a given abstract design. This gives even everyday concurrent programming practices a slightly more formal appearance than is usual in everyday sequential programming.

An implementation of this interface might maintain an internal instance variable, say `count`, which instances can use to assess whether they can perform an `inc` or `dec`. However, it is possible for action control in one object to depend on properties of other objects to which it in turn sends messages to assess state. For example, `BoundedCounter` could be implemented with a class that maintains a reference to a little helper object that maintains and reports the count value.

4.2.2 Logical State

Many objects maintain instance variables that together constitute a very large (or for all practical purposes infinite) state space, but maintain only a small finite logical state space for purposes of action control. For example, for purposes of `inc` and `dec`, `BoundedCounters` have only three logical states, not one state per value of their count:

State	Condition	inc	dec
top	`value == MAX`	no	yes
middle	`MIN < value < MAX`	yes	yes
bottom	`value == MIN`	yes	no

A bit of care is needed in characterizing these states. For example, if `MAX` is equal to `MIN+1`, then there is no distinct middle state. And if `MIN` is equal to `MAX`, then there is no way to distinguish top from bottom: neither method should ever fire.

Logical states are normally defined in terms of predicates — boolean expressions that distinguish particular ranges, values and/or other computable properties of instance variables, as seen in the table. They can be coded either as free-stand-

---

[1.] These are declared as `final` constants just for simplicity of illustration, and as `long` to allow easier generalization to any class that may require synchronized protection of instance variables.

ing internal boolean methods or simply as boolean conditions written inside methods relying on them. When state analysis becomes too big and unwieldy for such techniques, you can design and encode states using *StateCharts*, tables, decision trees, automata, and related tools of the trade for dealing with state machines (see the Further Readings).

4.2.2.1   *State variables*

Instead of relying on predicate expressions, you can represent logical state explicitly in a variable. Each distinct state can be labeled as an integer or any other discrete data type. The instance variable representing state must be re-evaluated upon each update so that it is always accurate. It is not strictly necessary to use a single variable: multiple variables can be used if object state can be partitioned on several independent dimensions. Common special cases include:

- *Role variables* control responses to all of a related set of methods (often those declared in a single interface). When objects may alternate among roles, a single variable may suffice to direct appropriate behavior. For example, an object may alternate between being a `Producer` and a `Consumer`. When in one role, it may ignore or delay responses to messages associated with the other.

- Rather than coding state as a value, you can code it as a reference to a *state-object*. For each state, write a class describing the behavior of the object when it is in that state. In the main class, create a reference instance variable, say `stateObject`, that is always bound to the appropriate state-object. This is an application of the *States as Objects* pattern described in the *Design Patterns* book; a variant is described in Chapter 8.

4.2.3   History and Execution State

Concise representations of logical state do not always suffice to implement state-dependent behavior. Action control can in principle be based on any aspect of an object's entire history, as well as that of any other object it might rely upon. The most extensive possible representation is a *history log*, recording all messages ever received and/or sent, along with all corresponding internal actions that have been initiated and/or completed. For example, some sort of message history log might be needed if you define a method that is triggered only if an object has not received the same request among its previous thirteen messages.

State encoding and even instance variables may be seen as optimized summaries of object histories that additionally encompass initial construction parameters. For example, in this sense, a `count` variable in a `BoundedCounter` implementation serves as a summary of the number of `inc` messages minus the number of `dec` messages processed, offset by the initial `MIN`.

It can be a challenge to balance design issues so that you maintain minimal, efficient representations, yet do not optimize away so much history that you cannot assess state accurately.

One compromise is to define *execution state variables* (sometimes known as *active state variables* and as particular forms of *meta-variables*). Execution state variables can represent the fact that a given message has been received, whether the corresponding action has been initiated, whether the action has terminated, and/or whether a reply to the message has been issued. The simplest and most common kind of execution state variable is a message counter, for example one recording the number of `inc` messages received.

Classes need to record enough state information to enable methods in expected subclasses to evaluate preconditions and postconditions. However, this is another matter of balance and judgment. For example, it would be silly for a class author to set up otherwise unused variables recording whether a certain message was received among its previous thirteen requests on the off chance that someone might want to build a subclass with a method relying on this condition. On the other hand, it would normally be a mistake for a class author not to provide `protected` (if necessary) accessors to internal logical state variables so that subclasses may specialize the ways in which they rely upon them.

4.3 Guarded Suspension

Guarded methods are those that block if the object is not in a state in which the associated actions can be executed:

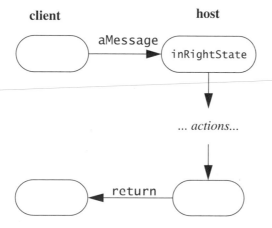

Guarded suspension plays a central role in concurrent software. This is reflected in the wide range of approaches to conceptualizing guards and in the many different notations and constructs available for designing concurrent software using guards. Before delving into Java implementation matters, it is worth stepping back to consider higher-level approaches and constructs that help organize designs relying on guarded suspension.

In one sense, guarded methods are customizable extensions of `synchronized` methods. The "guard" for a plain synchronized method is just that an object is in the *Ready* execution state. At the implementation level, this means that the current thread is in possession of the object's synchronization lock. Guarded methods further partition the *Ready* state by adding state-based conditions that are logically necessary for an action to proceed.

Guards may also be considered to be special forms of conditionals. In sequential programs, an `if` statement can check whether a condition holds upon entry to a method. When the condition is false, there is no point in waiting for it to be true; it can never become true since there are no other concurrent activities occurring in the program that could cause the condition to change. But in concurrent programs, asynchronous state changes happen all the time. Guarding can be thought of as an assertion that the required state changes will eventually occur; or if they do not, that it would be best never to proceed with the current activity. Guarded methods thus pose liveness issues that simple conditionals do not encounter.

Some high-level design methods express conditional waits using an `if`-like construct called WHEN, that can be useful in designing guarded methods. For example, here is a pidgin-Java version of a guarded counter class using WHEN:

```
pseudoclass BoundedCounterVW implements BoundedCounter {
  protected long count_ = MIN;

  public synchronized long value() {
    return count_;
  }

  public synchronized void inc() {
    WHEN (count_ < MAX)
      ++count_;
  }

  public synchronized void dec()
    WHEN (count_ > MIN)
      --count_;
  }

}
```

The idea here is that the BoundedCounter is obligated to keep the count value between MIN and MAX. If a dec message is received but the count cannot be decremented because it is already at MIN, the thread is blocked, resuming sometime later if and when the count becomes greater than MIN via an inc message performed by some other object running in some other thread.

Actions in guarded methods trigger only when both a certain message is received and the object is in a certain state. Because neither the message nor the state are necessarily primary, you might even conceptualize methods with the two parts inverted. This state-based style can be easier to use when logically designing classes in which several different methods are all triggered in the same states, for example when the object is assuming a particular role. This form also more clearly reflects state-based notations used in several popular high-level OO analysis and design methods.

Ada concurrency constructs can be used to express guards in this fashion. Expressed in Ada-like pidgin-Java, the BoundedCounter looks like:

```
pseudoclass BoundedCounterVAW implements BoundedCounter {
  protected long count_ = MIN;

  WHEN (true) ACCEPT public long value() {
    return count_;
  }

  WHEN (count_ < MAX) ACCEPT public void inc()  {
    ++count_;
  }

  WHEN (count_ > MIN) ACCEPT public void dec()  {
    --count_;
  }
}
```

In this sense, guarded methods define little localized *schedulers* in each object. Any Java object may itself control the conditions under which it initiates any requested task. This fact is exploited in the design of explicit schedulers, discussed in Chapter 8.

Going to the extreme, some designs are easier to reason about if you think of actions as *always* being requested, but triggering only when the object makes a state transition in to or out of a particular state. Some looping methods take this form. For example, you might design a special kind of counter with a continuously enabled mechanism that resets the count to zero whenever it reaches a certain value. This style is also seen in *concurrent constraint programming* (see Further Readings), where actions can only be triggered by state changes since there are no messages.

4.3.1 Implementation

There are at least as many ways to implement guarded methods in Java as there are ways to design them. But nearly all of these techniques can be considered as specializations of the following default strategy:

- For each condition that needs to be waited on, write a guarded `wait` loop.

- Ensure that every method causing state changes that affect the truth value of any waited-for condition invokes `notifyAll` to wake up any threads waiting for state changes.

This chapter deals with implementation options for designs in which both the conditions and actions for a method are managed by a single object. Considerations requiring the extensions presented in subsequent chapters are noted as they arise.

4.3.1.1 *Waits*

The standard coding idiom for expressing guarded waits is a simple `while` loop invoking `Object.wait`. To ensure that this is done correctly, it is sometimes helpful to encapsulate it in its own non-public method. For example:

```
public class GuardedClass { // generic code sketch
  protected boolean cond_ = false;

  protected synchronized void awaitCond() {
    while (!cond_) {
      try { wait(); }
      catch (InterruptedException ex) {}
    }
  }

  public synchronized void guardedAction() {
    awaitCond();
    // actions
  }

}
```

Except in very special cases, condition checks should always be placed in `while` loops. When an action is resumed, the waiting task doesn't know if the condition is actually true; it only knows that it has been woken up. So it must check again.

As a matter of programming practice, this style should be used even if the class contains only a single kind of wait, that waits for a single kind of condition. One reason is that otherwise, this code could fail just because some other unrelated object invoked `notifyAll` on the object by mistake. (These are `public` methods defined on all objects.) However, a more important consideration is that without re-evaluation, such code will start failing in peculiar ways if people define subclasses of your class that also use waits and notifications for other purposes.

Objects with guarded waits can be harder to think about than simple fully synchronized objects (Chapter 2). Methods with guarded waits are not completely atomic. A waiting method suspends without retaining its synchronization lock, thus allowing any other thread to begin executing any synchronized method on that object. (Other unsynchronized methods can still of course execute at any time.) Guarded methods need to be written so that objects are in consistent states upon entering `waits`. The simplest strategy for ensuring this stems from the general idea of using check-and-act policies. If you place guarded `waits` as the first statements of any method using them and do not change state in the process of checking it, then you cannot have changed state in any inconsistent way when entering the `wait`.

4.3.1.2 *Busy-Waits*

Implementing guards via `wait` is nearly always superior to the alternative of using a busy-wait "spin loop" of the form:

```
protected void spinWaitUntilCond() {
  while (!cond_)
    Thread.currentThread().yield();
}
```

Busy-waits have drawbacks that make them poor choices for implementing most guarded actions. The contrasts between the two techniques help explain why `wait` is defined in the way it is:

- Busy-waits can waste an unbounded amount of CPU time spinning uselessly. The `wait`-based version rechecks conditions only when some other thread provides a notification that the object's state has changed, thus possibly affecting the guard condition. Even if notifications are sometimes sent when enabling conditions do not hold, conditions are likely to be unproductively rechecked far less often than in a spin loop that continually, blindly rechecks.

- The `yield` in the spin-loop version is not guaranteed effective in allowing other threads to execute so they can change the condition. For example, if the spinning task is running at a high priority but the threads that change the condition run at low priority, the spinning task will still crowd out the others. In the `wait`-based version, the waiting task does not run at all, so cannot encounter such scheduling problems. (Although other scheduling problems can of course still arise; see Chapter 6.)

- Busy waits can miss opportunities to fire if they happen not to be scheduled to execute during times when the condition is momentarily true. Relying on conditions that are true only momentarily often leads to fragile constructions, but the need to do so does sometimes arise. The `wait`-based version always (eventually) executes when notified. The condition may still have changed if more than one thread waiting on the condition wakes up and changes the condition before others do. However, given reasonable priority assignments, all threads are guaranteed an opportunity to check. On the other hand, neither technique alone automatically guarantees *fairness* — that each potentially enabled thread will eventually proceed. It could so happen that one particular looping thread that repeatedly encounters the guard is always the one that proceeds, starving out all others.

- It is difficult (sometimes even impossible) to synchronize spin loops in the desired manner. For example, it would almost always be wrong to declare the method `spinUntilCond` as `synchronized`, since this would not allow any other `synchronized` method to change the condition. However, without synchronization, it is awkward at best to arrange that the object remains in the same state between the condition test and the associated action. The `wait`-based version automatically (via the Java run-time system) relinquishes the synchronization lock (for the host object only) upon `wait` and re-obtains the lock upon waking up. This is one reason that `wait` statements can be used only under synchronization. However, the fact that waiting tasks hold any locks at all can be the source of logistical difficulties, including the *nested monitor problem* discussed later in this chapter.

- Instance variables used in evaluating busy-wait conditions normally need to be marked as `volatile` (see Chapter 3).

4.3.1.3   *Interruptions*

In most respects, waking up from a `wait` is just like receiving control back from a method call. Waits and notifications are somewhat analogous to calls and returns. A guarded wait can be viewed as if it were an undirected call to objects running in other threads asking them to take any action at all that makes the condition true. A notification serves as a signal that the desired condition may have been attained.

In Java, this analogy is made stronger by the fact that a `wait` can also be broken by an `InterruptedException` caused by some object invoking `Thread.interrupt`. Interruptions can serve as notifications indicating that the required state changes can never occur, for example due to termination of certain threads. Possible responses to interruptions include:

- Ignore them (by re-evaluating the condition and re-waiting), which at least preserves safety at the possible expense of liveness. Most examples in this book use this option, mainly just for simplicity.

- Terminate the current thread (via `stop`). This also preserves safety, but in an inelegant (at best!) fashion.

- Exit the method, perhaps kicking the exception up to some caller that is prepared to handle it. This preserves liveness but may require that other objects re-establish consistent states to preserve safety.

- Take some pre-planned action; for example, perform some kind of cleanup and restart the main action of the program.

- Ask for user intervention before taking further action.

4.3.1.4 *Notifications*

Wait-based constructions make up the bulk of the safety side of guard translation. The first step to ensure liveness is to insert code that wakes up waiting threads when the conditions they are waiting for change value. Every time the value of any variable or object mentioned in a guard changes in a way that might affect the truth value of the condition, waiting tasks should be woken up so they can recheck guard conditions. The simplest way to do this is just to insert `notifyAll` in methods that cause state changes. In turn, the simplest way to do this is to define non-public utility methods that encapsulate assignment, issuing a notification upon any change in value.

Encapsulating assignments to instance variables representing logical state is a worthwhile practice even when not accompanied by notifications. Even if a base class does not require notifications of particular changes to an instance variable, subclass methods might, in which case they can override the assignment method to perform a `notifyAll`. Encapsulating assignment also helps prevent one of the most common programming errors in guard constructions, forgetting to call `notifyAll` when it is logically necessary. On the other hand, this may lead to too many useless signals and horrible performance (`notifyAll` is a relatively expensive operation) in classes that perform lots of assignments. However, as a design practice, it is sometimes a good idea to start out using blanket notifications within assignment methods, and then to minimize and reorganize them as discussed in the following sections and in later chapters.

For example, here is a first pass at implementing BoundedCounter:

```
public class BoundedCounterV0 implements BoundedCounter {
  protected long count_ = MIN;

  public synchronized long value() {
    return count_;
  }

  public synchronized void inc()  {
    awaitIncrementable();
    setCount(count_ + 1);
  }

  public synchronized void dec()  {
    awaitDecrementable();
    setCount(count_ - 1);
  }

  protected synchronized void setCount(long newValue) {
    count_ = newValue;
    notifyAll(); // wake up any thread depending on new value
  }

  protected synchronized void awaitIncrementable() {
    while (count_ >= MAX)
      try { wait(); } catch(InterruptedException ex) {};
  }

  protected synchronized void awaitDecrementable() {
    while (count_ <= MIN)
      try { wait(); } catch(InterruptedException ex) {};
  }

}
```

No matter how they are encapsulated, it is good practice always to place notifications as the final statement(s) of any method. This helps avoid having to think through the complexities that can occur when both the signaling method and the signaled task want to continue executing. When you cannot arrange to place notifications last, yet want to give unblocked threads a chance to run, you may be able to follow the notifyAll call with a yield, while also exiting any synchronized blocks held on the object.

4.3.1.5 *Single Notifications*

The BoundedCounterV0 class uses notifyAll because threads may be waiting either for the count to be greater than MIN or for it to be less than MAX. So it would not suffice to use notify, which only wakes up one thread (if one exists). The Java run-time system might pick a thread waiting for a condition that does not hold without picking the possibly many that could continue. However, notify can be used in designs in which:

- All possible waiting threads are necessarily waiting for conditions relying on the same notifications, usually the exact same condition.

- Each notification enables at most a single thread to continue. (Thus it would be useless to wake up others.)

A single notify is faster than notifyAll, and can be used to help improve performance when applicable. For example, in the AlternatingMessage-Printer class from Chapter 1, threads wait only for their turns. Each time a turn is taken, the turn changes. So even if multiple threads were for some reason generated, only one needs to be notified. This would, however, complicate construction of subclasses in which the conditions for using notify do not hold.

```
public class AlternatingMessagePrinter // from Chapter 1
            extends SimpleMessagePrinter {
  // ...

  public synchronized void turn() {
    turn_ = this;
    notify(); // unblock one thread
  }

}
```

The notify method is a more primitive operation than notifyAll and can be used to approximate the effects of notifyAll if further instrumentation is added to helper methods that encapsulate guards. For example, adding execution state variables to track the number of waiting threads allows you to write a loop that broadcasts a notification to all waiting threads, thus simulating notifyAll (although only approximately — notifyAll is an atomic primitive operation in Java):

```
public class GuardedClassV2 {
  protected boolean cond_ = false;
  protected int nWaiting_ = 0; // count waiting threads

  protected synchronized void awaitCond() {
    ++nWaiting_; // record fact that a thread is waiting
    while (!cond_)
      try { wait(); } catch (InterruptedException ex) {}
    --nWaiting_; // no longer waiting
  }

  protected synchronized void signalCond() {
    if (cond_)                      // simulate notifyAll
      for (int i = nWaiting_; i > 0; --i)
        notify();
  }
}
```

Other opportunities to use `notify` include *cascade* designs in which each notified thread wakes up the next one, even if it itself cannot proceed and thus must re-wait. However, the mechanics for doing a full cascade are error-prone and typically just as expensive, or even more so than using `notifyAll`.

All together, the conditions under which `notify` applies are rather special and fragile. Placing the waits and notifications in special helper methods both encapsulates the mechanics and permits overriding in subclasses. For example, you could create versions of `awaitCond` and/or `signalCond` in which notifications are guaranteed to be fair across a set of tasks. Similarly, you could define versions in which your own special-purpose priority indicators are attached to waits, so that the task with the highest priority is always awakened upon notification. This is not necessary with plain `notifyAll` constructions in the presence of different native Java priorities: if a set of tasks are all unblocked, one with the highest Java priority will generally run first relative to all the others. Chapter 8 discusses techniques that can be used to implement these and other specialized notification policies.

4.3.1.6 *Semaphores*

Variants of the bounded counter classes discussed in this book can serve as *semaphores*, which can in turn be used as low-level concurrency primitives. Semaphores play prominent roles in accounts of concurrent programming techniques in languages with less structured synchronization constructs than are available in Java (see the sources on non-object-oriented concurrent programming listed in Chapter 1). While there is rarely a compelling reason to do so, it is possible to create classes that emulate the effects of semaphores, and then use them to construct Java versions of programs relying on semaphore-based techniques.

For example, class `CountingSemaphore` is a Java implementation of a commonly used form of semaphore, a counter that is bounded in only one direction. The method traditionally called P is analogous to a dec operation, and V to an inc operation. This class is declared as `final` to emphasize and enforce the fact that P and V are the only operations supported. This fact also enables the use of `notify` in method V: (1) any waiting thread must be waiting for the count to become greater than zero in method P; (2) each V operation enables at most one waiting thread to resume.

```
public final class CountingSemaphore {
  private int count_ = 0;

  public CountingSemaphore(int initialCount) {
    count_ = initialCount;
  }

  public synchronized void P() {
    while (count_ <= 0)
      try { wait(); } catch (InterruptedException ex) {}
    --count_;
  }

  public synchronized void V() {
    ++count_;
    notify();
  }
}
```

Another common form of semaphore, a *binary semaphore*, can be obtained using any `BoundedCounter` implementation class (or simplification of one) in which MAX == MIN + 1. Since the count may take only two values, only one of dec and inc (or alternatively P and V) are enabled at any given time.

4.3.2 Tracking State

The most conservative strategy for writing guarded methods is to call `notifyAll` every time you change the value of any instance variable. This strategy is highly extensible. If all changes to all instance variables generate `notifyAll`, then any method in the class and all of its possible subclasses can define a guard clause that waits for any particular state. On the other hand, this practice can be very wasteful and inefficient when it generates notifications that cannot possibly affect the guard conditions of any waiting thread.

Some or all of these useless notifications can often be eliminated via logical state analysis. Rather than issuing notifications upon all changes in instance variables, you can arrange to issue notifications only upon transitions out of the logical states in which threads can ever wait.

To illustrate, consider again the logical states and transitions defined for BoundedCounter. Notice that the only transitions that could possibly affect *waiting* threads are those that step away from states bottom and top; that is, increment the count value away from MIN or decrement it away from MAX.

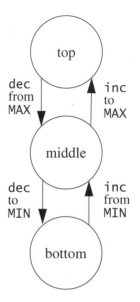

State	Condition	inc	dec
top	value == MAX	no	yes
middle	MIN < value < MAX	yes	yes
bottom	value == MIN	yes	no

These observations lead to the following concise implementation of BoundedCounter in which notifications are issued only when transitions are made out of the top and bottom states. Part of the conciseness is due to the convenience of *post*-increment and *post*-decrement Java coding idioms.

```
public class BoundedCounterVST implements BoundedCounter {
  protected long count_ = MIN;

  public synchronized long value() {
    return count_;
  }

  public synchronized void inc()  {
    while (count_ == MAX)
      try { wait(); } catch(InterruptedException ex) {};
    if (count_++ == MIN)// signal if was in bottom state
      notifyAll();
  }

  public synchronized void dec()  {
    while (count_ == MIN)
      try { wait(); } catch(InterruptedException ex) {};
    if (count_-- == MAX) // signal if was in top state
      notifyAll();
  }
}
```

This version can generate far fewer notifications than the original version in which every change to the count results in a notification. Since `notifyAll` is a slower operation than a simple conditional, this version will probably run faster. In cases where evaluating guards is itself computationally expensive, minimizing rechecks in this fashion results in even greater efficiency improvements.

While typically more efficient, this style of tracking can come at the price of greater fragility and inflexibility. It is impossible to build subclasses that include methods with guards waiting for any other property of the count than the particular ones sensed and tracked in this class without rewriting the methods from scratch.

For example, suppose we want to create a subclass that additionally contains methods `disable` and `enable`, where a `disable` message causes `inc` and `dec` to block until a subsequent `enable`. Support for these additional methods requires a different partitioning of logical state, which alters both the guard and the notification conditions for the base methods, which in turn leads to a total rewrite. This would not be a big deal here, but might be in anything beyond a toy textbook example.

4.3.2.1 *Bounded Buffers*

Bounded counters are not very interesting. However, the control strategies illustrated in this book with `BoundedCounter` apply to a number of commonly encountered concurrent components, including buffers and resource managers.

Bounded buffers have the same overall structure as bounded counters. In addition to a count, a buffer maintains a fixed array of elements. Instead of `inc`, it supports `put`, and instead of `dec`, it supports `take`. Also, the `MIN` is simply zero and the `MAX` is the capacity (declared as `int` to simplify use in array indexing):

```
public interface BoundedBuffer {
  public int    capacity(); // invariant: 0 <= capacity
  public int    count();    // invariant: 0 <= count <= capacity
  public void   put(Object x); // add only when count < capacity
  public Object take();     // remove only when count > 0
}
```

`BoundedBuffers` can be implemented with the classic technique (described in almost any data structures textbook) of using a fixed-sized array along with two indices that circularly traverse the array, keeping track of the next positions to put and take respectively. The following version is based on the same waiting and notification tactics used in `BoundedCounterVST`:

```
public class BoundedBufferVST implements BoundedBuffer {
  protected Object[] array_;        // the elements
  protected int putPtr_ = 0;        // circular indices
  protected int takePtr_ = 0;
  protected int usedSlots_ = 0;     // the count

  public BoundedBufferVST(int capacity)
   throws IllegalArgumentException {
    if (capacity <= 0)
      throw new IllegalArgumentException();
    array_ = new Object[capacity];
  }

  public int count() {
    return usedSlots_;
  }

  public int capacity() {
    return array_.length;
  }

  public synchronized void put(Object x) {

    while (usedSlots_ == array_.length) // wait until not full
      try { wait(); } catch(InterruptedException ex) {};

    array_[putPtr_] = x;
    putPtr_ = (putPtr_ + 1) % array_.length; // cyclically inc

    if (usedSlots_++ == 0) // signal if was empty
      notifyAll();
  }

  public synchronized Object take() {

    while (usedSlots_ == 0) // wait until not empty
      try { wait(); } catch(InterruptedException ex) {};

    Object x = array_[takePtr_];
    array_[takePtr_] = null;
    takePtr_ = (takePtr_ + 1) % array_.length;

    if (usedSlots_-- == array_.length) // signal if was full
      notifyAll();
    return x;
  }

}
```

4.3.2.2 *Tracking State Variables*

State tracking can sometimes be made both simpler and more extensible through the use of state variables. State variables represent the entire logical state of an object in (usually) a single instance variable. The variable is re-evaluated after any update to other relevant instance variables.

The most extensible way to implement state-variable designs is to isolate state re-evaluation in a single method, say checkState, that is called after each update method. After re-evaluating state, checkState can issue any notifications associated with the state change. As a simple conservative strategy, checkState can issue notifyAll after every state change. However, so long as this method can be overridden in subclasses, it does not hurt to specialize it to issue notifications only upon those changes that affect those guards actually defined in the class. Encapsulating all synchronization code within checkState allows subclasses to refine it in ways that are more specialized yet still consistent with the code relying upon it.

Common variants include those in which, instead of using checkState to reassess state, each method that performs updates also determines the correct next state and sends it as an argument to checkState, which can then still perform notifications upon change. This is sometimes more efficient, but harder to extend.

Using logical state variables restricts subclasses to those in which synchronization depends only on these logical states or subdivisions of these states. This is a highly defensible (although inflexible) practice, since it leads to subclasses that more clearly conform to the same abstract specifications with respect to logical state. This practice is recommended in several accounts of high-level OO analysis and design.

For example, adding a state variable in BoundedCounter leads to:

```java
public class BoundedCounterVSW implements BoundedCounter {
  static final int BOTTOM = 0;
  static final int MIDDLE = 1;
  static final int TOP    = 2;

  protected int state_ = BOTTOM;   // the state variable
  protected long count_ = MIN;

  protected synchronized void checkState() {
    int oldState = state_;
    if        (count_ == MIN) state_ = BOTTOM;
    else if (count_ == MAX) state_ = TOP;
    else                      state_ = MIDDLE;

    if (state_ != oldState &&    // notify on transition
        (oldState == TOP || oldState == BOTTOM))
      notifyAll();
  }
```

```
public synchronized long value() {
  return count_;
}

public synchronized void inc()  {
  while (state_ == TOP)
    try { wait(); } catch(InterruptedException ex) {};
  ++count_;
  checkState();
}

public synchronized void dec()  {
  while (state_ == BOTTOM)
    try { wait();} catch(InterruptedException ex) {};
  --count_;
  checkState();
  }
}
```

4.3.3 Latches

Latch-based waiting and notification is a common special case of guarded method design and implementation. Latches (sometimes called *permanent* conditions) are variables of atomic types that change value *at most once, ever.* Examples include:

- Instance variables holding references to other objects, initialized to `null` in a constructor but ultimately bound (assigned) exactly once later. In the terminology of managed resources (Chapter 2), this corresponds to a constrained ownership protocol in which at most one transfer ever occurs. (This is also known as a kind of *single static assignment.*)

- Completion indications; for example, a boolean variable and associated accessor `done` in a thread-based class that is set to `true` when the service completes.

- Timing thresholds. Time never un-elapses. To wait for a time-latch, you can use `sleep` rather than hand-crafted loops that recheck the time. Unless broken by an `InterruptedException`, you can be sure that the specified time has elapsed upon return.

- Event indications. A particular instance of an event either has not yet occurred or has occurred. By nature, once it occurs, it never un-occurs. For example, one kind of event is reception of a message sent from another object.

- Global program states such as deadlock and the lack of any references to an object.

- Instance variables representing the fact that an object is in a special state that it can never leave. For example, an end-of-file indicator for a non-rewindable file can serve as a latch.

The use of latches can simplify the design, implementation and understandability of guarded methods because the surrounding variables, conditions, and/or objects behave immutably after the latch has been set.

Latched properties are by far the simplest kinds of conditions in guarded methods that rely on other objects. When guarded methods depend on the state of objects other than a host, it is difficult to synchronize both objects so that the other object's state does not change between the test and the action. (Strategies for doing so are described in Chapter 8.) In fact, in some distributed systems, the synchronization required is all but impossible to implement, so the *only* kinds of properties ever worth trying to detect are those that remain true forever.

Some concurrent programming languages restrict wait-style constructs to those based on latches, or otherwise specially support latch-based forms. Even though Java does not specially require or support any such usage, the resulting simplicities can be exploited whenever they are present. Conversely, you can define latch-style instance variables to obtain these simplicities.

It is not always necessary to use synchronized constructions for latches. If a latch variable has been set, there is no need to lock the object when accessing it. (If it hasn't changed and you are waiting for the latched value, then you still need to `wait`.) Avoiding synchronization when waiting is not necessary can enhance performance and help ensure liveness.

For example, consider a class with a constructor generating an initialization thread to establish a helper object. The reference to the helper is never changed once it is set:

```
class Helper { // an internal helper class
  void help() { /* ... */ }
}

class HelperInitializer implements Runnable {
  protected HelpedServer s_;

  HelperInitializer(HelpedServer s) {
    s_ = s;
  }

  public void run() {
    Helper h = new Helper(); // create
    s_.initializeHelper(h);  // call back server
  }
}
```

```
public class HelpedServer {
  protected Helper helper_; // latch, unique

  public HelpedServer() {
    helper_ = null;
    new Thread(new HelperInitializer(this)).start();
  }

  // callback from initializer
  synchronized void initializeHelper(Helper h) {
    if (helper_ == null) {
      helper_ = h;
      notifyAll();
    }
  }

  // get helper reference; if null, wait for it.
  protected Helper helper() {
    if (helper_ == null)   {
      synchronized(this) {
        while (helper_ == null)
          try { wait(); } catch(InterruptedException ex) {}
      }
    }
    return helper_;
  }

  // Use helper, for example in:
  public void delegatedAction() {
    helper().help();
  }

}
```

Latch properties are common and exploitable enough to deserve routine annotation within class declarations. Similar opportunities may exist for properties that are not permanent but are stable with respect to guards; that is conditions that cannot change value again until the action waiting for a particular value is triggered.

Documentation of other, more specialized categories along these lines may permit further refinements. For example, it can be helpful to know that a numeric variable, for example a counter, increases monotonically (never decreases in value) across the lifetime of an object. This property may allow conditional removal of synchronization for guards involving accessors that need only return a lower bound on the value. Similar considerations apply to collections that grow monotonically (never have elements removed).

4.3.3.1 *Using Suspend and Resume*

In closed designs, pairs of objects may know so much about each other that they can exert more precise control over latch-based suspension and resumption. In these situations, latch-style notifications can be performed implicitly using the fragile but slightly more efficient `Thread.currentThread().suspend` instead of `wait`, and `otherThread.resume` instead of `notifyAll` (where `otherThread` is a reference to the thread that the notifying action knows is waiting for the condition to become true).

This usage of `suspend` and `resume` is applicable only when objects know so much about the state of the activity running in a thread (often including timing information) that they can be sure that continuation is possible. Also, if the target object invokes `suspend` itself within a synchronized block or method, it must be acceptable for it to retain the lock while suspended, thus blocking out all other synchronized methods invoked from other threads during its suspension. Conversely, if the target object invokes `suspend` outside of synchronized code, it must be acceptable for other threads involving the object to continue.

The resulting constructions are too delicate for use outside of specialized contexts (see Chapter 8). But just to illustrate usage even though it would not be a good choice here, a suspend/resume protocol can be applied to a variant of `HelpedServer` in which the constructor explicitly suspends its thread until the initialization thread completes:

```
public class HelpedServerV2 { // fragments
  protected Helper helper_; // latch, unique
  protected Thread ctor_thread_;

  public HelpedServerV2() {
    ctor_thread_ = Thread.currentThread();
    new Thread(new HelperInitializer(this)).start();
    ctor_thread_.suspend();
  }

  // callback from initializer
  public synchronized void initializeHelper(Helper h) {
    if (helper_ == null) {
      helper_ = h;
      ctor_thread_.resume(); // beware: possible race condition
    }
  }

  // ...

}
```

4.3.4 Nested Monitors

Use of classes with guarded waits is constrained by synchronization issues usually described as *the nested monitor problem* (also known as a particular form of *lockout*). To illustrate, consider the following minimal classes:

```
class Inner {
  protected boolean cond_ = false;

  synchronized void methodAwaitingCond() {
    while (!cond_)
      try { wait(); } catch(InterruptedException ex) {}
    // any other code
  }

  synchronized void methodSignallingCond(boolean c) {
    cond_ = c;
    notifyAll();
  }
}

class Outer {
  protected Inner inner_ = new Inner(); // fixed, unique

  synchronized void rely() {
    inner_.methodAwaitingCond();
  }

  synchronized void set(boolean c) {
    inner_.methodSignallingCond(c);
  }
}
```

In Java, a thread that is waiting in a wait queue retains all of its locks except that of the object placed in the queue. For example, suppose that in thread *T* a call is made to `outer.rely` causing it to block within `inner`. The lock to `outer` is retained while *T* is blocked: no other thread will ever get a chance to unblock it via `outer.set`.

This usage of the `Inner` class is suspicious to begin with. Guarded suspension makes sense when you believe that other threads could eventually unblock a `wait`. But here, the `Outer` class structurally precludes other threads from executing code that could do so.

Nesting constraints can lead to unexpected deadlock conditions when otherwise ordinary-looking synchronized methods invoke other equally ordinary-looking synchronized methods that happen to use wait queues. As with all policies for handling state-dependent behavior, you need to document and advertise the wait

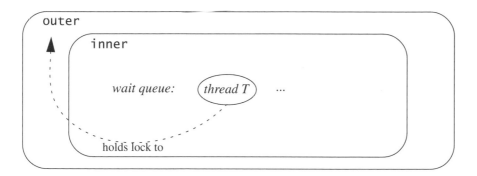

policies employed in a class so that people trying to use them have a chance to address potential problems.

Some monitor-based concurrent programming languages support monitor *condition queues* that can help avoid one-level nesting problems, but do not address problems at multiple levels. Some other languages employ special lock-based or copy-based protocols in nested constructions.

Java does not provide any special support for dealing with nested monitors. However, there are two general approaches to avoiding nesting problems in Java. While neither of these alone guarantees freedom from lockouts, they avoid its most common causes:

- Ensure that objects using guarded waits are referenced and used by multiple outer objects. If there are multiple paths to an inner object, no one of them will necessarily lock out others. (They still might, but under invocation sequences that could deadlock for other reasons as well.)

- If an instance of an `Inner` class must be held uniquely by an outer object, invoke all inner methods that may wait *without* synchronization on the outer object. Java requires that the sections of inner methods containing `wait` be synchronized, which requires, in this case, that outer callers not be synchronized. This applies in a natural way when hosts serve only as *pass-throughs* (see Chapter 3), or always invoke helper methods using new threads (see Chapters 6 and 8).

Chapter 8 presents techniques that circumvent nested monitor problems in some particular cases in which they would otherwise be encountered.

4.4 Balking

A balking method first checks the preconditions for an action and, if they do not hold, returns a failure indication to the client. Inaction designs are simplified versions of balking applying when clients need not be informed of failure:

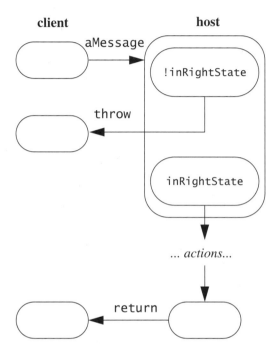

Balking is a familiar and common policy in both sequential and concurrent programming. Balking is internally less committal than guarding. A balking method makes no assumptions about whether an action could ever be enabled; it simply reports that the action is not currently possible. Decisions about what to do about this are left to clients (or to policy control objects — see Chapter 5).

To implement balking methods:

- Taking into account the severity and consequences of failure and the kinds of clients that will need to deal with them, define appropriate exception types to be thrown, global clean-up actions to be initiated, and/or failure indications to be returned.

- Check preconditions and conditionally return failure before taking any irreversible action in the method. In cases where precondition checks simply test properties of argument values (for example, against `final` constants), the check need not be in a synchronized region of code. The need for synchronization in other cases varies according to other policies.

- To the extent reasonable, make public accessor methods so that clients can avoid or minimize failures and can take appropriate evasive actions when they occur.

For example, here is a balking version of a counter:

```java
public class CannotIncrementException extends Exception { }

public class CannotDecrementException extends Exception { }

public class BalkingBoundedCounter {
  protected long count_ = BoundedCounter.MIN;

  public synchronized long value() {
    return count_;
  }

  public synchronized void inc()
   throws CannotIncrementException {
    if (count_ >= BoundedCounter.MAX)
      throw new CannotIncrementException();
    else
      ++count_;
  }

  public synchronized void dec()
   throws CannotDecrementException {
    if (count_ <= BoundedCounter.MIN)
      throw new CannotDecrementException();
    else
      --count_;
  }

}
```

4.4.1 Timed Waits

Time-out designs are mixtures of balking and guard-based strategies. Rather than waiting forever for a condition to become true in a guarded method, you can place an upper bound on how long any given `wait` should remain suspended and/or on how many times its guard condition can be re-evaluated. To implement this, you can use `wait(long millisec)` instead of the standard no-argument version, and/or limit the number of times a guard loop may execute. A failure exception can be thrown upon time-out.

The parameters controlling wait time and/or number of re-evaluations are completely arbitrary, and often require some trial and error. It is usually not too hard to provide values that will catch true liveness problems without false-alarming on waits that just happen to be slow. Since most such failures will at some point require human intervention, policies can be backed up via mechanisms that query users about remedial actions.

Chapter 8 describes one of the more common applications of timed waits. Special-purpose `Lock` classes can serve as substitutes for `synchronized` methods, where time-outs are used as a heuristic strategy for sensing deadlock and other liveness problems.

Time-out values may also be controlled by clients. For example, the following implementation of `BoundedBuffer` supports an overloaded version of `take` accepting a time-out value indicating the maximum time that a client wishes to wait for an item. In keeping with the most common policy used in balking buffers and queues, rather than throwing an exception, the method returns `null` upon time-out. For illustration, this version also returns `null` on interruption.

In this version, the `wait` is placed in a loop in order to deal with the fact that unrelated notifications may occur. This loop is slightly messy but has identical rationale as versions without time-outs. The condition being waited on is always checked first after waking up from the `wait`, no matter how the `wait` is broken. This helps avoid cases in which a wait is broken by a time-out, but other contending threads execute before the woken-up thread gets a chance to resume. One of those threads could have changed the condition, in which case it would not be necessary to return a failure indication. If the condition does not hold the time-out is checked and, if necessary, adjusted for use in the next iteration:

```
public class BoundedBufferVTO extends BoundedBufferVST {

  public BoundedBufferVTO(int capacity)
   throws IllegalArgumentException {
    super(capacity);
  }

  // returns null on time-out or interrupt
  public synchronized Object take(long maxWaitMillis) {
    if (usedSlots_ == 0) {
      long waitTime = maxWaitMillis;
      long startTime = System.currentTimeMillis();
      for (;;) {
        try {
          wait(waitTime);
        }
        catch(InterruptedException ex) {
          return null;
        }

        if (usedSlots_ > 0) // recheck condition
          break;
        else {
          long now = System.currentTimeMillis();
          long timeSoFar = now - startTime;
          if (timeSoFar >= maxWaitMillis)  // timed out
            return null;
          else // adjust time-out for next time
            waitTime = maxWaitMillis - timeSoFar;
        }
      }
    }

    // otherwise, same code as VST version
    Object x = array_[takePtr_];
    array_[takePtr_] = null;
    takePtr_ = (takePtr_ + 1) % array_.length;

    if (usedSlots_-- == array_.length)
      notifyAll();
    return x;
  }

}
```

4.5 Optimistic Control

In check-and-act designs, objects refuse to engage in actions unless they are known to be in states that allow the action to succeed. In optimistic, try-and-see designs, objects proceed with actions without necessarily checking to see if all preconditions hold. But they also possess strategies and mechanisms for detecting failures and, when necessary, undoing the effects of any actions that led to failure.

The basic idea can be seen as an extension of check-and-act protocols. Fallible actions are allowed to occur before performing state checks (but in the pure versions considered here, *not* after the checks). The form analogous to balking is shown in the interaction diagram. The form analogous to guarding is the same except that instead of terminating with an exception throw, the entire method is retried.

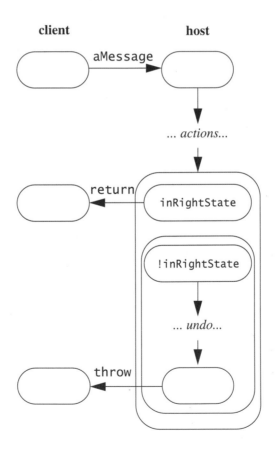

Optimistic control has roots in database update schemes for systems in which the likelihood of failures due to interference and other forms of contention is very low. It is more efficient on average to assume that contention will not occur and to fall back upon more expensive processing when it does. Variants are also seen in approaches to fault tolerance based upon detection of mismatches in the results of multiple processes or failed remote objects. Smaller-scale versions are employed in low-level operating-system support for multiple processors relying only on simple primitive instructions that can sometimes be implemented in hardware. Similar techniques stem from *design for testability*, in which objects perform self-checks to see if operations have the intended effects.

All optimistic control techniques share three basic features:

- A means of detecting failure, for example by tracking and assessing logical state via instance variables or catching downstream exceptions.

- A policy for dealing with failure: inaction, throwing exceptions or retrying actions.

- A means of dealing with the consequences of actions leading to failure. This can be achieved in a forward or backward direction, or any mixture of the two:

    - *Provisional action*. Only "pretending" to act, delaying commitment of effects until the possibility of failure has been ruled out. Provisional action is usually easier to manage for methods that only update instance variables. Since there is no way to undo an assignment statement, values of variables must somehow be held in *shadow* copies that are committed to as necessary.

    - *Rollback/Recovery*. Undoing the effects of each performed action. Rollback techniques are used for actions that must be undone, including actions resulting from sending other messages. Every message sent within an optimistic method should have an inverse *antimessage*. For example, a `credit` operation might be undone via `debit`.

Some kinds of operations can neither be provisionally attempted nor undone via antimessages, and thus cannot be used in optimistic designs. This rules out methods with externally visible effects that irrevocably change the real world by performing I/O or actuating physical devices (unless it is possible to undo the actions without harm). In the case of I/O, conventions can be adopted to allow the conceptual equivalent of rollback. For example, if methods log actions in a log file and the log file supports a "please disregard log entry XYZ" option, then this can be invoked in case of failure.

4.5.1   Loosening Synchronization

Optimistic control can be used as a means of loosening synchronization policies. Rather than treating even the possession of a synchronization lock as a precondition for action, optimistic methods can proceed without synchronization, but detect and deal with any interference that occurs. This strategy leads to a family of techniques that allow most parts of most methods to proceed without any synchronization control by:

- Isolating state changes into atomic updates.

- Tracking the current *version* of maintained state.

- Failing to complete and/or undoing effects of methods that would lead to version conflicts.

- Arranging or allowing that failed operations be retried.

The remainder of this section concentrates on designs of this form, since they can be used as the foundations for other optimistic control strategies. For example, it is easy to mix in or adapt methods that rely on exceptions to detect failure. It is also possible to adapt strategies originating from check-and-act designs (such as state tracking) to deal with postconditions instead of preconditions. However, discussion of optimistic control strategies that apply to transactional designs involving the actions of multiple independent objects is postponed to Chapter 8.

The central idea in this form of optimistic control is to isolate all instance variable updates of a class in a single atomic update method, which is normally designed to be the last statement called in any method that updates state. (Some concurrent languages syntactically require that each method be defined in this way.)

While there are several possible variants, the most common and usable form is a `commit` operation (also known as `compareAndSwap` and a variant form of `become`). This operation takes as arguments the assumed object state and the new state that should result if the current state is actually the same as that assumed. If the assumption is correct, the update succeeds. In this way, version mismatch serves as the failure detection condition.

```
class Optimistic { // generic code sketch
  private State currentState_; // State is any type

  synchronized boolean commit(State assumed, State next) {
    boolean success = (currentState_ == assumed);
    if (success)
      currentState_ = next;
    return success;
  }

}
```

Classes using `commit` operations isolate the *stable* states of objects into versions and ensure that each update proceeds from one stable version to another by prohibiting, aborting and/or retrying those that don't. For most people, the resulting designs are not especially natural or easy to program, but may be worth consideration because of their superior liveness properties.

There are three principal steps to building classes based on this form of optimistic control: structuring state, structuring methods, and implementing update policies (exceptions, retries, and/or synchronization). Each has prerequisites that can limit applicability.

4.5.1.1 *Structuring State*

All local state must be encapsulated as a single unit representing the version of the state. This is an extreme form of the instance variable regrouping techniques discussed in Chapter 3. It can be accomplished in several ways, including:

- Define an immutable helper class holding values of all instance variables. The host class holds a reference to an instance of this class to maintain its state. Note that this makes subclassing more difficult when the subclasses must add new instance variables, since in this case both the host class and the instance variable holder classes must be subclassed.

- Define a representation class, but make it mutable (allow instance variables to change), and additionally include a *version number* (or *transaction identifier*) field or even a sufficiently precise *time stamp*. The version identifier is changed (if a number, just incremented) upon each update. This version identifier can then be used as the assumed state argument to `commit`.

- Embed all instance variables, plus a version number, in the host class, but define `commit` to take as arguments all assumed values and all new values of these variables.

- Various mixtures of the above, such as using two independent helper objects. This might apply, for example, if an object maintains two independent aspects of state in which changes to one never affect the other. On the other hand, if the host class maintains two strictly independent aspects of state, it is likely that splitting it into two distinct objects will lead to a simpler and better design.

All accessor methods that report this state can be defined as unsynchronized, since callers of these methods will never see transient values.

4.5.1.2 *Structuring Updates*

The main actions of each method must be structured according to the form (momentarily ignoring failure issues):

```
State assumed = currentState();
State next = ...
commit(assumed, next);
otherActionsDependingOnNewStateButNotChangingIt();
```

All permanent state updates must be performed in a single atomic unit, by swapping in a new version of the representation. This requirement might not hold for update methods that in turn call other update methods (via self-calls), each of which changes only one aspect of state, or those that invoke methods on otherwise independent helper objects. Heavier variants of this technique can still be made to work in such cases via *nested* control, described in Chapter 8.

Because commit can fail, operations cannot be allowed to have irrecoverable effects that occur before commitment. On the other hand, if a method encounters an exception condition before commitment, it can exit without worrying about rolling back state.

4.5.1.3 *Exceptions*

Under exception-based failure policies, an exception is thrown upon commitment failure. Methods take the form:

```
State assumed = currentState();
State next = ...
if (!commit(assumed, next)) {
    rollBackAnyNonStateBasedActions();
    throw new InterferenceException();
}
otherActionsDependingOnNewStateButNotChangingIt();
```

In practice, the commit operation itself is usually designed to perform the roll-back actions upon failure.

Uncommitted optimistic methods result in full, clean failures: they leave the object in the same state as it would have been if the method had not been called in the first place. Responsibility for evasive action is then placed upon the client.

4.5.1.4 *Retries*

In retry-based schemes, provisional updates are repeated until they commit, using methods of the form:

```
for(;;) {
  State assumed = currentState();
  State next = ...
  if (!commit(assumed, next))
    rollBackAnyNonStateBasedActions();
  else
    break;
}
otherActionsDependingOnNewStateButNotChangingIt();
```

This is risky unless there is some independent assurance that the method will eventually succeed. Otherwise, it can result in a version of *livelock,* the optimistic analog of indefinitely postponed guarded methods. The action will never complete and will probably expend a lot of CPU resources repeatedly attempting to do so.

Algorithms that can be proven eventually to succeed after a bounded number of attempts are (somewhat deceptively) called *wait-free* (and/or in some cases *lock-free*). Not very many provably wait-free algorithms are currently known (see the Further Readings). When eventual success cannot be assured, a maximum number of retries may be specified, ultimately leading to an exception. This is analogous to using a time-out in check-and-act designs.

Methods with retries are disguised versions of busy waits. To ensure that they are well behaved in a concurrent setting, the retry loops should normally include `yield` calls. If local state information is accessed directly, the associated variables may need to be marked as `volatile`.

4.5.1.5 *Synchronization*

Even when some methods in a class are programmed using failures or retries, others can use standard lock-based techniques, in particular, partial synchronization of the form:

```
synchronized (this) {
  State assumed = currentState();
  State next = ...
  commit(assumed, next); // cannot fail
}
otherActionsDependingOnNewStateButNotChangingIt();
```

4.5.1.6 *Example*

Here is an optimistic version of a Dot class similar to the one in Chapter 3. It relies on an immutable Point class to maintain state. For illustration, several minor variants are shown in different update methods:

```
public class Point { // From Chapter 3
  private int x_,  y_; // fixed

  public Point(int x, int y) {
    x_ = x;
    y_ = y;
  }

  public int x() {
    return x_;
  }

  public int y() {
    return y_;
  }
}

public class InterferenceException extends Exception {}

public class DotV2 {
  protected volatile Point loc_;

  public DotV2(int x, int y) {
    loc_ = new Point(x, y);
  }
  // unsynchronized accessor
  public Point location() {
    return loc_;
  }

  // the atomic update method
  protected synchronized boolean commit(Point assumed,
                                        Point next) {
    boolean success = (assumed == loc_);
    if (success)
      loc_ = next;
    return success;
  }
```

```
// Exception-based
public void shiftXY(int deltaX, int deltaY)
 throws InterferenceException {
  Point assumed = location();
  Point next = new Point(assumed.x() + deltaX,
                         assumed.y() + deltaY);
  if (!commit(assumed, next))
    throw new InterferenceException();
}

// automatic retry
public void shiftX(int deltaX) {
  Point assumed = null;
  Point next = null;
  do {
    assumed = location();
    next = new Point(assumed.x() + deltaX, assumed.y());
  } while (!commit(assumed, next));
}

// partially synchronized
public Point shiftY(int deltaY) { // returns new location
  synchronized(this) {
    Point assumed = location();
    Point next = new Point(assumed.x(), assumed.y() + deltaY);
    commit(assumed, next); // no need to check failure
  }
  return location();
}

// fully synchronized
public synchronized void move(int x, int y) {
  Point assumed = location();
  Point next = new Point(x, y);
  commit(assumed, next); // no need to check failure
}

}
```

4.6 Further Readings

State-based reasoning has a long history in computer hardware and software design. The texts on real-time programming and discrete event simulation listed in Chapter 1 are good sources for advanced state-based design techniques as well as for many scheduling and resource allocation issues. Extensions to some of the state-based techniques mentioned in this chapter are described in several recent technical papers and design patterns, including:

Sane, Aamod, and Roy Campbell. "Object-Oriented State Machines", *OOPSLA 95 Proceedings,* ACM, 1995.

Java waiting and notification constructs are derived from *monitors*, first described by C. A. R. Hoare. A survey of monitor policies and usage may be found in:

Buhr, Peter, Michel Fortier, and Michael Coffin. "Monitor Classification", *ACM Computing Surveys*, 1994.

Papers describing several approaches to constraint-based programming can be found in the Agha, Wegner, and Yonezawa collection listed in Chapter 1. Similar non-concurrent constraint-based techniques are used in `java.awt` layout managers and related support classes.

Unity and its follow-ons helped popularize specification and design using conditions described here as latches. See the text by Chandy and Misra listed in Chapter 1.

The theory of wait-free algorithms is described in:

Herlihy, Maurice. "Wait-free synchronization", *ACM Transactions on Programming Languages and Systems*, vol. 13, no. 1, 1991.

Work on wait-free algorithms is still scattered across the technical research literature, and guaranteed wait-free algorithms are known for only a small number of common design problems, for example simple queues and lists. Implementations of these algorithms tend to outperform more standard algorithms only on multiple CPUs supporting special machine instructions. The on-line supplement to this book contains a Java adaptation of a wait-free queue class otherwise similar to (and based on an algorithm described in the same paper as) the `TwoLockQueue` class from Chapter 3. It also contains links to descriptions of wait-free algorithms implemented in other languages, as well as additional examples of semaphores and related synchronization tools.

CHAPTER 5

Concurrency Control

Layered composition (also called *superimposition*) forms the basis for implementing policy over mechanism. Layering is seen in almost every large concurrent OO program and framework, and many small ones as well.

The term *concurrency control* has come to refer to the layering of synchronization and control policies over base mechanisms. This chapter describes three different approaches to concurrency control, based on three different object-oriented structuring techniques:

- Adding policy control in subclasses.

- Controlling delegated actions.

- Representing messages as objects.

Each of these compositional techniques require that the *ground* classes providing base functionality be amenable to the desired form of control; for example, that they possess sufficient accessors for assessing logical state. Higher layers can then regulate the ground objects by tracking their execution state, intercepting their messages, and taking different courses of action in accord with particular policies. Well-structured compositional design often requires planning to ensure that ground classes and objects are usable in this fashion. Extensive retrofitting is sometimes needed when they are not.

This chapter is organized as a series of loosely connected pattern-based presentations of issues and techniques surrounding the imposition of synchronization policies. Several sample policies are used to illustrate the composition techniques that are usually, although not necessarily, best suited for expressing the given policies. The chapter concludes with a discussion of object models that places these techniques in a broader perspective.

5.1   Subclassing

Subclassing can be used to implement new concurrency control policies over existing mechanisms, or even vice versa. This can be achieved via adaptations and extensions of the *Template Method* pattern (see *Design Patterns*) in which:

- Basic ground-level action code is defined in non-public methods. Somewhat less flexibly, these methods need not be declared non-public if they are instead designed to be overridden in subclasses.

- Public methods implement the synchronization policy of choice, performing basic actions by forwarding to the non-public implementation code.

There are two resulting programming styles that exploit this arrangement in which public methods intercept messages in order to surround ground-level actions with *before/after*-style concurrency control measures:

- You can define ground code in base classes and then add public methods in subclasses. This style typically applies best when you are adding different forms of control to the same ground-level methods.

- You can arrange that the public code in base classes calls `abstract` or default-implemented ground-level methods. This sets up a framework facilitating construction of subclasses that vary on either dimension.

5.1.1   Adding Synchronization

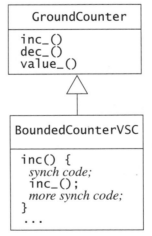

The simplest application of subclass-based control is adding synchronization and/ or guarded waits to all of the methods of a class. For example, to impose subclass-based synchronization in the running `BoundedCounter` example, start with a

GroundCounter class that does not even know the invariant rules, and thus cannot possibly know what to do if they do not hold. (By convention, non-public ground-level methods have names ending with underscores.) A usable and properly synchronized version can then be created as a subclass:

```java
public class GroundCounter {
  protected long count_;

  protected GroundCounter(long c) {
    count_ = c;
  }

  protected long value_() {
    return count_;
  }

  protected void inc_() {
    ++count_;
  }

  protected void dec_() {
    --count_;
  }
}

public class BoundedCounterVSC extends GroundCounter
                          implements BoundedCounter {
  public BoundedCounterVSC() {
    super(MIN);
  }

  public synchronized long value() {
    return value_();
  }

  public synchronized void inc() {
    while (value_() >= MAX)
      try { wait(); } catch(InterruptedException ex) {};
    inc_();
    notifyAll();
  }

  public synchronized void dec() {
    while (value_() <= MIN)
      try { wait(); } catch(InterruptedException ex) {};
    dec_();
    notifyAll();
  }
}
```

Conversely, we could have started with a version of `BoundedCounterVSC` in which `inc_`, etc., were declared as `abstract`, and then created a subclass implementing the code in `GroundCounter`. Or we could have done both at once, in which case future subclasses could change either the functionality or the policy.

5.1.2   Inheritance Anomalies

Some concurrent OO programming languages (see the Further Readings) syntactically require separation between non-public methods defining functionality and public methods defining synchronization policies. Even though Java does not require separation, it is an attractive option for writing extensible classes and frameworks:

- It enables either action or synchronization code to be varied independently in subclasses, avoiding constructions that would make it impossible for the subclass to obtain desired functionality without rewriting nearly every method.

- It avoids the need to mix execution state variables used solely for purposes of synchronization with logical state variables required for base functionality. Instead, these variables can be introduced in subclasses.

- It supports the notion of internal self calls. When one action in a class invokes another, it need not go through `public synchronized` methods that are designed for external access. This can also be more efficient than explicit delegation.

- It avoids problems surrounding exclusive control, access to internal variables and methods, object identity, nested monitors, and interface adaptation sometimes encountered with other layering techniques. Subclassing extends objects rather than composing multiple objects. For example, no special considerations are needed to guarantee unique ownership of the base "part" of an object.

Perhaps the main advantage of subclassing as an implementation technique for imposing policy is that as long as all relevant variables and methods are declared as `protected`, a subclass can perform all necessary modifications to base-level code in order to support a given policy. Despite the best intentions by class authors, extensive surgery on method code in a subclass is sometimes the only way to salvage a class to work under a given policy. Although `protected` access has some clear drawbacks as a design convention, in concurrent settings the resulting ability for subclasses to alter policy control can outweigh concerns about abuse of superclass representations. For this to work, necessary invariants must be well-documented.

But this form of subclassing does have its limitations. When people first started using experimental concurrent OO languages, several researchers noticed that it can be difficult or even impossible to define subclasses for concurrent objects that add or extend commonly desired functionality or policy to superclasses. Similar concerns have been expressed in accounts of high-level OO analysis and design methods.

Some constructions in purely sequential classes are hard to extend as well, for example those declaring variables or methods as `private` or `final` for no good reason. But enough additional snags are encountered in concurrent OO programming for this state of affairs to have been labeled the *inheritance anomaly*. The issues and problems covered by term "inheritance anomaly" are only loosely related. Examples seen already in this book include:

- If a superclass does not explicitly represent and track those aspects of its state on which subclass methods depend, then all methods that need to track and check that state must be recoded (see page 87).

- If a subclass partitions logical state in a different way than represented by a superclass state variable, superclass methods that refer to the state variable must be recoded (see page 101).

- If a subclass includes guarded waits on conditions that superclass methods do not provide notifications about, then these methods must be recoded (see page 99).

- If a superclass uses `notify` instead of `notifyAll`, and a subclass adds features that cause the conditions for using `notify` to no longer hold, then all methods performing notifications must be recoded (see page 95).

- If an instance variable is treated as fixed in a superclass but assigned to in a subclass, then all methods taking advantage of immutability must be recoded (see page 44). Similar problems occur with assumption mismatches about uniqueness.

Taken together, these kinds of problems serve as a warning that without more care than usually necessary in sequential settings, it is too easy to write concurrent classes that programmers (including you) will not be able to extend easily or usefully. Although there is no catchy name for the issue, similar obstacles may be encountered when trying to aggregate, compose, and delegate concurrent objects.

Just as in sequential OO programming, there are no universally valid rules for making classes that can serve as useful superclasses for all possible extensions or can be used without modification in all possible contexts. Most guidelines for writing classes that avoid obstacles boil down to two well-known design rules:

1. Avoid premature optimization.

2. Encapsulate design decisions.

Both of these rules can be surprisingly hard to follow. More often than not, avoiding optimization requires more abstraction and scaffolding than optimizing for known situations. Similarly, you cannot encapsulate a design decision unless you are aware that a decision has been made. This requires contemplation of alternatives that may not occur to you upon first writing a class.

Rules such as these are perhaps most commonly applied retrospectively, during cleanup of existing code in efforts to make it more reusable. In an ideal world, you might be able to anticipate all the ways a class needs to be opened up to make it more extensible. The world is almost never this ideal. Retrospective refactorings and iterative reworkings are honorable and routine aspects of OO development.

5.1.3 Layering Guards

Basic data structure classes are often written in balking form so that they can be used in purely sequential settings. For example, consider a simple `Stack`:

```
public class StackEmptyException extends Exception { }

public class Stack { // fragments
  public synchronized boolean isEmpty() { /* ... */ }
  public synchronized void push(Object x) { /* ... */ }
  public synchronized Object pop() throws StackEmptyException {
    if (isEmpty())
      throw new StackEmptyException();
    // else ...
  }
}
```

Balking on attempts to take an element from an empty stack is attractive since it makes the class usable in sequential settings where it would be pointless to wait for a `pop`: if no other threads can add an element, the program will just stall forever. On the other hand, some clients of a `Stack` in concurrent contexts might want to hold up and wait for an element to appear. One inefficient and ineffective approach is to `try` to perform `pop`, and if a `StackEmptyException` is caught, to try again. This is a disguised form of busy-waiting.

A version that directly supports guarded usage can be built using a straightforward variant of subclass-based coordination in which base methods are not even non-public. The ones that need further coordination are overridden:

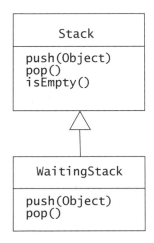

```
public class WaitingStack extends Stack {
  public synchronized void push(Object x) {
    super.push(x);
    notifyAll();
  }

  public synchronized Object pop() throws StackEmptyException {
    while (isEmpty())
      try { wait(); } catch (InterruptedException ex) {}
    return super.pop();
  }

}
```

The subclass version shown here has the mildly annoying property that pop still declares that it can throw StackEmptyException even though it never does. Defining it to be an unrelated class that delegates its actions to the underlying simple Stack would remove this obligation, but would also remove opportunities to reuse client code written to use simple Stacks. One way to avoid some of these problems (though perhaps cause others) would be for the subclass to define a new method, say waitingPop, so that clients could use either or both styles on the same object. These snags are typical of the interface definition and usage problems that arise when attempting to support multiple policies for handling state-dependent actions.

Life would have been simpler here if the original Stack had instead been a raw GroundStack class, supporting neither balking nor even synchronization. In that case, the versions supporting the two different policies could have been more easily defined as sibling subclasses of GroundStack.

5.1.4 Conflict Sets

Subclassing can be used to provide more fine-grained synchronization and control by keeping track of the progress of actions associated with received messages. Subclass methods can keep track of the logical execution state of ground-level operations and use this information to decide what to do about new incoming requests. (Similar designs can be constructed using the other compositional strategies described in this chapter.) This style of concurrency control applies best when relations among activities can be mapped out at design time, with full knowledge of all pairs of actions that can or cannot co-occur.

To illustrate, consider a ground-level `Inventory` class with methods to `store` and `retrieve` objects. Suppose that these operations are somewhat time-consuming, but are implemented in a way that does not require low-level synchronization. In the classic context for this form of policy control, basic functionality is arranged via database transactions, but here is a version using `java.util.Hashtable`. For simplicity of illustration, it relies on the assumption that each item has a unique description:

```
public class GroundInventory {
  protected Hashtable items_ = new Hashtable();
  protected Hashtable suppliers_ = new Hashtable();

  protected void store_(String description, Object item,
                        String supplier) {
    items_.put(description, item);
    suppliers_.put(supplier, description);
  }

  protected Object retrieve_(String description) {
    Object x = items_.get(description);
    if (x != null)
      items_.remove(description);
    return x;
  }
}
```

Even though `GroundInventory` objects don't need low-level protection on instance variables, there are still some semantic constraints on the `store` and `retrieve` operations in multithreaded contexts:

- A `retrieve` operation should not run concurrently with a `store` operation since the `store` might be in the process of adding exactly the item requested, in which case you don't want to return a failure indication.

- Two or more `retrieve` operations should not execute at the same time, since one may be in the process of removing the item requested by the others.

Several formal and semiformal notations have been devised to help represent this kind of information. The simplest and most widely used method, that suffices for most concurrency control problems of this kind, is based on *conflict sets* — sets of pairs of actions that cannot co-occur. For example, here the conflict set is just:

{ (store, retrieve), (retrieve, retrieve) }.

This information can serve both as documentation of class semantics and as a guide for implementing these semantics.

5.1.4.1 *Tracking Execution State*

Implementation of policies based on conflict sets requires execution state tracking. The easiest and most common way to do this is:

- Declare counter variables to represent whether methods are in progress.

- Surround ground-level code with counter updates.

- Guard methods to prevent new ground-level operations from executing until all conflicting operations terminate.

For example:

```
public class Inventory extends GroundInventory {
  protected int storing_ = 0;    // number of in-progress stores
  protected int retrieving_ = 0; // number of retrieves

  public void store(String description, Object item,
                    String supplier) {

    synchronized(this) {
      while (retrieving_ != 0) // don't overlap with retrieves
        try { wait(); } catch (InterruptedException ex) {}
      ++storing_;                          // record exec state
    }

    store_(description, item, supplier); // ground action

    synchronized(this) {                  // signal retrieves
      if (--storing_ == 0) // only necessary when hit zero
        notifyAll();
    }

  }
```

```
public Object retrieve(String description) {

  synchronized(this) { // wait until no stores or retrieves
    while (storing_ != 0 || retrieving_ != 0)
      try { wait(); } catch (InterruptedException ex) {}
    ++retrieving_;
  }

  Object x = retrieve_(description);    // ground action

  synchronized(this) {                  // signal others
    if (--retrieving_ == 0)
      notifyAll();
  }
  return x;
}

}
```

The same ideas also apply to optimistic control methods, in which case conflicts are often termed *invalidation relations*. These are implemented by aborting conflicting operations before commitment rather than waiting until it is safe to perform them.

More extensive notation can be used to represent conflict at an arbitrarily fine level of detail, covering cases such as those in which, say, some methodA conflicts with methodB only if it occurs after methodC. Similarly, in the Inventory class, we might want to use a more precise notation in order to state that a store operation can commence if a retrieve is in progress, but not vice versa. A range of notation has been devised for such purposes (see the Further Readings), enabling more detailed representation of conflicts while still allowing semi-automatic implementation via execution state tracking variables. However, in the extreme, it may be that nothing short of a full history log suffices to implement a given policy.

Implementations based on conflict sets and related analyses can suffer the same kinds of fragility and non-extensibility problems seen when tracking ordinary state predicates and variables, and even more so. Since conflict sets are based on the methods actually defined in a class rather than on logical representations of their semantics, they are difficult to extend when changing or adding methods in subclasses.

For example, if a sort method is introduced to re-order the items in some fashion, or a search method to check if an item exists, they can conflict in different ways from those currently handled, requiring rework. The Readers and Writers pattern and related constructions described next alleviate these problems by classifying operations into extensible categories.

5.1.5 Readers and Writers

The Readers and Writers pattern is a family of concurrency control designs having a common basis but differing in matters of policy governing control of threads invoking inspective accessors ("Readers") versus those invoking mutative, state-changing operations ("Writers").

While other forms of composition can be used to implement this pattern, subclassing provides a simpler and more straightforward mechanism for extending classes to support policies that may apply when any number of Reader threads can be executing simultaneously so long as there are no Writers, but Writers require exclusive access. In particular, the pattern applies when:

- The ground-level methods of a class can be cleanly separated into read methods and write methods, where write methods may internally call read methods, but never the opposite. For illustration, `read_` and `write_` are used as stand-ins for these ground-level methods. However, there may be any number of methods of each form.

- You would like to loosen synchronization for read-methods so that multiple threads can perform read-methods, while still providing full exclusion for write-methods. This can minimize the potential for deadlock and eliminate synchronization-based bottlenecks for heavily used resources such as central database files.

Beyond its intrinsic utility, the Readers and Writers pattern is a good model for arranging any kind of policy that can be implemented by mixing together subclass-based before/after concurrency control and counters recording messages and activities. For example, very similar techniques apply to classes that require certain categories of messages to occur in ordered pairs (as in enforcing, say, `read`, `write`, `read`, `write`, and so on).

5.1.5.1 *Policies*

Before putting control mechanisms in place, you must first establish a set of policies governing their use. Readers and Writers policies are a generalization of the kinds of concurrency-control policies seen, for example, in the `Inventory` class: rather than dealing with particular methods, they deal with all methods having the semantics of reading versus writing. But the details are still situation-dependent. Considerations include:

- If there are already one or more active (executing) Readers, can a newly arriving Reader immediately join them even if there is also a waiting Writer? If so, a continuous stream of entering Readers will cause Writers to starve. If not, the throughput of Readers decreases.

- If both some Readers and some Writers are waiting for an active Writer to finish, should you bias the policy toward allowing Readers? a Writer? Earliest first? Random? Alternate? Similar choices are available after termination of Readers.

- Do you need a way to allow Readers to upgrade access to be Writers without having to give up access?

Although there are no right answers to these policy matters, there are some standard solutions and corresponding implementations. The remainder of this section illustrates a common policy choice:

- Block incoming Readers if there are waiting Writers.

- "Randomly" choose among incoming threads. (This is random only in that it depends on the order in which the native Java scheduler happens to resume unblocked threads, which may in fact be fully deterministic.)

- No upgrade mechanisms.

5.1.5.2   *Tracking Execution State*

Implementing any kind of method-based concurrency control policy requires that you track execution state. For the most flexible possible solution, you could maintain your own special-purpose queues and take over all aspects of scheduling yourself (see Chapter 8). However, most policies can be established with less instrumentation overhead, simply by maintaining counts of threads that are actively engaged in the read and write operations, plus those that are waiting to do so. Tracking *waiting* threads represents the main extension here of the techniques seen in typical implementations of conflict sets.

To structure the corresponding implementations, control code can be factored out into method pairs that surround the actual read and write code, which must be defined in subclasses. This *before/after* method design allows simple construction of any number of public read-style and write-style methods, where each public method invokes the non-public one within the pairs.

The following version is written in a generic fashion, so that minor variants would be simple to implement in subclasses. In particular, the count of waiting readers is not really necessary in this version, since no policy depends on its value. However, its presence allows you to adjust policies by changing the predicates in the `allowReader` and `allowWriter` methods to rely on them in some way. For example, you might alter the conditionals to give preference to whichever count is greater. (Chapter 8 presents further refinements along these lines.)

```
public abstract class RW {
  protected int activeReaders_ = 0;   // threads executing read_
  protected int activeWriters_ = 0;   // always zero or one
  protected int waitingReaders_ = 0;  // threads not yet in read_
  protected int waitingWriters_ = 0;  // same for write_

  protected abstract void read_(); // implement in subclasses
  protected abstract void write_();

  public void read() {
    beforeRead();
    read_();
    afterRead();
  }

  public void write() {
    beforeWrite();
    write_();
    afterWrite();
  }

  protected boolean allowReader() {
    return waitingWriters_ == 0 && activeWriters_ == 0;
  }

  protected boolean allowWriter() {
    return activeReaders_ == 0 && activeWriters_ == 0;
  }

  protected synchronized void beforeRead() {
    ++waitingReaders_;
    while (!allowReader())
      try { wait(); } catch (InterruptedException ex) {}
    --waitingReaders_;
    ++activeReaders_;
  }

  protected synchronized void afterRead()  {
    --activeReaders_;
    notifyAll();
  }
```

```
protected synchronized void beforeWrite() {
  ++waitingWriters_;
  while (!allowWriter())
    try { wait(); } catch (InterruptedException ex) {}
  --waitingWriters_;
  ++activeWriters_;
}

protected synchronized void afterWrite() {
  --activeWriters_;
  notifyAll();
}

}
```

5.2   Adapters and Delegation

When standardized interfaces are defined after designing one or more concrete classes, these classes often do not quite implement the desired interface. For example, the names of their methods might be slightly different from those defined in the interface. Even if you cannot modify these concrete classes to fix such problems, you can still obtain the desired effect by building an Adapter class that translates away the incompatibilities.

For example, suppose you have a `Performer` class that supports method `perform` and meets all the qualifications of being usable as a `Runnable` except for the name mismatch. You can build an Adapter so it can be used in a thread by some other class:

```
class AdaptedPerformer implements Runnable {
  private Performer performer_;

  public AdaptedPerformer(Performer p) {
    performer_ = p;
  }

  public void run() {
    performer_.perform();
  }
}
```

This is only one of many common contexts for building Adapters (also called *views* and *wrappers*), which form the basis of several related patterns in the *Design Patterns* book (for example, Composites and Proxies). Adapters are also among the simplest *Host-Helper* composite object designs, in which a host object obtains some or all of its functionality by coordinating the actions of one or more helper objects.

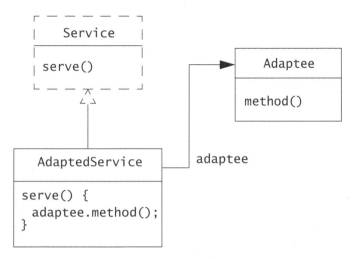

In this delegation-based style of class composition, the publicly accessible outer class forwards all methods to one or more inner delegates and relays back replies, perhaps doing some light translation (name changes, parameter coercion, result filtering, etc.) before and/or after the inner calls.

This form of delegation can even be used as a substitute of sorts for subclassing by having each "sub" class (Adapter) hold a reference to an instance of its "super" class (Adaptee), forwarding it all "inherited" operations. Such Adapters often have exactly the same interfaces as their delegates, in which case they are sometimes referred to as simple kinds of *Proxies*. Delegation can also be more flexible than subclassing, since "derived" objects can even change their "bases" (by re-assigning the delegate reference) dynamically.

However, delegation is both less powerful and less attractive than subclassing in some other respects. For example, self-calls in "superclasses" are not automatically bound to the versions of methods that have been "overridden" in delegation-based "subclasses". Adapter designs can also run into snags revolving around the fact that the inner and outer objects are different objects. For example, object reference equality tests must be performed more carefully since a test to see if you have the inner version of an object fails if you have the outer version, and vice versa.

Most of these problems can be avoided via the extreme measure of declaring all methods in inner classes to take an "apparent self" argument referring to the Adapter, and always using it instead of `this`, even for self-calls, locking, waiting, and identity checks (for example by overriding `Object.equals`). Some people reserve the term *delegation* for objects and classes written in this style rather than the forwarding techniques that are almost always used to implement simple Adapters. (Delegation techniques used in the transactional classes discussed in Chapter 8 more closely approximate this "selfless" form.)

In summary, Adapter-based designs are preferable to other forms of composition when:

- One or more ground classes providing the base functionality contain methods that should not be present (or should be renamed) in the coordinated one. Otherwise, you can normally use subclassing instead. However, Adapters may still be used if desired, in which case they take the form of Proxies — Adapter classes that have the same interfaces as their delegates.

- You can tolerate the identity-change issues surrounding any kind of Adapter; that is that the wrapper is not the same object as (has a different reference from) the object to which it is controlling access.

- When required, the Adaptee classes contain sufficient public accessors for the Adapters to assess their states. (Adapters have no privileged access.)

- You can ensure unique containment: no other object can directly access the delegate. If this is not true, then you may need to use one of the transactional forms described in Chapter 8. Containment requirements for delegation-based designs stem from the fact that Adapters cannot always know and/or do much about internal concurrency control decisions made within the classes of the objects to which they are attempting to delegate. In the absence of exclusive control via containment, very little can be guaranteed about the resulting designs.

5.2.1 Synchronized Adapters

Adapters can be used to wrap bare unsynchronized ground objects within fully synchronized objects. This leads to the simplest possible delegation-style designs; those specializing the containment strategies described in Chapter 2. Synchronized methods in Adapters just forward all messages on to their delegates.

Synchronized Adapters can often be used to enclose "legacy" code originally written for sequential settings. An Adapter can provide a single safe entry point into a heavily optimized (perhaps even into `native` code), computationally intensive set of functionality that, for the sake of efficiency, performs no internal concurrency control.

Given one or more ground classes, you can define a Synchronized Adapter with an instance variable, say `delegate`, holding a reference to a ground object, to which it forwards requests and relays replies. (Note that if any ground method contains a reply of the form `return this`, it should be translated as `return this` in the Adapter.) Delegate references need not be fixed, but if they are assignable, care must be taken that the Adapter obtains exclusive access. For example, an Adapter might occasionally assign the reference to a new internally constructed delegate.

5.2.1.1 *Wrapping Classes with Public Variables*

Synchronized Adapters can be used to place synchronized access and update methods around a class containing `public` instance variables. This effect cannot be achieved via subclassing in Java since you cannot remove the "publicness" of raw access. For example, you can build an Adapter around a wide-open point class:

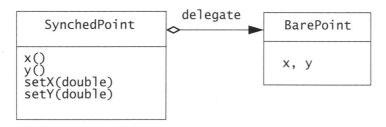

```
public class BarePoint {
  public double x, y;
}

public class SynchedPoint {
  protected BarePoint delegate_ = new BarePoint();

  public synchronized double x() {
    return delegate_.x;
  }

  public synchronized double y() {
    return delegate_.y;
  }

  public synchronized void setX(double v) {
    delegate_.x = v;
  }

  public synchronized void setY(double v) {
    delegate_.y = v;
  }
}
```

137

5.2.1.2 *Adding Guarded Methods*

Suppose you have a simple `BareCounter` class that maintained counts:

```java
public class BareCounter {
  private long count_;

  public BareCounter(long c) {
    count_ = c;
  }

  public long value() {
    return count_;
  }

  public void add(long c) {
    count_ += c;
  }

}
```

A `BoundedCounter` can be layered on by adding `wait/notifyAll` control. The strategy is identical to the subclass version except for those differences stemming from the use of delegation versus subclassing, here allowing `inc` to be translated into add:

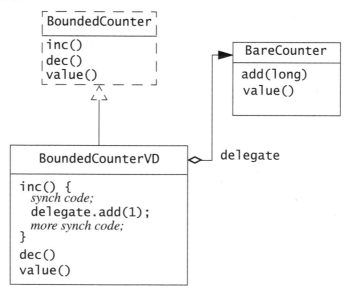

```
public class BoundedCounterVD implements BoundedCounter {
  private BareCounter delegate_ = new BareCounter(MIN);

  public synchronized long value() {
    return delegate_.value();
  }

  public synchronized void inc()    {
    while (delegate_.value() >= MAX)
      try { wait(); } catch(InterruptedException ex) {};
    delegate_.add(1);
    notifyAll();
  }

  public synchronized void dec()    {
    while (delegate_.value() <= MIN)
      try { wait(); } catch(InterruptedException ex) {};
    delegate_.add(-1);
    notifyAll();
  }
}
```

In more flexible variants of this approach, you can encapsulate the *before* and *after* operations within methods that can be either overridden in subclasses or plugged in dynamically via *hooks*. The resulting Decorator and Strategy designs (see the *Design Patterns* book) enable the implementation of multiple policies using the same Adapter class and/or its subclasses.

5.2.2 Read-Only Adapters

Synchronized Adapters allow objects to be used as if they were themselves synchronized. Read-Only Adapters allow objects to be used as if they were immutable. Rather than supplying synchronization, Adapters can control *visibility* to methods that could cause delegates to change state. This allows you to implement policies that eliminate all possibility of unsynchronized changes, while still forwarding access to other methods.

Transient immutability is most frequently needed with ordinary data structure classes — tables, lists, and so on. For example, a method may be sent a modifiable list of some sort with the intent that it traverse the list without otherwise modifying it, and the client may have no good strategy on what to do if the method does modify it. Synchronization is typically not the main concern in such contexts. Instead, the goal is to avoid any changes at all, often because you do not completely trust the method being handed the object.

Read-Only Adapters provide a solution that may be applicable when:

- The alternative of making deep copies of transmitted objects is undesirable for performance or functionality reasons.

- Similarly, it is undesirable to write a totally unrelated immutable class along with a constructor that creates one out of an updatable representation. This alternative is seen, for example, in the immutable `java.lang.String` class that supports conversion from mutable `java.lang.StringBuffer`.

- You can ensure that the Adapter maintains exclusive control of the wrapped object.

5.2.2.1 *Design Steps*

- (Optional) Use a convention to provide a name for this immutability property. For example, define an empty interface `Immutable` so that, by convention, such classes declare `implements Immutable`.

- Define a base interface describing some non-mutative functionality. The listed methods may include those constructing new objects that are the same as the target object except for some stated difference. For example, for a `String` class, this could be a method that returns a new `String` which is the same as the current one except that it has a newline appended.

- Define a subinterface that supports additional update methods.

- Implement the updatable interfaces in any way you like.

- Declare that the immutable versions are `final` classes and support only the operations described in the interface. The use of `final` means that when you think you have an immutable object, you really do — it's not of some subclass that supports mutable operations as well.

- Define the immutable class to have an instance variable, say `delegate`, of the base interface type, and define each method to forward the message to `delegate`. However, for the sake of efficiency, methods that would otherwise cause the construction of new objects can sometimes instead be implemented using lazy updates and other algorithmic cleverness.

For example, these steps can be applied to a simple Account class:

```
public interface Immutable {}

public class InsufficientFunds extends Exception {}

public interface Account {
  public long balance();
}

public interface UpdatableAccount extends Account {
  public void credit(long amount) throws InsufficientFunds;
  public void debit(long amount) throws InsufficientFunds;
}
```

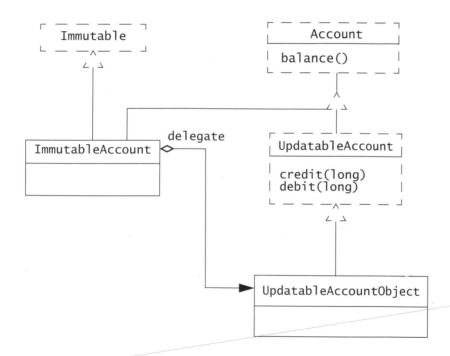

```
// Sample implementation of updatable version
public class UpdatableAccountObject
              implements UpdatableAccount{
  private long currentBalance_;

  public UpdatableAccountObject(long initialBalance) {
    currentBalance_ = initialBalance;
  }

  public synchronized long balance() {
    return currentBalance_;
  }

  public synchronized void credit(long amount)
   throws InsufficientFunds {
    if (amount >= 0 || currentBalance_ >= -amount)
      currentBalance_ += amount;
    else
      throw new InsufficientFunds();
  }

  public synchronized void debit(long amount)
   throws InsufficientFunds {
    credit(-amount);
  }
}

public final class ImmutableAccount // the adapter class
                   implements Account, Immutable {
  private Account delegate_;

  // create a fresh immutable account
  public ImmutableAccount(long initialBalance) {
    delegate_ = new UpdatableAccountObject(initialBalance);
  }

  // hold an existing account immutably
  ImmutableAccount(Account delegate) {
    delegate_ = delegate;
  }

  public long balance() { // forward the immutable method
    return delegate_.balance();
  }
}
```

These classes could be used, for example, in:

```java
public class AccountRecorder { // A logging facility
  public void recordBalance(Account a) {
    System.out.println(a.balance()); // or record in file
  }
}

public class AccountHolder {
  private UpdatableAccount acct_ = new UpdatableAccountObject(0);
  private AccountRecorder recorder_;

  public AccountHolder(AccountRecorder r) {
    recorder_ = r;
  }

  public void acceptMoney(long amount) {
    try {
      acct_.credit(amount);
      recorder_.recordBalance(new ImmutableAccount(acct_));//(*)
    }
    catch (InsufficientFunds ex) {
      System.out.println("Cannot accept negative amount.");
    }
  }
}
```

Use of an immutable wrapper at line (*) might seem an unnecessary precaution. But the precaution guards against what might happen if someone were to write the following subclass and use it in the constructor for an AccountUser:

```java
public class EvilAccountRecorder extends AccountRecorder {
  private long embezzlement_;
  // ...
  public void recordBalance(Account a) {
    if (a instanceof UpdatableAccount) {
      UpdatableAccount u = (UpdatableAccount)a;
      try {
        u.debit(10);
        embezzlement_ += 10;
      }
      catch (InsufficientFunds quietlyignore) {}
    }
    super.recordBalance(a);
  }
}
```

143

5.2.3 Extending Atomicity

Adapters can sometimes be used to "extend the range" of existing synchronization policies for specialized purposes.

For example, suppose you had a TwoLockQueue (Chapter 3) and would like to instrument it to print a message after every put and take. You might just add print statements, as in:

```
public class Producer implements Runnable {
  private TwoLockQueue b_; // balking queue class from Chapter 3

  public Producer(TwoLockQueue b) {
    b_ = b;
    new Thread(this).start();
  }

  public void run() {
    int i = 0;
    for (;;) {
      Object x = new Integer(i++); // or whatever
      b_.put(x);
      System.out.println("put " + x); // print after each put
      // do something else ...
    }
  }

}

public class Consumer implements Runnable {
  private TwoLockQueue b_;

  public Consumer(TwoLockQueue b) {
    b_ = b;
    new Thread(this).start();
  }

  public void run() {
    for (;;) {
      Object x = b_.take();
      if (x != null) { // print after each successful take
        System.out.println("take " + x);
        // use x ...
      }
    }
  }

}
```

However, this could lead to confusing results. The printlns are not at all guaranteed to follow put and take atomically. It could happen that a take message is printed before its corresponding put message.

One possible solution is to enclose the put;print and take;print sequences in synchronized blocks holding the lock for the queue. However, the success of this construction hinges on knowledge of the particular synchronization policies of the put and take methods, which might not be amenable to this kind of control. Here, the TwoLockQueue class does not even rely on synchronization on the queue object itself for the take operation.

Delegation-based designs do not encounter such problems. The synchronization lock used for methods in an Adapter controls only *access* by participants to the delegate. It cannot otherwise interfere with any of its internal synchronization policies. (On the other hand, this form of delegation can lead to the nested monitor problems discussed in Chapter 4 if delegate methods use guarded waits. This is not an issue with TwoLockQueue. Solutions applying to cases where it is an issue are described in Chapter 8.)

For example, the Producer and Consumer classes could be reworked to rely on class PrintingBuffer:

```
public class PrintingBuffer {
  private TwoLockQueue b_ = new TwoLockQueue();

  public synchronized void put(Object x) {
    b_.put(x);
    System.out.println("put " + x);
  }

  public synchronized Object take() {
    Object x = b_.take();
    if (x != null)
      System.out.println("take " + x);
    return x;
  }

}
```

5.3 Acceptors

Layering is closely associated with the notion of *reflection* via *meta-objects* that oversee, represent, manipulate, reason about, and/or otherwise control ground objects. However, the concurrency control strategies presented so far in this chapter have focused on cheaper compositional techniques based on subclassing and delegation. These techniques achieve sufficient control and separation of control without needing to explicitly represent other messages, methods, or objects.

But subclassing and delegation techniques tend to break down as the code needed to intercept messages, track execution states, and schedule activities overwhelms that for normal ground-level actions. Reflective techniques provide a basis for full separation between concurrency control and ground-level processing, although at the cost of passing around *representations* (also known as *reifications*) of messages rather than just performing normal invocations.

A meta-object receives messages in some form or another that it decodes into method calls to one or more underlying normal ground objects. Although not always characterized as such, among the most common meta-object designs are *event frameworks*, in which messages are explicitly represented as events. More generally, reflective designs can be based around just about any kind of message representation, including:

- An integer representing a key press, mouse click, or service code.

- A string representation of an incoming request and its arguments (as used in `Applet.getParameter`).

- An `Event` class used to represent user input, as seen in the Java AWT. Or one that represents simulated physical occurrences, as in a discrete event simulation system. Or perhaps even a set of subclasses, one per event type. (This allows decoding and dispatching via `instanceof`.)

- A CORBA Request packet received from an external process.

- A `Runnable` object, in which case execution simply amounts to telling the object to `run`.

- A `Class` object, in which case "execution" entails creation of a `newInstance` of the associated class.

The basic interface for any object participating in such a framework contains a method that accepts a message representation, decodes it somehow, and causes the corresponding action to be executed:

```
public interface Acceptor {
  public void accept(MessageType msg);
}
```

A common alternative is to use a boolean flag as a return value indicating whether the message has been processed. Common alternative names for the operation itself include `handle`, `action`, `perform`, `post`, and `execute`.

You can structure an Acceptor in any of the countless ways that you can structure any ordinary object, plus more because Acceptors have more chances to "think about" and manipulate messages before ultimately executing the ground actions. While only a few of these are illustrated here and in subsequent chapters, the range of options includes Acceptors that:

- Support `accept` as well as corresponding ground-level methods themselves, in which case the Acceptor implements `accept` by decoding the message and forwarding to its own ground-level methods.

- Delegate `accept` to one or more other objects.

- Map requests to actions using a dispatch table.

- Use a thread-per-message design in which `accept` processes each request in a new thread.

- Explicitly represent and manipulate any state-based conditions (for example using `Constraint` classes) required for the associated actions to trigger, or even represent the entire receive-check-act sequence using `EventConditionAction` classes.

- Schedule multiple execution agents.

- Maintain history logs of messages to enable undoing and replay.

- Filter or transform messages on their ways to other Acceptors.

Acceptors can provide basic synchronization control on behalf of the ground objects, exactly as in subclass-based and Adapter-based designs. In a sense, using meta-objects for concurrency control is the ideal design form, since it provides the most flexible control mechanisms. The `accept` method can look at the entire state of the program if need be when deciding whether a given object should perform a given method, otherwise perhaps queuing the message for later. However, in practice the overhead and awkwardness of "going meta" is usually too overwhelming unless you already need to create an event framework to organize a reactive application or simulation system, or unless processing is already so computationally intensive that the added overhead is not an issue. This may hold for example in applications performing expensive transaction control.

Acceptor objects can themselves locally maintain references to other acceptor objects, forming a chain or tree of acceptors. This cascading Chain of Responsibility strategy (see the *Design Patterns* book) is seen in the `java.awt.Component` event-handling framework, where each `Container` object may try to dispatch events locally to each of its members, or may just choose to handle them all itself. If all event acceptors are maintained according to a strict containment policy, events can be quickly dispatched to the appropriate Acceptor.

5.3.1 Proxy Encoders

Some languages (for example, CLOS) and tools (for example, SOM) provide syntactic support for meta-object-level programming. For example, they allow you to create a meta-object that handles all messages of a certain form using the same kind of before/after processing. These must be programmed "manually" in Java, which takes a bit more work but also provides a bit more flexibility. In Java, you can define the representation of messages in any way you like. Once you do, you can bypass normal native message-passing styles when necessary by constructing explicit message representations and forwarding them to an appropriate Acceptor.

Usually, the best way to establish the required structure is to use proxies that perform this encoding and dispatch. Designs based on Proxy Encoders take typical form:

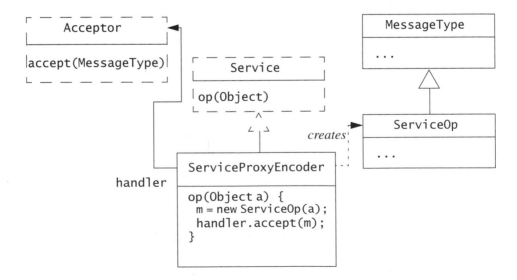

```
public interface Service {   // fragments
  public void op(Object arg);
}

public class ServiceOp extends MessageType {
  private Object arg_:
  // ...
}

public class ServiceProxy implements Service { // ...
  protected Acceptor handler_;
  public void op(Object arg) {
    MessageType m = new ServiceOp(arg); // encode
    handler_.accept(m);                 // relay
  }

}
```

5.3.2 Event Loops

In the java.applet framework, applets with a handleEvent or action method translate button presses and the like to method calls on the objects implementing their main functionality. Here, the main event-gathering loop is common to an entire Java program. It dispatches incoming user events to the per-applet handlers.

The same need arises in other event-processing problems as well, in which case you can construct your own event loops. Event loops continuously accept request messages from local objects and dispatch them to other objects or methods that are the first stages of flows that service the underlying requests (see Chapter 7).

Events often take a simple, specialized form, for example, integers representing mouse events. However the same design applies across classes based on just about any message type. And once you have an event-handling system in place, you can use it for several extended forms of event handling. For example, you may choose to post "artificial" events to help control responses to events representing user input.

Buffered event loops run asynchronously with respect to objects posting events, although not necessarily with respect to those servicing them. Asynchronous service could be obtained by creating a new thread to run each command, but it is often both easier and more efficient instead to maintain a buffer along with a single thread that continually executes deposited commands.

5.3.2.1 *Design Steps*

To create an Event Loop, use, adapt, or write the following classes:

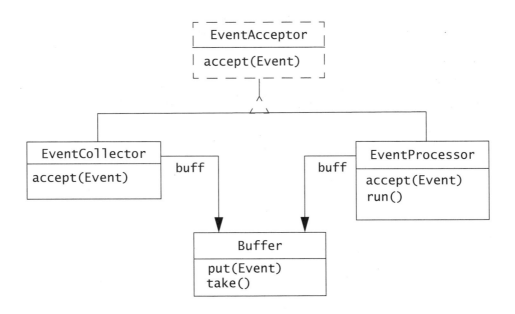

Event. Any appropriate representation of events, for example the one defined in
java.awt.Event.

Buffer. Any kind of data structure holding Events, minimally with methods of
the form put and take.

EventCollector. The class describing objects with which event producers
communicate. It supports a method invoked by clients that accepts events and
deposits them in a buffer.

EventProcessor. A class with an accept method that performs the action
associated with the event, along with a run method with a loop to pull requests
continuously from the buffer (waiting if there are no requests) and then execute
them.

5.3.2.2 *Example*

Here is a simple version using a `BoundedBuffer`. Because the buffer is bounded,
event producers may sometimes stall if the `EventProcessor` is lagging too far
behind (see Chapter 7).

```
public abstract class Event { // minimal Event class
  public abstract int eventCode();
}


public class EventCollector implements Acceptor {
  protected BoundedBuffer buff_;

  public EventCollector() {
    buff_ = new BoundedBufferVST(100);
    new EventProcessor(buff_);
  }

  public synchronized void accept(Event e) {
    buff_.put(e);
  }

}


public class EventProcessor implements Runnable, Acceptor  {
  protected BoundedBuffer buff_;

  public EventProcessor(BoundedBuffer b) {
    buff_ = b;
    new Thread(this).start();
  }

  public void accept(Event e) {
    switch (e.eventCode()) {
      // ... dispatch ...
    }
  }

  public void run() {
    for (;;) {
      accept((Event)(buff_.take()));
    }
  }

}
```

5.3.2.3 *Table-Based Handlers*

The simplest kinds of EventProcessors are born knowing how to handle each
incoming event. More flexible versions can be constructed by recasting accept to
work off tables or other adjustable mechanisms that delegate event-handling
actions to dynamically installed handlers. For example, using a hash table:

```
public interface EventHandler {
  boolean handle(Event e); // return false if could not handle
}

public class TableDrivenEventProcessor extends EventProcessor {
  protected Hashtable table_ = new Hashtable();

  public TableDrivenEventProcessor(BoundedBuffer b) {
    super(b);
  }

  public void accept(Event e) {
    Integer i = new Integer(e.eventCode());
    Vector b = (Vector)(table_.get(i));
    if (b != null) { // run each handler
      for (Enumeration p = b.elements(); p.hasMoreElements(); )
        ((EventHandler)(p.nextElement())).handle(e);
    }
  }

  public void addHandler(Event e, EventHandler h) {
    Integer i = new Integer(e.eventCode());
    Vector b = (Vector)(table_.get(i));
    if (b == null) { // if no handler list, make one
      b = new Vector();
      table_.put(i, b);
    }
    b.addElement(h);
  }

}
```

To maximize flexibility, the table entries here themselves hold Vectors of
handlers, allowing more than one handler per event type. Within accept, all handlers associated with the received event are tried. One alternative design is to continue trying handlers until hitting the first one that returns true. Another alternative
is to restructure the entire class to use a cascade strategy in which each Handler
itself forwards unhandled events to others, leading to a push-based flow design of
the sort described in Chapter 7.

5.3.3 Listeners

Most Java programs communicate with other programs. Even the act of firing up an applet intrinsically involves communication among different programs typically residing on different machines. Additionally, each of these Java programs typically involves several concurrent threads.

Listeners are probably the most common forms of meta-object in concurrent OO programs that deal with external processes. A Listener serves as a shared meta-object that accepts external messages and then executes them by dispatching to ground-level objects. Listener-based objects are also sometimes called *Reactors*, *Object Adapters*, *Guardians*, *Skeletons*, *Executives,* and *Demultiplexers.*

The general form of a Listener is an interpreter loop that continually pulls messages from a stream and feeds them to an event-handling method:

```
public class Listener implements Acceptor, Runnable {
  MessageInputStream s; // any kind of input stream or connection

  void accept(MessageType m) {
    // call some method on some object
  }

  public void run() {
    for (;;) {
      accept(s.readMessage());
    }
  }
}
```

There is again considerable room for variation. Options include Listeners that:

- Serve as Parsers and Builders (see *Design Patterns*), transforming raw input into internal representations of messages.

- Pass the message input stream to the execution handler so that it can read other embedded arguments and data mixed in with commands.

- Are fired up using a *thread-per-channel* policy, where a new Listener is started in its own thread whenever a stream connection is opened.

Meta-level control strategies are overkill for many everyday concurrency problems. But they are nearly indispensable in designs that deal with external programs. They help organize the interaction of objects with their environments by addressing *naming* and *messaging* issues encountered in any distributed system:

5.3.3.1 *Naming*

One of the primary tasks in establishing a distributed object system is dealing with *handles* (sometimes known as references, locators and channels) that name objects across different machines. Java object references serve as handles inside single Java programs, but they have no external form. So they cannot be used for distributed messaging. For purposes of developing most distributed object systems, this restriction is a feature rather than a bug in Java, since usually you don't want the normal Java objects in a program to receive external messages directly.

In fact, it suffices to have exactly one Listener object per Java program. The Listener can accept any kind of external message and then internally relay it to any ground-level object to perform the indicated action. This approach restricts interprocess communication to interactions among meta-objects, not ground objects, limiting the cases and senses in which you must deal with external naming issues. Only the Listeners need external handles. When there is exactly one Listener, the entire issue almost disappears, since you can then just use standard Internet-style addresses and ports for handles. For example, this is how http works. Machines that serve http traffic almost always have a single handle (`http://internet.addr:80`) corresponding to a single Listener object that may relay requests to other internal or external helpers (for example, replicate processes and CGI programs). It takes only a little more work to generalize this to incorporate more than one Listener, and use one per externally available service provided by the process. This is how CORBA systems are usually organized.

5.3.3.2 *Messaging*

Messages sent across processes must be encoded into a network-compatible format, which requires some kind of decoding. A Listener-based design can use nearly any external message format for communication among processes, but uses standard built-in Java messaging for communication among the internal ground objects. Listeners must be paired with encoders and transporters that allow ground objects to send external-format messages to Listeners in external processes.

5.3.3.3 *Applications*

Even small examples of Listener-based designs would require too much additional infrastructure to illustrate implementation techniques here. In addition to encoding, transport, decoding, and connection management mechanisms, distributed object systems and the code using them must deal with distributed faults, failures, and security, which are all beyond the scope of this book. However, the range of applicability of Listener-based designs encompasses the following kinds of distributed frameworks:

Ad hoc networking. Nearly every Java server program that opens a `Socket` includes at least a simple Listener that listens for incoming messages and dispatches them to worker objects, for example `ContentHandlers`.

Structured requests as messages. In remote method invocation (RMI) systems (whether native to Java or part of a framework such as CORBA), normal-looking messages are passed to remote servers by first encoding them into Request objects of fixed known format, usually with the help of Proxy Encoders that serve as internal stand-ins for external objects. Proxies send Requests through network transport mechanisms to a Listener that determines which local object and method to dispatch the message to. It ultimately returns replies in a similar manner.

Classes as messages. The Java class-loading framework uses a message-passing strategy in which entire classes are treated as messages. In Java, `Class` objects have a predefined external format (the "`.class`" format). This forms the basis for the Java applet framework:

- `Class` objects are encoded by compiling source code.

- They are transported using http or other standard network mechanisms.

- They are decoded using the Java `ClassLoader` utilities attached to a master listener loop.

- At least in the case of applets, they are executed via `cls.newInstance`. This constructs an instance of `cls` (the decoded `Class`) and sets it in motion, thus executing the command. The command may of course amount to the execution of any functionality that can be bundled as an applet.

Objects as messages. Rather than sending classes, you can send objects as messages. In the most straightforward version of this scheme, the `Listener.accept` method just asks a transported `Runnable` command object to run itself. The use of command objects (sometimes known as *smart messages, active messages,* and *closure-based messages*) exploits the "meta" aspects of the Listener framework by relying on the built-in Java interpreter to execute the commands. Command-based messaging requires the ability to ship descriptions of full objects across wires. While you could encapsulate messages as singleton `Classes` and then use the Java class loader framework, this scheme would be too heavy for most message-passing applications. However, it is possible to scale down each of the required capabilities to form a more attractive basis for command-based distributed messaging systems. For example, you can build a facility around serialization mechanisms that pack objects into transportable messages:

- Clients construct commands as instances of `Runnable` objects, which are then serialized. In the most ambitious versions of this approach, commands represent entire threads, capturing the dynamic state of running objects.

- Serialized commands are transported via streams (in turn tied to `Sockets` or whatever).

- Listeners continuously pull commands from an input stream and decode them by unserializing them, thus constructing new local ground objects.

- Execution consists of asking the unpacked object to `run` itself.

5.4   Models and Mappings

The nature, role, and properties of compositional layering techniques and policy control are intimately tied to basic models of what's going on in concurrent Java programs. The remainder of this chapter surveys broader notions of *models* — formal, semiformal, or conventional descriptions of how objects are structured, created, and used for computation — and *mappings* — descriptions of how object models are implemented on actual computers.

5.4.1   Models

Different object models[1] make different assumptions about how objects are structured, created, and used. These models can be expressed at just about any level of formality and precision. Nearly all share at least the following commonalities. Different models specialize and/or more carefully specify different features in different ways.

Statics. The static structure of each object is described (normally via a class) in terms of internal attributes and states, links (references) to other objects, local (internal) methods, and methods or ports for accepting messages from other objects.

Encapsulation. Objects have membranes separating their insides and outsides. The degree of enforcement of encapsulation can vary. For example, when objects reside on different computers, the separation is usually "physical". Within

---

[1]. Beware that the term "object model" is sometimes applied in senses different from that used here, ranging from rules for laying out storage locations in particular languages to primitives in abstract calculi.

concurrent programming languages like Java, it is arranged via scoping and access control constructs such as `private`.

Identity. New objects of a certain form (again, normally as described via a class) can be constructed and/or activated at any time (subject to system resource constraints) and by any other object (subject to access control). Once constructed, each object maintains a unique identity that persists over its lifetime, thus allowing it to be referenced from other objects.

Communication. Objects communicate only via message passing, that is, by invoking accessible methods on other objects.

Computation. Objects perform actions in accord with a computation loop along the lines of:

- Accept a message.

- Execute a method corresponding to an accepted message: perform some sequence of internal operations, possibly varying according to current internal state and taking any of three forms:

  - Update internal state.

  - Send a message.

  - Create a new object.

5.4.2 Mappings

As Gregor Kiczales has noted, software engineering, like all forms of engineering, is fundamentally concerned with the control of physical processes. So let's start at the bottom. Well, perhaps not the very bottom, but close enough to see the issues involved in building a system to support sequential and concurrent object-oriented programming.

Consider a typical computer containing memory cells and a single CPU (among other components ignored for present purposes). Each of the memory cells is an object according to the above generic model, an impoverished object in most respects but still an object. Each maintains state and accepts read and write messages (although usually only to/from the CPU).

The CPU is also an object, although a much more complicated one, mainly because of its programmability. Its messages take the form of machine instructions telling it to sequentially emulate the behavior of any other arbitrary object. With the help of memory cells dedicated to maintaining its program text, the CPU can pretend that it is any kind of object, up to and including a different kind of CPU, for example the Java Virtual Machine. Also, unlike typical memory cells, the CPU can deal with messages to and from external objects (via interrupts, ports, and the like), as well as all the memory cell objects, which it may group together, re-assign roles for, and otherwise manage in just about any fashion.

These observations immediately lead to a mapping for the high-level object model characteristic of sequential non-object-oriented programming, where a smart CPU-based object (the program) coordinates the actions of all the dumb memory cell objects (its data variables). But any number of other models can be mapped to the same hardware. While all reasonable models are presumably equivalent at some theoretical level, it's worth pursuing those that better mirror the ground rules for programming with concurrent objects.

5.4.3 Active and Passive Objects

Most run-of-the-mill objects are clearly not exactly like either memory cells or CPUs. Unlike memory cells, most programming-level objects maintain more than one bit (or word or whatever) of state, communicate directly with others, and support a number of operations beyond simple reads and writes. But unlike CPUs, they have no need to support dynamic programmability. Once created, objects (at least Java `Objects` except perhaps for those of class `Class`) are meant to retain the same structural form throughout their lifetimes.

As a reflection of this, essentially all OO models include both memory-like and CPU-like features. These are mapped by allowing each object to carve out its own piece of a computer. Each object uses some memory cells to represent state and method bodies, uses a memory address (or something that can be mapped to one) to represent its local identity, and uses a CPU for computation.

Different ways of looking at this have led to two kinds of object models. *Passive* models view objects as smart memory cells; *active* models view objects as dumb CPUs.

5.4.3.1 *Passive Models*

Purely passive object models restrict computation to sequential message passing, in fact just the kinds of messaging natively supported by normal Java invocation mechanisms. In the most primitive passive scheme:

- Objects cannot prevent themselves from acting upon new messages. When an invocation is performed, the method body is immediately triggered.

- Upon sending a message, further actions in a sender's method body suspend until the recipient completes the associated action and issues a `return` or `throws` an `Exception`.

The resulting programming models have been highly successful in purely sequential OO languages where there is only one CPU-like object, the one associated with the main action of the program. In this case, there's no reason to remove either kind of limitation.

5.4.3.2 *Active Models*

Active object models (also known as *per-object concurrency* models and as *actor* models) lift either or both of these restrictions:

- At least in the most straightforward active object models, each object is a single CPU-like entity that can only do one thing at a time. While an active object may or may not be able to prevent itself from *receiving* a request, it can control which (if any) messages it is *acting* upon at any given time based on its current state. The object may postpone actions associated with a particular message because it is not currently in a state that logically permits any action.

- In addition to using procedural[2] message-passing protocols, objects may issue messages without waiting for replies. Asynchronous *oneway* messages are usually construed as the basic mechanism for obtaining concurrency of different activities across different objects. In most active object models, asynchronous messages are viewed as more primitive and fundamental than synchronous ones. A procedural interaction can be constructed via a pair of asynchronous messages (a request and a reply), along with guards that cause the client to wait for the reply before proceeding.

The resulting programming models have been highly successful in purely distributed settings and networking applications in which each different object resides on a different computer (or, often enough, essentially *is* the entire computer). In this case, you cannot do with much less. Incoming messages from networks must be accepted and decoded from network packet form, queued, and scheduled according to particular policies and protocols. And outgoing messages must be sent without any obligation to wait for replies that never arrive because the recipient computer fails.

5.4.4 Concurrent Objects

The realm of concurrent programming, the entire middle ground between the extreme forms of passive and active models, applies when some objects have at

---

2. The term *procedural* is used in this book only in the sense of request/reply-style communication. It is *not* used as a synonym for "non-object-oriented".

least some of the characteristics of active objects. This arises when any combination of multiple physical and virtual CPUs run, in the case of Java, a generic interpreter-style computation loop based upon two kinds of instructions:

1. Instructions that perform ground-level object constructions, state updates and method invocations.

2. Instructions that construct, update, and allow communication among interpreters (threads) themselves.

The resulting diversity of object forms along the passive-active dimension defies capture by any one model. Instead, there are gradations in models applying to familiar *policies* such as:

Synchronized objects. Objects living within procedural restrictions, but also using Java synchronization locks to prevent multiple conflicting methods from being triggered by multiple active objects.

Balking objects. Objects that cannot actively delay execution of a procedural request if they are not in the right state, but can at least arrange to do nothing at all beyond report failure to comply.

Guarded objects. Objects that, in addition to enforcing one-method-at-a-time rules, delay action upon methods until they are in the proper state.

Versioned objects. Objects that can pretend that they are in different states, only sometimes committing to them.

Concurrency policy controllers. Objects that explicitly represent and manipulate the execution state of ground objects.

Acceptors. Objects that represent, store, and manipulate messages ultimately translated down to primitive invocations.

5.4.4.1   *Open Implementations*

No matter how you go about implementing concurrency control, you are intrinsically dealing with the object modeling and mapping issues associated with different concurrency policies. Composition and layering are among the best engineering strategies for coping with diversity of models and the never-ending trade-offs encountered when choosing among them. Concurrent programming often involves determining the least powerful object forms needed to carry out a given task. For example, in general, an active form is strictly necessary only when creating a new asynchronous activity, which is what Java `Threads` do best.

High-level OO analysis and modeling are usually easier and more productive if you start out using the most powerful active object models available. But detailed design and implementation are often easier and more productive if you use a more bottom-up approach. While it is usually possible to construct more powerful forms out of less powerful ones, the opposite is less often true. And even when it is, it is usually wasteful. All else being equal, why use a smart but expensive object when a dumb cheap one will do? In principle, you might be able to optimize down a smart but slow object into a dumber but faster one. But in a world of self-contained components, you do not always have the opportunity to do so.

In larger applications, compositional approaches often lead to designs with at least three discernible layers of classes:

- Ground objects that provide raw functionality. These objects are structured to be amenable to concurrency control but do not themselves provide any kind of synchronization or even self protection.

- Objects that implement synchronization and control policies on top of other objects so that they can be used in multithreaded settings.

- Objects that accept requests from and implement policies for dealing with the *external* world — other processes, users, databases, and so on.

The associated techniques differ from non-OO black-box layering schemes in supporting to varying extents, *open implementation* strategies in which:

- Classes providing mechanism can be extended and otherwise varied independently of those at higher layers.

- Classes providing policy may be reconfigured to deal differently with those at lower layers.

Open implementations help deal with the range of policy and mapping decisions made along the path from concept to implementation. Making object characteristics and trade-offs explicit, allowing for both static and dynamic alternatives, and, when affordable, using intrinsically reflective designs all help prepare for inevitable changes in policies and mappings over time.

5.5 Further Readings

Layering policy over mechanism is an extremely common structuring principle in systems of all sorts. For discussions from an architectural perspective, see the books by Garlan and Shaw and by Buschmann *et al* listed in Chapter 1. Open implementation designs that avoid extensibility and usability problems associated with pure black-box layering are described in:

Kiczales, Gregor. "Beyond the Black Box: Open Implementation", *IEEE Software*, January, 1996.

More thorough discussions and further examples of inheritance anomalies can be found in the collection edited by Agha, Wegner, and Yonezawa listed in Chapter 1, as well as in papers presented at recent OO conferences such as *ECOOP*, and in:

McHale, Ciaran. *Synchronization in Concurrent Object-Oriented Languages*, PhD Thesis, Trinity College, 1994.

The *Composition-Filters* system is an example of an OO development framework that requires separation of functionality from synchronization control. It also includes a more extensive notation than conflict sets for representing concurrency control constraints. See for example, papers by Mehmet Aksit and others in the collection edited by Guerraoui, Nierstrasz, and Riveill listed in Chapter 1.

Other extensions of conflict set notation, for example *path expressions*, are described in the text by Andrews as well as in most of the sources on database systems listed in Chapter 1.

The Readers and Writers pattern is one of several patterns presented here in this book that are also discussed in just about any non-object-oriented account of concurrent programming, although not in the context of design patterns.

The object-oriented language Self is among the few that directly support a pure delegation style of programming without requiring explicit message forwarding. See:

Ungar, David. "The Self Papers", *Lisp and Symbolic Computation*, 1991.

More general accounts of reflection and meta-level programming can be found in books on Lisp, Scheme and CLOS (the Common Lisp Object System); for example:

Abelson, Harold, and Gerald Sussman. *Structure and Interpretation of Computer Programs*, MIT Press, 1996.

Kiczales, Gregor, Jim des Rivieres, and Daniel Bobrow. *The Art of the Metaobject Protocol,* MIT Press, 1993.

SOM is an example of a framework that automates message representation and encoding chores in a way that simplifies definition and manipulation of meta-object methods. See:

Forman, Ira, and Scott Danforth. "Composition of before/after metaclasses in SOM", *OOPSLA '94 Proceedings*, ACM, 1994.

Structured distributed infrastructures and tools for Java are rapidly emerging; see the on-line supplement for pointers to current information. Design patterns for establishing infrastructures supporting distributed object systems may be found in papers by Doug Schmidt and colleagues, including those in the *Pattern Languages of Program Design* series.

Most active object models rely on asynchronous communication. Many non-object-oriented concurrency models are instead based on synchronous communication among processes (which may be construed as active objects). Under synchronous *rendezvous*-style communication rules, a message sender cannot proceed until the recipient is ready to accept the message. Synchronous communication plays a central role in languages (including Ada) and models based on process calculi such as CSP and CCS — see the books by Hoare and Milner listed in Chapter 1. It is possible to implement versions of synchronous communication channels in Java using variants and extensions of the flow-based techniques described in Chapter 7.

Many books and research papers discuss object models (see the sources on object-oriented design and on research in OO systems listed in Chapter 1). However, few discuss multiple layers or gradations of object models. The most notable exceptions lie outside the technical concurrency literature. See, for example:

Dennett, Daniel. *Darwin's Dangerous Idea*, Simon and Schuster, 1995.

Winograd, Terry and Fernando Flores. *Understanding Computers and Cognition: A New Foundation for Design,* Addison-Wesley, 1986.

CHAPTER 6

Services in Threads

THIS chapter presents more details and options about how and when to create and invoke thread-based services than have been described so far in this book.

6.1 Styles and Policies

Java thread mechanics provide a way to obtain the effect of the pseudocode:

```
execute server.op(arg) in a new Thread
```

However, you cannot just write lines of code of this form. Java does not support any kind of syntax for sending the names of methods as arguments. So you cannot pass a string or symbol to a Thread to indicate the method(s) to run or the arguments to run them with. Instead, you must use the same method name for all activities run in threads, so that the native Thread.start mechanism can always invoke a known method. Thread.start is the only programmable message in Java that can be sent non-procedurally (without waiting for completion). It is in turn hard-coded to call run of a Runnable. *Runnable Commands* are classes that implement Runnable in a fashion amenable for use with Java thread facilities.

While run is most commonly used as the name of the method to run in a thread, it can also be used in any other context requiring that an arbitrary self-contained method be invoked. It serves as a standard way of implementing most instances of the Command pattern described in the *Design Patterns* book. Runnable Commands are highly specialized Adapters that serve to repackage any kind of functionality to conform to the most minimal form of message possible in the language. In this sense, Runnable Commands are canonical representations (or *reifications*) of Java messages. They are often the most convenient message type (see Chapter 5) for meta-level designs in which messages are passed around, stored, and so on, in addition to actually being executed.

A special Runnable class is necessary for each distinct kind of action needing to be run in a Java Thread. Runnable classes are more awkward to set up than just sending method names would be, but not at all hard to implement. And even though they require more coding, these classes do not add much overhead, especially when the `Runnable` objects simply act as relays. Most languages that support such constructs natively (via *closures* or *blocks*) do so in exactly the same way. The only difference is that they do not require that programmers explicitly define these helper classes. It is possible to build tools in Java to define common forms of `Runnable` classes automatically (even at run time) to achieve this effect.

There are a number of common forms and styles for defining and using `Runnable` commands and related utility classes. Choices among them sometimes just amount to matters of taste. But they should also be based on considerations of the particular activities of interest and the need to establish regular conventions so that threads in a system are created in a compatible, predictable manner.

6.1.1   Invocation

The first consideration is whether the client or the server controls the form of the interaction. Client-controlled forms are a bit more flexible. Server-controlled forms are a bit easier to use.

Depending on the nature of the activity of interest and the other party's choice of conventions, each side can treat the invocation as a procedural call, a fully independent thread, or as a thread that later interacts with the other party to convey the results of the activity.

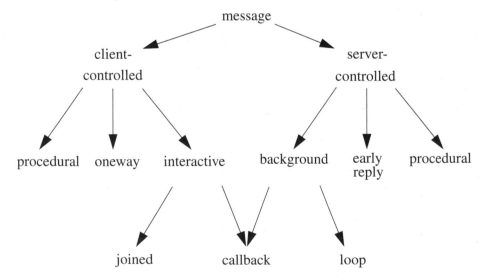

6.1.2 Interfaces

The second consideration surrounds interfaces and usage of the server-side classes:

- A client can invoke a thread-based service by invoking run. The service may already be defined as a *Runnable Service*, that is a class with run as its primary method. Otherwise, an Adapter can be defined to force a service to conform to interface Runnable.

- A Proxy (also known as a *Protocol Adapter*) can be defined to force thread-based versions to support the same (or at least similar) client invocation syntax as procedural versions.

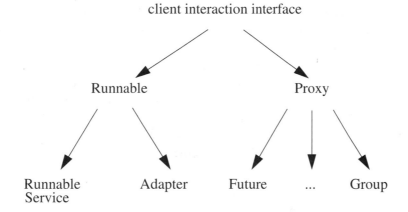

6.1.3 Subclassing

The third stylistic consideration revolves around class relations for any class, say RC, that implements the Runnable interface. There are three options:

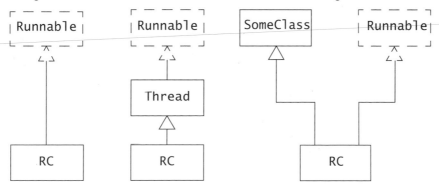

- A new standalone class implementing `Runnable`.

- A subclass of class `Thread`. (`Thread` itself implements `Runnable`.)

- A subclass of some other service class, mixing in `Runnable`.

While any of these can be made to work, the first approach is generally preferable. In Java, any method can access the `Thread` it is running within via:

```
Thread mythread = Thread.currentThread();
```

This means that any `Runnable` can include code performing operations on the `Thread` it is running within without itself having to *be* a `Thread`. Subclassing `Thread` provides no functionality advantages unless you need to override `Thread` methods. But since most `Thread` methods except for `run` are `final native`, you cannot override them. On the other hand, if a new extension of `Thread` were made available (for example, an `AutoReprioritizingThread` subclass) a `Runnable` would still be executable within it, but a `Thread` subclass normally would not be.

Also, maintaining a distinction between class `Thread` and the objects participating in threads tends to make designs a bit easier to implement and understand. For example, if you isolate thread control from other concurrency control mechanics, you don't even need to be aware of the fact that class `Thread` internally uses `notifyAll` (mainly to implement `join`).

Adding `Runnable` as a *mixin* subclass of an existing class (other than `java.lang.Object`, the base of all Java objects) is often the simplest option. For example:

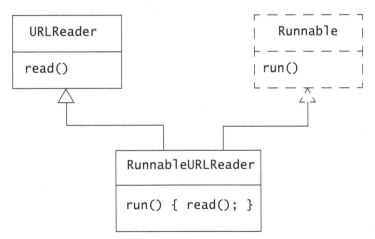

```
public class URLReader {
  protected String url_;
  protected byte[] buffer_;

  public URLReader(String url, byte[] buffer) {
    url_ = url;
    buffer_ = buffer;
  }

  public void read() { /* read into buffer */ }
}

public class RunnableURLReader extends URLReader
                            implements Runnable {

  public RunnableURLReader(String url, byte[] buffer) {
    super(url, buffer);
  }

  public void run() {
    read();
  }
}
```

This style of subclassing has somewhat limited applicability. If other ordinary methods in the class remain accessible, you need to be careful about potential interference. For example, unless the action is intrinsically parameterless, you may need to add parameter-holding instance variables that lock in a particular call to a particular method to be performed in run. These fixed settings often make no sense when the object is executing the method as a response to a normal invocation. It is usually easier to avoid such problems by making standalone classes.

6.2 Commands

The remainder of this chapter presents selected patterns resulting from the design space generated by considerations of invocation styles, class interfaces, thread usage, and Java implementation techniques. Presentations are interleaved with a few Java-specific implementation matters that are most closely associated or first encountered with each pattern, but also frequently apply to others.

This section focuses on *commands* — services that never convey results to or otherwise interact with clients. The following sections deal with completion dependence and with services run in multiple threads. The chapter concludes with a discussion of arrangements that can help thread-based services coexist with their environments.

6.2.1 Runnable Services

A run method can encapsulate a well-defined service, often involving other internal helper methods also defined in the Runnable class. The Runnable Service pattern is a set of design and implementation conventions for encoding a single method as a standalone service. Instead of invoking the method by calling it, clients set it in action by starting it in a thread:

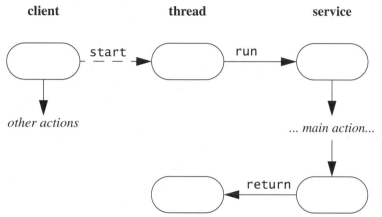

Runnable Services are often constructed as transformations of existing classes. Usually, these existing classes were not originally defined as Runnables, but contain time-consuming operations that should normally be executed in their own threads. Thread-based execution of existing methods in existing classes can always be arranged using Runnable Adapters that relay the calls. However, if a single service method can be factored into its own Runnable service class, it becomes easier to invoke, control, and use in a standardized fashion.

6.2.1.1 *Example*

For a classic example, suppose you start out with a class that reads and writes files.[1]

```
public class FileIO {
  //...
  public void writeBytes(String fileNm, byte[] data) { /*...*/ }
  public void readBytes(String fileNm, byte[] data) { /*...*/ }
}
```

[1.] While this makes a good example of how to build Runnable Services, it would be a somewhat odd class in Java since it doesn't mesh well with java.io classes that are already structured in ways that make I/O convenient to perform within threads.

Both of these methods might be good candidates for transformation into service threads. File I/O can be time-consuming, but can often be done independently of callers. In fact, file and network I/O are probably the most common kinds of activities routinely encapsulated within threads.

6.2.1.2 *Representing Arguments and Results*

The single method `FileIO.writeBytes` can be transformed into a simple service class. All data otherwise passed as arguments to `writeBytes` are instead sent as constructor arguments and are held by internal instance variables:

```
public class FileWriter implements Runnable {
  private String nm_; // hold arguments
  private byte[] d_;

  public FileWriter(String name, byte[] data) {
    nm_ = name;
    d_ = data;
  }

  public void run() {
    // write bytes in d_ to file nm_ ...
  }

}
```

Because the `run` method can neither take arguments nor return results, all control information must be held and managed by the `Runnable` command object itself, normally with the help of non-public instance variables. The simplest way to arrange that parameters be sent is to define a constructor that initializes instance variables corresponding to all target objects for relayed messages, and all arguments needed by any component operations.

Most Runnable Services are best designed as *one-shot* objects, `run` either just once or always with the same set of parameters. Their resulting immutability means that you don't need to worry about synchronization or state conflicts in the `Runnable` objects themselves, and can treat all instance variables as *thread-specific storage* that cannot be interfered with by other threads.

When the `Runnable` class is designed to be `run` more than once with different parameters, it must support `synchronized` assignment-based methods that assign control parameters one by one, to be called between each use. This may also require synchronization of the `run` method itself, and possibly other precautions. (Even though each instance of class `Thread` can `run` only one activity at a time, different `Threads` may be constructed around the same `Runnable`.)

6.2.1.3 *Client-Controlled Activation*

The `FileWriter` class could be used, for example, by an object that needs to save picture data in a file while at the same time rendering it:

```
public class PictureManipulator { // fragments
  public void processPicture(byte rawPicture[]) {
    Runnable r = new FileWriter("PictureCache", rawPicture);
    Thread t = new Thread(r);
    t.start();
    renderPicture(rawPicture);
    //  ...
  }

  void renderPicture(byte[] rawPicture) { /* ... */ }
}
```

This is an example of *client-controlled activation*, in which the object that constructs a `Runnable` object also constructs and starts an associated thread. Client-controlled activation takes the form:

```
Runnable action = new SpecialRunnable();
Thread t = new Thread(action);
t.start();
```

or, more concisely:

```
new Thread(new SpecialRunnable()).start();
```

Client-controlled activation policies allow clients to construct `Runnable` objects in one phase and set them in motion in another. Clients may also set any of the control parameters defined for threads (see Chapter 1) before starting them up.

6.2.1.4 *Server-Controlled Activation*

Instead of relying on other objects, a `Runnable` object itself can create a thread in its constructor or any other method using:

```
new Thread(this).start()
```

This can be a better option, for example, in situations in which it would be nonsensical or wrong for the `Runnable` ever to execute `run` more than once, so it is worth sacrificing flexibility to ensure conformance to this non-reentrancy constraint without relying on programmer convention. This applies when the `run` method is designed to support a single activity that is initiated upon construction of the `Runnable` object itself. If a `Thread` is established in a constructor, the `run` method can check to see that it is in fact using the one established by the object itself, as in:

```
public class AutoStartOneShotRunnable implements Runnable {
  protected Thread me_;

  AutoStartOneShotRunnable() {
    me_ = new Thread(this);
    me_.setDaemon(true);
    me_.start();
  }

  public void run() {
    // (Use while instead of if here for looping actions.)
    if (Thread.currentThread() == me_) // ensure one thread
      mainAction();
  }
}
```

To achieve this effect when Threads are not created in constructors, a Runnable can ensure that run is executed at most once by detecting the Thread reference used in its first call.

There is no way to associate an exception with such unintended usages without breaking the run signature (which lists no exceptions). The best you can do while still conforming to the Runnable interface is return with no effect. Alternatively, you can wrap such constructions in a second-level Adapter class that associates, say, NoMultipleThreadsException with the analog of the run method.

Guards can be used to ensure that a set of otherwise asynchronous activities run in different threads do not overlap. For example to avoid creating a new Thread activating a Runnable until another is finished, you can use a guard construction based on the convention that a maintained Thread reference is nulled out after completion. Or rather than using guarded suspension, you could use an analogous inaction construction that just ignores requests to start new threads while another is in progress. This is seen in applets with threads that are initiated when users click buttons and the like. A request that a new activity be started when another is already in progress is treated as a harmless, quietly ignored error.

Instead of limiting to exactly one thread, you can keep a fixed array or other collection of them as a *thread pool*, stalling new requests until one of them completes its run. This is a very common strategy in languages and systems in which initial construction of thread objects is time-consuming enough to be avoided via recycling, but it does not seem to impact performance much in current implementations of Java. The main reason for considering thread pools is to limit total thread usage to some fixed number (see Chapter 7).

6.2.2   Thread-Per-Message Proxies

Thread-based Proxies are protocol adapter classes that force activities invoked in threads to obey a "nicer" interface than just `Runnable`, typically the same interface as a non-thread-based version of the class. In Java, the use of Proxies requires construction of second-level relay-style classes that in turn invoke `Runnable.run`. This takes more work to arrange, but simplifies and standardizes usage while also providing a single locus for `Thread`-based activation mechanics, for example, those controlling priorities and `ThreadGroups`.

Proxies that repackage a set of methods that have been split into different Runnable Services are sometimes known as *Gateways*. In a thread-per-message Gateway class, each method is implemented by constructing and starting an associated thread. Gateways thus serve as midpoints between client-controlled and server-controlled activation policies:

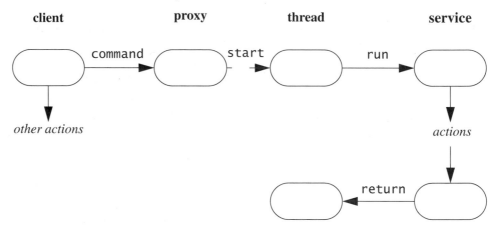

For example, assuming construction of a `FileReader` service class, a Gateway version of the original `FileIO` class can be defined as:

```
public class FileIOV2 {
  public void writeBytes(String fileName, byte[] data) {
    new Thread (new FileWriter(fileName, data)).start();
  }

  public void readBytes(String fileName, byte[] data) {
    new Thread (new FileReader(fileName, data)).start();
  }
}
```

Objects that accept messages from other processes are often structured as Gateways, leading to a thread-per-incoming-external-message design. Spawning a thread to perform a self-contained but time-consuming service ensures that the main object is ready to receive other incoming requests almost immediately. This minimizes service latency and avoids network bottlenecks. This is a common way of setting up general-purpose servers. It is also a useful strategy for structuring applets in which each user event leads to a new activity in a new thread.

Gateway designs may also be seen as thread-based analogs of the Factory design pattern (see *Design Patterns*). The Gateway serves as a Factory for arbitrary worker objects that do the real work. The main difference is that a Factory constructs an object and then returns a handle to it, while a Gateway constructs an object and then runs it. However, when it is better to have clients, not the Gateway itself, control Thread mechanics, it is possible to structure such classes instead as straight Factories, returning references to Runnables that clients can then start.

6.2.2.1 *Standardizing Interfaces*

Proxies can be useful whenever the operation being performed does not intrinsically take the form of Runnable.run because it requires arguments or returns results. Usually, there is a natural way to express Proxy interfaces, using meaningful operation names. But when Proxies are designed to be used across a broad range of contexts, they must rely on blander, standardized interfaces.

Interface Runnable standardizes the name of any parameterless, resultless action. You can take the same tactic for actions with one argument, one result, one argument and one result, and so on. While there are an infinite number of such interfaces, any given framework will need only a few of them. Commonly useful interfaces include:

```
public interface Procedure { // apply any operation
  public void    apply(Object x);
}

public interface Generator { // return an object
  public Object  next();
}

public interface Function { // apply operation; return object
  public Object  map(Object x);
}

public interface Predicate { // test some property
  public boolean test(Object x);
}

public interface Combiner  { // return result of binary op
  public Object  combine(Object x, Object y);
}
```

6.2.3 Waiters

Many `run` methods are defined to initiate a service via calls to some particular method(s) on some other independent object(s). Here, the sole purpose of the `Runnable` is to allow a client to run the method(s) in a new thread when it does not want or need to block waiting for a normal method call to a server to complete.

In distributed programming, protocols in which the call proceeds forever independently are usually called *oneway* messages. Runnable Adapters provide the means for obtaining the effects of oneway and other kinds of asynchronous message-passing constructs within the confines of a single Java program.

The simplest kinds of Runnable Adapters are *Waiters*, which just wait out completion of a conceptually oneway *send-and-forget* resultless method. Waiters are classes with:

- Instance variables holding a reference to the target object and each argument to the target method; also, when applicable, instance variables and associated accessor methods holding any return values or exceptions from the called method.

- A constructor that initializes these variables.

- A `run` method that invokes the target method with the supplied arguments and places any results in instance variables.

- In the normal case where the waiter object is designed to be run only once, optional safeguards that help enforce this.

6.2.3.1 *Example*

For a generic example, suppose you have a class supporting some resultless action that you want to run in a thread:

```
class AClass { // ...
  public void anAction(int arg1, Object arg2) { /* ... */ }
}
```

A minimal Runnable helper class that arranges that `anAction` be performed would have instance variables, constructor, and `run` method as follows:

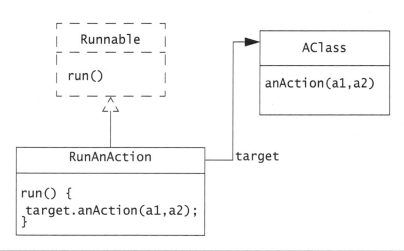

```
class RunAnAction implements Runnable {
  private AClass target_;
  private int    arg1_;
  private Object arg2_;

  RunAnAction(AClass target, int arg1, Object arg2) {
    target_ = target;
    arg1_ = arg1;
    arg2_ = arg2;
  }

  public synchronized void run() {
    target_.anAction(arg1_, arg2_);
  }
}
```

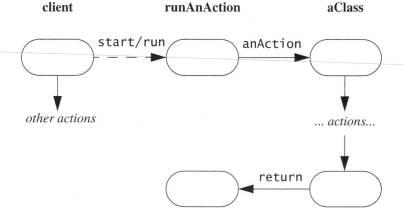

6.2.4   Composites

If you need to perform multiple actions within the same `run` method but the exact set or sequence of methods to call cannot be determined until run time, you can build an instance of the Composite pattern (see the *Design Patterns* book) that maintains a sequence of other `Runnable`s and contains a `run` method that executes all of them in order.

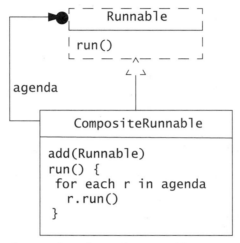

Here is a minimal example using a `java.util.Vector` to hold commands:

```java
public class CompositeRunnable implements Runnable {
  protected Vector agenda_ = new Vector();

  synchronized void add(Runnable r) {
    agenda_.addElement(r);
  }

  // plus possibly other similar methods to remove, reorder, etc

  public synchronized void run() {
    Enumeration e = agenda_.elements();
    while (e.hasMoreElements())
      ((Runnable)(e.nextElement())).run();
  }
}
```

This notion can be extended to allow non-sequential execution as well; for example, by using tree or graph data structures accommodating branching, loops, and undo methods that are performed upon failures. You can even write entire programs consisting only of such commands using the flow-based organizing strategies described in Chapter 7.

6.2.5 Early Replies

Some methods are designed to be triggered as asynchronous background activities whenever an object receives a particular kind of message. One way to conceptualize the associated forms of Runnables is through the notion of an *early reply,* a construct found natively in some concurrent programming languages. Early replies mesh nicely with the synchronous nature of normal OO message sends, while at the same time supporting concurrency. To illustrate, suppose for a moment that Java had a REPLY construct, as in:

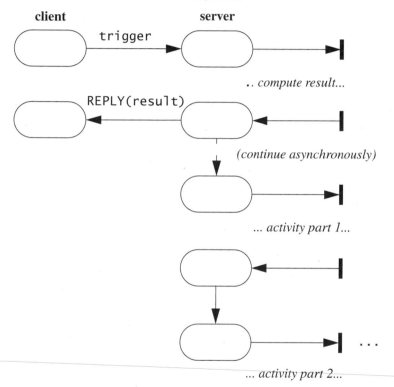

```
pseudoclass ERServer {
  public synchronized int triggerActivity() {
    int result = computeResult();
    REPLY result;
    activityPart1();
    activitypart2(23);
  }
  int computeResult() { /* ... */ }
  void activityPart1() { /* ... */ }
  void activityPart2(int j) { /* ... */ }
}
```

The idea is that at the REPLY point, one thread of control returns to the caller and another runs activityPart1 followed by activityPart2, asynchronously with respect to the caller.

One application of early reply methods is implementing time-consuming resultless methods that are designed to be called from external processes. Sending back a quick acknowledgment reply before starting on the main action tells the client that the object has received the request without holding up the client until the method actually finishes. Sending acknowledgments is a simple way to help the client ensure that requests are properly sequenced. If the client sends a series of requests sequentially, waiting for each *ack* before sending out the next one, then the client can be more confident that the server starts (although doesn't necessarily finish) handling each request in the order in which it was issued.

One danger of using early replies is that they can break expectations of clients (or rather their programmers) who equate replies with completion of the activity of interest for synchronization purposes. Since early reply constructions do not maintain the conventional relationship between return and completion, they can be the source of subtle design errors.

6.2.5.1   *Design Steps*

Java does not support early replies directly, but it does supply a built-in method that uses early reply, the start method in class Thread. This turns out to suffice for programming all other forms of early replies. (In fact, it is the basis for *all* asynchrony in Java.) To arrange that an activity be runnable as a single background task, you can define a Runnable class with:

- An instance variable holding a reference to the service object, instance variables holding each argument to the activity method, and a constructor that initializes variables.

- A run method that calls back the service object to run the activity. If this activity involves multiple calls, then you can define run to perform them all, or alternatively define a method in the Server itself that runs them all, called by run. In the special case where there is only one plausible parameterless background activity, you can define the server class itself to implement Runnable, thus avoiding the need for a helper class.

For example, applying these steps to the pseudocode ERServer leads to classes:

```
class ServerActivity implements Runnable { // helper class
  private ERServer s_; // target object
  private int j_;        // argument to activityPart2

  ServerActivity(ERServer s, int j) {
    s_ = s;
    j_ = j;
  }

  public void run() {
    s_.doActivities(j_);
  }

}

public class ERServer {

  public synchronized int triggerActivity() {
    int result = computeResult();
    new Thread(new ServerActivity(this, 23)).start();
    return result;
  }

  synchronized void doActivities(int j) {
    activityPart1();
    activityPart2(j);
  }

  protected int computeResult() { /* ... */ }
  protected synchronized void activityPart1() { /* ... */ }
  protected synchronized void activityPart2(int j) { /* ... */ }
}
```

6.2.6 Autonomous Loops

Background activities designed to run forever (or until stopped by another object) have run methods of the form:

```
for (;;) { doSomething(); }
```

Even though it would be logically equivalent, it is a bad idea to define run as infinitely recursive or, even worse, to follow each iteration with construction of a new Thread to run the next iteration. Since current implementations of Java do not optimize tail recursion, such practices could cause the program to exhaust all memory.

Common applications of autonomous loops include:

- Models of autonomous objects that, upon construction, fire up a thread that forever executes an update loop causing the object to continually change state independently of any other object.

- Continuous animation loops in applets.

- Simulations of random processes.

- Event Loops and Listeners (Chapter 5).

- Checkpointing mechanisms that persistently save object states on a periodic basis.

6.2.6.1   *Example*

Here is a mini-framework for autonomous objects that can be drawn in applets. This is slightly tricky to pull off using `java.awt` classes. One way to do it is to provide a *loopback* so that when an autonomous object changes in a way that requires a screen update, it asks its controlling applet to do a `repaint`, which in turn requests that the autonomous object paint itself. (One reason for using this loopback design is that the applet receives the `Graphics` object from the screen updater that is needed by `paint`. There are other ways to accommodate this as well, for example initially handing the object a `Canvas` to use for all subsequent drawing.)

To scaffold this framework, we can define the following abstractions:

```
public interface AutonomousGraphic extends Runnable {
  public void paint(Graphics g);
}

public abstract class AutonomousGraphicApplet extends Applet {

  // Subclasses responsible for returning their model
  protected abstract AutonomousGraphic model();

  public void start() {
    new Thread(model()).start();
  }

  public void paint(Graphics g) { // relay paint call to model
    model().paint(g);
  }

}
```

These allow creation of different kinds of AutonomousGraphic implementations, controlled by different subclasses of AutonomousGraphicApplet. For example, we could instantiate the autonomous graphics as:

```
public class ChangingText implements AutonomousGraphic {
  private String msg_;              // message to display
  private Rectangle drawingArea_;   // where to display it
  private Color color_;             // current color
  private Applet app_;              // for loopback

  public ChangingText(Applet app, Rectangle area, String msg) {
    app_ = app;
    msg_ = msg;
    drawingArea_ = area;
    color_ = Color.black;
  }

  protected void changeColor() {
    color_ = new Color((int)(Math.random() * 255.0),
                       (int)(Math.random() * 255.0),
                       (int)(Math.random() * 255.0));
  }

  public void run() {
    for (;;) {
      changeColor();

      app_.repaint(); // request a repaint from applet

      // do nothing for a while
      try { Thread.currentThread().sleep(1000);  }
      catch(InterruptedException ex) { return; }
    }
  }

  public void paint(Graphics g) {
    g.setColor(color_);
    // code to clip and center to fit nicely in rectangle ...
    g.drawString(msg_, drawingArea_.x, drawingArea_.y);
  }

}
```

This class can be controlled by an applet such as:

```
public class ChangingTextApplet extends AutonomousGraphicApplet{
  protected AutonomousGraphic model_;

  protected AutonomousGraphic model() { return model_; }

  public void init() {
    Rectangle area = new Rectangle(10, 10, 200, 40);
    model_ = new ChangingText(this, area,"Hello");
  }
}
```

6.2.7 Polling Watches

A Polling Watch is a looping daemon thread that occasionally checks to see if an action needs to be performed and if so, executes it.

Polling Watches are simple and common utility classes. However, because they are based on busy-waits, they require care to set up and have a restricted range of applicability. They can be used when:

- You can tolerate the possibility of missing opportunities to perform the action.

- It is not essential to perform the action precisely when it is triggerable.

- You can either tolerate or preclude false alarms in which the action fires after the condition has already changed. Usually, the best way to evade false-alarm problems in this context is to define the action as a synchronized balking method.

- You can tolerate the overhead of continuous polling for conditions, normally because polling is infrequent.

6.2.7.1 *Design Steps*

A Polling Watch can be constructed as a thread-based service or autonomous loop-based class, say `Daemon`, with:

- Instance variables referencing all participants, plus any other values necessary to evaluate conditions and perform actions, all initialized in a constructor.

- A method, say `checkAndAct`, that checks for conditions and, if they hold, performs the associated action.

- A `run` method that continuously invokes `checkAndAct`, interposed with `sleep`s of appropriate duration. The method either exits upon success (in the case of one-shot actions) or loops forever (in the case of continuously enabled actions).

- Normally, a constructor that initiates the associated thread.

To reduce overhead, sets of watches can be collected into aggregate daemons that check the triggering conditions of a possibly large number of actions. This can be done by housing each `checkAndact` method in a separate object, maintained in an *agenda* as in Composite Adapters. The daemon periodically runs through the entire collection, perhaps in a prioritized order. Alternatively, the daemon could optimize items into an order such that those with multiple conditions are skipped over if those with simple conditions implying them are false.

6.2.7.2 *Example*

Consider a transfer daemon for bank accounts designed to run once a day. The daemon tries to transfer some predetermined amount from a checking account to a savings account (perhaps so it can earn interest). Here is a skeletal implementation in which `BankAccount` stands for any class with operations to reveal and change a balance. (Some techniques for implementing the `BankAccount` class are described in Chapter 8.)

```
public class TransferDaemon implements Runnable {
  static final long recheckInterval = 86400000; // 24 hrs
  protected BankAccount checking_;     // participants
  protected BankAccount savings_;
  protected long amountToTransfer_;    // transfer argument
  protected Thread me_;

  public TransferDaemon(BankAccount checking,
                        BankAccount savings,
                        long amount) {
    checking_ = checking;
    savings_  = savings;
    amountToTransfer_ = amount;
    me_ = new Thread(this);
    me_.setDaemon(true);
    me_.start();
  }

  protected void transfer() { /* do the transfer */ }

  protected void checkAndAct() {
    if (checking_.balance() > amountToTransfer_) // bad idea (*)
      transfer();
  }
```

```
public void run() {
  for (;;) {
    checkAndAct();
    try { Thread.sleep(recheckInterval); }
    catch (InterruptedException ex) { return; }
  }
}

}
```

The line marked (*) in checkAndAct is very suspect and should be reworked. The method attempts to perform a transfer only if the checking account has sufficient balance. However, this check is not synchronized with the transfer itself. The transfer can still fail if the balance decreases between the check and action. In addition, opportunities to perform the transfer may be missed if the balance increases between the check and the action. To avoid these problems, the transfer operation should be written in a balking style so that it can be invoked unconditionally here (see Chapter 8).

6.3 Completion

Actions run in threads cannot return results directly since Runnable.run has a void return type. Other mechanisms must be used to simulate this aspect of procedural control when it is needed. These can apply even when the methods being run themselves have void return types. Sometimes an indication of *completion* of the activity is itself a useful result.

Viewed somewhat differently, even when the activity running in a thread does not produce results, the actions of client may in some way be dependent on its completion. For example, consider an applet that cannot proceed until a user presses a button in a dialog window that terminates a helper thread. The client's continuation activity is implicitly state-dependent in the sense of Chapter 4: the triggering condition for further actions is that the helper thread has terminated.

Usually the best way to deal with termination dependency is to avoid threads all together and just use standard Java invocations that cause the client to wait for a reply. However, this does not apply in designs where clients are only loosely coupled to servers. Thread-based designs allow clients to proceed independently for a while before engaging in termination-dependent activities.

A simple but rarely useful strategy for dealing with termination is to have the client continually poll, calling the built-in method Thread.isAlive to find out if the thread has been started but not stopped. As a minor variant, a one-shot Runnable of an otherwise resultless action can maintain a latch variable and associated access method, say `boolean done`, that the client can invoke to check if an action has completed. Similarly, if the `run` method is defined in the same class as the client (for example as an early reply thread), the `run` method can change a local instance variable upon completion. For example, it could set a `workerThread` variable to `null`.

These polling-based techniques face limitations stemming from the need for clients to *busy-wait* for termination, which is usually too wasteful. Additionally, they do not always supply sufficient means for clients to obtain results from actions upon completion.

6.3.1 Joining Threads

Join-based techniques help solve both of the problems associated with client polling for termination. They represent the analogs of `wait/notifyAll` constructions for termination-based notifications. In fact, under the covers, they are implemented by the Java run-time system using forms of `wait` and `notifyAll`. You can even simulate `join` by hand with your own notification-based constructions, but there is no reason to do so in the situations that `join` handles automatically.

Join-based techniques extend one-shot Waiter constructions. All results of a service run in a thread should be maintained in instance variables and associated accessor methods in a helper class. A client that starts a thread asynchronously but later needs to use the results of the call or otherwise relies on completion can use statements of the form:

```
waiterThread.join();        // wait for thread
result = waiter.result(); // invoke accessor
```

These constructions apply most readily in designs where a single thread is started and later waited out in the same client method. Alternatives based on Completion Callbacks and Group Proxies presented later in this chapter are usually more appropriate when multiple client methods and/or server threads are involved.

6.3.1.1 *Example*

Suppose you have one or more classes that include a method for rendering pictures, and a client that would like to run this method independently, later displaying the resulting picture when it is ready. Assuming the existence of a suitable implementation of the `PictureRenderer` interface, this could be accomplished using `Thread.join` as follows:

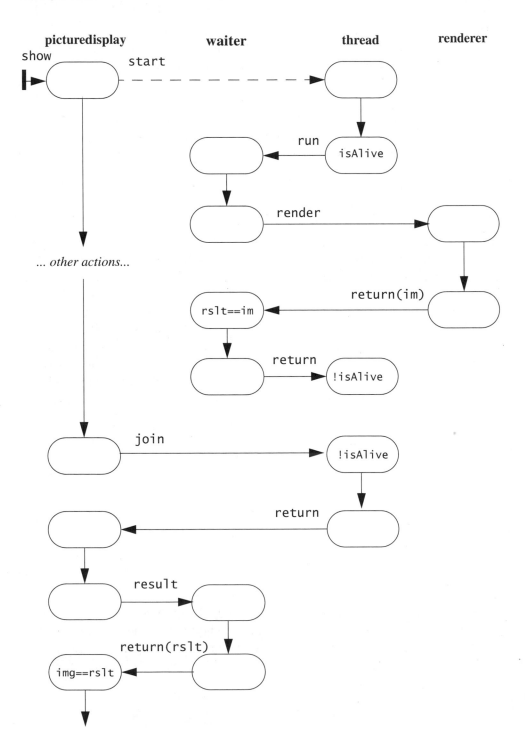

```
public class Picture { /* ... */ }

public interface PictureRenderer {
  public Picture render(byte[] rawPicture);
}

class RenderWaiter implements Runnable {
  private PictureRenderer r_;    // service object
  private byte [] arg_;          // arguments to its method
  private Picture rslt_ = null; // results from its method

  RenderWaiter(PictureRenderer r, byte[] raw) {
    r_ = r;
    arg_ = raw;
  }

  synchronized Picture result() {
    return rslt_; // return saved result
  }

  public void run() {
    rslt_ = r_.render(arg_);
  }
}

public class PictureDisplayV1 {
  private PictureRenderer myRenderer_;
  // ... assume other methods invoked below

  public void show(byte[] rawPicture) {
    // create and start thread
    RenderWaiter w = new RenderWaiter(myRenderer_, rawPicture);
    Thread t = new Thread(w);
    t.start();
    // do some other things, such as:
    displayBorders();
    displayCaption();

    try {     // wait for thread to complete
      t.join();
    }
    catch(InterruptedException ex) {
      cleanUp();
      return;
    }
    Picture img = w.result(); // get the result from the waiter
    displayPicture(img);      // use result
  }
}
```

6.3.2 Futures

At the small price of a small loss in flexibility, you can obtain more transparent usage of `join` based constructions by packaging more of the mechanics inside protocol adapter classes. *Futures* are Proxies that closely mimic "wait-by-necessity" constructs in other concurrent languages in which clients only wait for completion of threads when they actually try to use their results.

While it is not possible to remove *all* syntactic differences between `join` based forms and normal invocations in Java, future-style classes can make them more convenient to use. To build one, define a `result` method in an Adaptor or Proxy class. The `result` method should block using `join` until the activity terminates. All other details are the same as those in other Adapter and Proxy classes.

For example, client-side usage of the following `FutureRenderer` differs from non-thread-based invocation of `PictureRenderer.render` only in that the method is declared as `void`. Results must be obtained by calling the `result` method. (This class also illustrates a few minor safeguards that help deal with unintended usages.)

```
public class FutureRenderer implements Runnable {
  private PictureRenderer r_; // same setup as Waiter version
  private byte [] arg_ = null;
  private Picture rslt_ = null;
  private Thread thread_ = null;

  public FutureRenderer(PictureRenderer r) {
    r_ = r;
  }

  public synchronized void render(byte[] raw) {
    // safeguard in case of overlapping calls
    while (thread_ != null)
      try { wait(); } catch (InterruptedException ex) {}

    arg_ = raw;
    rslt_ = null;
    thread_ = new Thread(this);
    thread_.start();
  }

  public void run() {
    // safeguard in case run not called via render
    if (Thread.currentThread() == thread_)
      rslt_ = r_.render(arg_);
  }
```

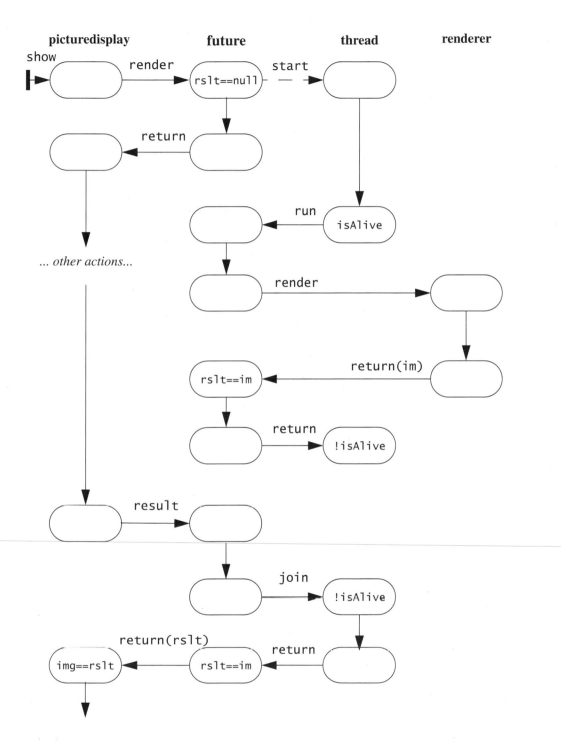

```
    public synchronized Picture result() {
      // safeguard in case render not called first
      if (thread_ == null)
        return null;

      try { thread_.join(); }
      catch(InterruptedException ex) { return null; }

      thread_ = null;
      notifyAll(); // unblock new requests
      return rslt_;
    }

}

public class PictureDisplayV2 { // sample usage
  private PictureRenderer myRenderer_;
  // ...

  public void show(byte[] rawPicture) {
    FutureRenderer r = new FutureRenderer(myRenderer_);
    r.render(rawPicture);
    displayBorders();
    displayCaption();
    displayPicture(r.result());
  }

}
```

6.3.3 Time-Outs

The Java `Thread.join(long milliseconds)` method returns when the thread is terminated, or the indicated time has elapsed, or it receives an `InterruptedException`. This allows implementation of calls with time-outs using code of the form:

```
waiterThread.join(timeOutValue);
waiterThread.stop(); // stop it even if not done
if (waiter.done()) result = waiter.result();
```

For example, suppose we want to cancel a `PictureRenderer.render` call if it does not complete in one second (counting time from the `join` call, not the `start` call). For simplicity of illustration, rather than using a separate method to distinguish normal termination from a time-out, the class just relies on the fact that `RenderWaiter.result` is `null` until the method completes successfully.

```
public class PictureDisplayV3 { // time-out version
  private PictureRenderer myRenderer_;
  // ...

  public void show(byte[] rawPicture) {
    // create/start thread
    RenderWaiter w = new RenderWaiter(myRenderer_, rawPicture);
    Thread t = new Thread(w);
    t.start();

    // do other things
    displayBorders();
    displayCaption();

    // wait for either completion or time-out
    try {
      t.join(1000);
    }
    catch(InterruptedException ex) {
      cleanUp();
      return;
    }

    t.stop(); // no effect if already done
    Picture img = w.result(); // will be null if didn't complete

    // take appropriate action
    if (img == null)
      cleanUp();
    else
      displayPicture(img);
  }
}
```

6.3.4 Completion Callbacks

In Completion Callback designs, `Runnable` objects invoke special methods to inform other objects when their services complete. Completion Callbacks are analogs of `return` statements and/or exception `throws` for actions that are run in threads, which cannot otherwise support replies.

A callback method is just an ordinary method that is designed to be called in some special circumstance by a server. Here, callbacks are restricted to *continuations* — invocations that lead to the continuation of client-side activities in the event of success or failure termination. (For more general versions, see Chapter 8). Completion Callbacks are a bit more flexible than join-based techniques but a bit less controllable. They are appropriate when:

- One or more arbitrary actions must be performed upon completion rather than, or in addition to, simply making the results (if any) known.

- The completion actions are not necessarily embedded in a particular call context, but can be expressed as free-standing methods.

- Logical completion need not coincide with thread termination, because the activity conceptually completes either before or after actual thread termination. For example, if a server uses an early reply form, in turn spawning yet another thread, then server thread termination is not a reliable indication of actual completion of the activity of interest, so `join` cannot be used.

- The completion actions may be performed by objects that are in no way aware of the object issuing the callback.

- The design context supports an asynchronous, notification-based programming style.

For example, consider a service-style `Runnable` class designed to read the contents of a file into a byte array:

```
public class FileReaderV0 implements Runnable {
  private String nm_;
  private byte[] d_;

  public FileReaderV0(String name, byte[] data) {
    nm_ = name;
    d_ = data;
  }

  public synchronized void read() { /* try to read file */  }

  public void run() {
    read();
  }

}
```

It is hard to picture any use for this class because of the following problems:

1. The `read` method has to be written in a way that catches all possible `IOExceptions` associated with the read, and quietly fails if any are thrown. This is rarely an acceptable solution.

2. A client running this in a thread cannot reliably tell if or when the read has successfully completed so it can start using the data.

Both problems can be solved by associating callbacks with the different kinds of termination:

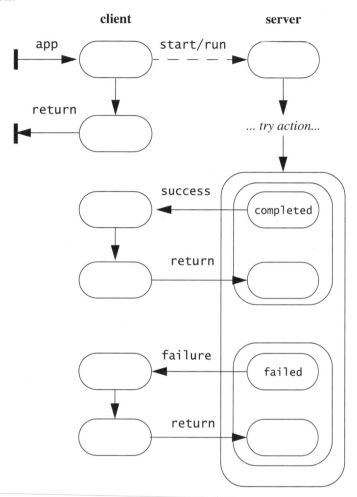

6.3.4.1 *Design Steps*

- Decide upon the interesting kinds of completion for the run action. Often, these entail two kinds of callbacks, one for successful completion, the other for failures. However, these could be combined into one, or subdivided.

- Establish interfaces describing the callback methods, so that the action can be initiated by any kind of class that supports those methods. Alternatively, you can use the blander Generic Callback variant described next that just relies on interface Runnable. And no interface is required when the callback action is to invoke `notify` or `notifyAll` (or any other method defined for any `java.lang.Object`).

- Add references to the object(s) to be called back to the `Runnable` Command class constructor, and arrange that `run` invokes them under the conditions indicated.

- Optionally, supply an alternative no-callback version of the service (via an alternative constructor). This way, clients that do not need notification need not support the interface. In any case, be prepared for this argument to be `null`.

- Arrange that appropriate clients support the callback methods. Alternatively, instead of `this`, the client could pass a reference to a handler object that deals with completion events.

6.3.4.2 *Example*

To continue the file example, suppose we'd like to let `FileReader` clients be notified when the file has been read in so they can start using the read-in data, while also alerting them if any problems arise in the attempted read. Each of these can be encoded as callbacks:

```java
public interface FileReaderClient {
  public void readCompleted(String filename);
  public void readFailed(String filename, IOException ioerr);
}

public class FileReaderApp implements FileReaderClient {
  private byte[] data_;

  public void readCompleted(String fn) {
    // ... use data ...
  }

  public void readFailed(String fn, IOException ioerr) {
    // ... deal with failure ...
  }

  public void app() { // main method...
    FileReader f = new FileReader("afile", data_, this);
    new Thread(f).start();
  }

}
```

```
public class FileReader implements Runnable {
  protected String nm_;        // hold arguments
  protected byte[] d_;
  protected FileReaderClient client_; // callback target

  // constructor for callback version
  public FileReader(String name, byte[] data,
                    FileReaderClient c) {
    nm_ = name;
    d_ = data;
    client_ = c;
  }

  // constructor for no-callback version
  public FileReader(String name, byte[] data) {
    this(name, data, null);
  }

  public synchronized void read() {
    try {
      // ... perform I/O  ...
      if (client_ != null)
        client_.readCompleted(nm_);
    }
    catch (IOException ex) {
      if (client_ != null)
        client_.readFailed(nm_, ex);
    }
  }

  public void run() {
    read();
  }
}
```

6.3.4.3 *Generic Callbacks*

Specialized interfaces usually provide the simplest and best ways to support callbacks in Java. However, it is sometimes desirable to use blander, less-situation-dependent callback arguments so as to apply them over a wider range of contexts. For example, returning to FileWriter, suppose we want to allow any parameterless method of any object to be called when the write completes successfully, and similarly for a method to be called upon failure.

This context is exactly the same as that leading to the construction of Runnable classes themselves, and exactly the same solution applies: use Runnables. Java Runnables are most commonly tied to the use of threads, but they work fine even if the callback method is not run in a thread.

As always, applying this idea requires definition of a special Runnable class for each distinct way you use it. For example, a better (although bulkier) version of the original FileWriter class can be defined as follows:

```
class SuccessfulWriteHandler implements Runnable {
  PictureManipulator target_; // just relay callback to target

  public SuccessfulWriteHandler(PictureManipulator x) {
    target_ = x;
  }

  public void run() {
    target_.successfulWrite();
  }

}

class FailedWriteHandler implements Runnable {
  PictureManipulator target_;

  public FailedWriteHandler(PictureManipulator x) {
    target_ = x;
  }

  public void run() {
    target_.failedWrite();
  }

}

public class FileWriterV2 implements Runnable {
  protected String nm_;
  protected byte[] d_;
  protected Runnable successCallback_;
  protected Runnable failureCallback_;

  public FileWriterV2(String name, byte[] data,
                      Runnable successCallback,
                      Runnable failureCallback) {
    nm_ = name;
    d_ = data;
    successCallback_ = successCallback;
    failureCallback_ = failureCallback;
  }
```

```
  public synchronized void write() {
    // ... try to write the file ..
    if (/* any problems */ ) {
      if (failureCallback_ != null)
        failureCallback_.run();
    }
    else {
      if (successCallback_ != null)
        successCallback_.run();
    }
  }

  public void run() {
    write();
  }

}

public class PictureManipulator { // main client

  void successfulWrite() { /* do something */ }
  void failedWrite()     { /* do something */ }
  // ...

  public void processPicture(byte rawPicture[]) {
    Runnable s = new SuccessfulWriteHandler(this);
    Runnable f = new FailedWriteHandler(this);
    new Thread(new FileWriterV2("PictureCache",
                                rawPicture, s,f)).start();
    renderPicture(rawPicture);
    // ...
  }

}
```

The Runnable classes here could be primed with additional information. For example, they could hold instance variables (initialized in a constructor) indicating the FileWriter or file name associated with the call, and send them as added arguments to re-parameterized versions of the successfulWrite and failedWrite methods so that the client could figure out exactly which write failed or succeeded.

Also, rather than having two different Runnables here, you could get away with only one that had a boolean flag initialized via a constructor argument and used in the run method to call either successfulWrite or failedWrite depending on how it was initialized.

6.3.4.4 *Guarding Callback Methods*

In some applications, clients can process completion callbacks only when they are
in particular states. For example, suppose that a client initiates a number of service
threads with callbacks, but can process them only in the order in which they were
created. When the state-based conditions can be hard-coded, you can evade the
problem by using `join` constructions in which the client waits for the thread at
some particular point in some particular method.

Otherwise, the callback methods themselves should contain guards that suspend processing of each incoming callback until the client is ready to process it,
using a standard `wait/notifyAll` construction.

6.3.4.5 *Example*

Suppose we have a `FileReaderClient` that initiates a set of asynchronous file
reads and needs to process them in the order issued. This construction mimics
how remote procedure calls (RPCs) are usually handled: typically each RPC
request is assigned a sequence number. Replies are processed in sequence order.
This can be a risky strategy, since it will cause indefinite suspension of ready callbacks if one or more of them never completes. This could be addressed by associating time-outs with the waits.

```
public class FileApplication implements FileReaderClient {
  private String[] filenames_;
  private int currentCompletion_; // index of ready file
  private byte[][] data_;

  public synchronized void readCompleted(String fn) {

    // wait until ready to process this callback
    while (!fn.equals(filenames_[currentCompletion_])) {
      try { wait(); } catch(InterruptedException ex) { return; }
    }

    // ... process data_[currentCompletion_] ...

    // wake up any other thread waiting on this condition
    ++currentCompletion_;
    notifyAll();
  }

  public synchronized void readFailed(String fn, IOException e) {
    // similar...
  }
```

```
public synchronized void readfiles() {
  currentCompletion_ = 0;
  for (int i = 0; i < filenames_.length; ++i) {
    FileReader f = new FileReader(filenames_[i],data_[i],this);
    new Thread(f).start();
  }
}
// ...
}
```

6.4 Group Services

Even on a single-CPU machine, the overall performance and liveness characteristics of an application can sometimes be improved by creating additional threads. But this is not always as easy as it may sound. To reach beyond those opportunities for exploiting concurrency that occur naturally in reactive programs, you need to somehow *partition* functionality so that activities can be run independently. Coming up with good partitioning strategies is among the primary tasks of parallel (as opposed to concurrent) program design, where the goal is to maximize use of multiple processors.

In most concurrent settings, a few simple coarse-grained partitionings almost always suffice to achieve performance and/or functionality goals. For example, a class serving as an entry point for a database search facility may generate several threads, each searching a different part of the database. Or, if the database is replicated for the sake of fault tolerance, the class may even generate several otherwise identical threads, each attempting to connect to and search a replicated version of the database.

Group Proxies provide a framework for designing and implementing partitioned concurrent activities in Java. A *group* consists of all the members of some arbitrary set. Group Proxies are protocol adapters that manage multiple threads controlled by multiple objects. Group Proxies maintain some kind of collection of delegates, sometimes enabling members to *join* and *leave* groups dynamically by adding and removing them from collections representing membership.

Group-based designs make it easy to increase parallelism transparently when there are multiple CPUs, but also apply whenever there is a good reason to partition a problem into parts that can be run concurrently; for example, when they are all I/O-bound, or when multiple algorithms can be applied to a problem and you'd like to use the results of whichever one finishes first.

Group Proxies also encapsulate the thread-based mechanics needed to implement Java analogs of execution constructs found in other concurrent, parallel, and distributed languages. They can be used to emulate *cobegin/coend* concurrent programming, *barrier synchronization* parallel programming, and *multicast-based* distributed programming.

Most design and implementation issues surrounding Group Proxies result from the need to perform *multithreaded delegation* (also known as a form of *scatter/gather* processing). The general form of a typical class and delegated operation is:

```
public interface AnInterface {
  public ResultType op(ArgType arg);
}

pseudoclass GroupProxy implements AnInterface {
  // ...
  public ResultType op(ArgType arg) {
    // "Scatter" phase
    split the problem into parts;
    for each part {
      start up a thread performing its actions;
    }

    // "Gather" phase
    wait for some or all threads to terminate;
    collect and return results;

  }
}
```

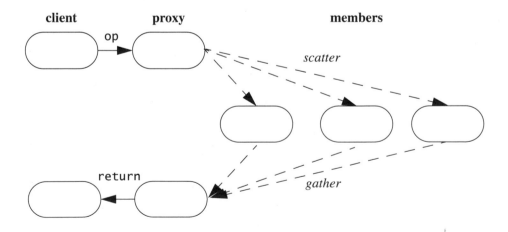

When the different threads all perform resultless independent oneway-style actions, then only the *scatter* part about firing up the threads applies. However, when actions must be waited out and/or results must be collected, you need to establish a *cotermination* policy. The policy ordinarily stems from the nature and semantics of the operation of interest. Three common policies are:

AND Termination. Wait for *all* threads to terminate

OR Termination. Wait for *any* thread to terminate.

Incremental. Collate and present results to clients as they arrive.

Multithreaded delegation also requires management of concurrently executing threads themselves rather than, or in addition to, the objects running in threads. You could use `ThreadGroups` for this purpose. But in very small-scale applications involving only a couple of threads, group membership can be handled implicitly, without bothering to track members in an array, `ThreadGroup` or other collection. Another occasionally applicable technique for tracking group members is to maintain a collection as a `static` in the class that describes all members, adding each new instance to the collection upon construction. For example, all members of an `Applet` subclass might be registered in a common `ControlPanel` held as a `static`.

6.4.1 AND Termination

Designs relying on AND termination can be based on the join-based techniques seen in one-thread designs. For example, suppose you anticipate that multiple CPUs will be available and split a picture-processing task into two halves so they can be done concurrently, continuing only when both have completed.

To implement this in Java, first note that since the group here has only two fixed members, it is not worth recording membership in any kind of collection. A pair of instance variables works fine. The corresponding class uses a straightforward extension of single-thread `join` constructions. Exactly the same `Render-Waiter` objects can be used as in the one-thread version. But here, every step happens in pairs.

Since the Group Proxy `SplitRenderer` itself implements the `PictureRenderer` interface, it can be used transparently by any object needing a `PictureRenderer`. For example, you might build an application with a `RendererFactory` that hands out `SplitRenderers` if it is operating on a multi-CPU platform but non-concurrent versions otherwise.

```
public class SplitRenderer implements PictureRenderer {
  PictureRenderer renderer1_; //  group member 1
  PictureRenderer renderer2_; //  group member 2
  // assume other methods used below ...
  public Picture render(byte[] rawPicture) {
    // split
    byte[] rawLeft = leftHalf(rawPicture);
    byte[] rawRight = rightHalf(rawPicture);

    // start threads
    RenderWaiter leftRenderer =
      new RenderWaiter(renderer1_, rawLeft);
    RenderWaiter rightRenderer =
      new RenderWaiter(renderer2_, rawRight);
    Thread leftthread = new Thread(leftRenderer);
    Thread rightthread = new Thread(rightRenderer);
    leftthread.start();
    rightthread.start();

    // join both of them
    try {
      leftthread.join();    // (order doesn't matter)
      rightthread.join();
    }
    catch(InterruptedException ex) {
      leftthread.stop();
      rightthread.stop();
      return null;
    }

    // use results
    Picture leftImg = leftRenderer.result();
    Picture rightImg = rightRenderer.result();
    return combinePictures(leftImg, rightImg);
  }
}
```

6.4.2 OR Termination

Join-based constructions apply to AND-style termination in which all threads must terminate before the client can continue. However, they do not apply to OR-style termination in which the client can continue when *any* thread terminates.

For example, suppose you want to implement a parallel search facility that tries to find a string in either of two databases using two different threads. Once either thread finds an answer, the other can be terminated and the client can continue. This is the most common strategy for implementing parallel search algorithms where each thread looks at a different subset of a database.

OR-style termination control can be obtained using a Completion Callback design in which the underlying methods running in the different threads issue a callback message upon finding the answer, at which point the other thread is terminated.

For example, here is the relevant code for a simple search method that assumes the existence of appropriate Runnable SearchDB classes. The Searcher.search method is itself here defined to be single-threaded (that is, only one search request is processed at a time). To allow multiple searches, a version of this class could be used inside a thread-per-message gateway that in turn fires up a new Searcher for each new search request.

```java
public class Searcher {
  protected Thread t1_ = null;      // one of the threads
  protected Thread t2_ = null;      // the other thread
  protected String answer_ = null;  // non-null after answer
  // ...

  public synchronized String lookup(String target) {
    // wait for any previous request to terminate
    while (t1_!= null && t2_ != null)
      try { wait(); } catch (InterruptedException ex) {}

    // fire up threads
    t1_ = new Thread(new SearchDB1(target, this));
    t2_ = new Thread(new SearchDB2(target, this));
    t1_.start();
    t2_.start();

    while (answer_ == null)  // wait for answer
      try { wait(); } catch (InterruptedException ex) {}

    String ans = answer_;    // record in local to later return
    answer_ = null;          // reset state for next request
    t1_ = null;
    t2_ = null;
    notifyAll();             // signal any new requests
    return ans;
  }

  synchronized void answer(String ans)  { // callback
    answer_ = ans;
    if (t1_ != null) t1_.stop(); // stop the other thread
    if (t2_ != null) t2_.stop();
    notifyAll();                 // allow lookup to proceed
  }
}
```

This example illustrates a common, although slightly messy construction seen in callback designs: the callback method (here `answer`) is used to unblock a `wait` buried in the middle of another method (here `lookup`) that cannot continue until the callback has been received.

This is sometimes called a *half-synch/half-asynch* design, since the client-accessible method acts like a normal synchronous call even though it is controlled via asynchronous techniques. Join-based solutions superficially avoid the need for such constructions. But internally, they are implemented in a similar fashion. In particular, a `notifyAll` is issued upon `Thread` termination by the Java run-time system.

6.4.3   Incremental Methods

Suppose you have a set of pictures and want to render them all in threads, displaying each as it becomes available. Like OR-termination, this effect cannot be obtained using `join`, but can be arranged using callback constructions, as seen in the following example.

For illustration, the example holds up completion of the `show` method itself until all pictures have been displayed. This avoids errors that could occur if it were to start another group of renderers while one is already in progress. Analogous safeguards would apply if there were methods to add new group members or remove old ones. These actions should not take place during a group operation, since counts and/or indices could become incorrect in the midst of operations.

Also just for illustration, this version creates a `ThreadGroup` for all the renderer threads.

```
public interface NotifyingRendererClient { // callback interface
  public void renderDone(Picture result);
}

public class GroupPictureRenderer
            implements NotifyingRendererClient {
  private PictureRenderer myRenderer_;
  private int activeRenderers_ = 0;
  private NotifyingRenderWaiter[] waiter_ = null;
  // ...

  public synchronized void renderDone(Picture result) {
    displayPicture(result); // use results
    if (--activeRenderers_ == 0)
      notifyAll();
  }
```

```
  public synchronized void show(byte[] [] rawPictures) {
    // only support one call at a time; even if blocked below
    while (waiter_ != null)
      try { wait(); } catch(InterruptedException ex) { return; }

    // create waiters
    activeRenderers_ = rawPictures.length;
    waiter_ = new NotifyingRenderWaiter[activeRenderers_];
    ThreadGroup tg = new ThreadGroup("Renderers");

    // fire up threads
    for(int i = 0; i < rawPictures.length; i++) {
      waiter_[i] = new NotifyingRenderWaiter(this, myRenderer_,
                                                 rawPictures[i]);
      new Thread(tg, waiter_[i]).start();
    }

    // wait until receive all callbacks
    while (activeRenderers_ != 0)
      try { wait(); } catch(InterruptedException ex) { return; }

    // reset for next request
    waiter_ = null;
    notifyAll(); // unblock new show() call
  }

}

public class NotifyingRenderWaiter implements Runnable {
  private PictureRenderer r_;
  private byte [] arg_;
  private Picture rslt_ = null;
  private NotifyingRendererClient caller_;

  public NotifyingRenderWaiter(NotifyingRendererClient caller,
                              PictureRenderer r, byte[] raw) {
    caller_ = caller;
    r_ = r;
    arg_ = raw;
  }

  public Picture result() {
    return rslt_;
  }

  public synchronized void run() {
    rslt_ = r_.render(arg_);
    caller_.renderDone(rslt_);
  }
}
```

Countless variants and extensions of this basic design form can be obtained by using more flexible data structures and traversal mechanisms for results. For example, instead of using a simple internal array for tracking both the tasks and their results, you can make the results of multiple threads available stream-style by supporting the `java.util.Enumeration` interface, where each result is obtained via a `nextElement` method that returns a completed result, blocking if none are available but are expected.

These techniques in turn allow you to implement any number of *collation* strategies, for example those that incrementally merge results together in some application-specific way, those that wait for a particular result, those that traverse through the enumeration looking for the best result, and those that assign responsibility for handling each result to a different helper object. Yet further extensions apply to *consensus* problems, establishing protocols that attempt to force activities run in different threads to agree upon results (see the Further Readings).

6.5   Coexistence

You cannot absolutely guarantee liveness of a thread-based service in the broadest possible sense of the term *live*. For example, you cannot prevent electrical power outages or other physical failures in the computers that the services run on. The best you can do is arrange that services be live across the widest possible set of contexts you need or want them to be used in.

Efforts to maximize service liveness necessarily take place at many levels. For example, at the hardware level, you might invest in uninterruptable power supplies and redundant fault-tolerant computer systems. However, the goal of maximizing liveness of any particular service should be viewed within a realistic context. For example, it would surely improve liveness to run a picture rendering task redundantly on every computer on the Internet. But this would be costly; worse, most people would be unable to use the service, since all the computers (and perhaps even all the electrical power!) would be tied up.

These examples are extreme versions of the two kinds of measures that help services coexist with other physical and computational processes in their environments:

Protection. Limiting the ability of other processes to harm a service.

Citizenship. Minimizing the resource demands of a service.

6.5.1 Protection

One or more threads comprising a Java application or applet may be running concurrently with other unrelated threads in other applets and applications. Further, the process running these threads may be running concurrently with other programs on the same computer. This computer may in turn be concurrently interacting with others.

Java includes security measures that can be used to protect threads against direct (perhaps malicious) threats to liveness by other threads, processes, and computers. Basic Java safety provisions help prevent other threads from crashing the machine. `ThreadGroups` can be used to prevent unrelated threads from killing your threads via `stop`.

At a more localized level, you can impose structural containment policies to help protect one thread from direct intervention by others. Thread-based containment is an extended form of the containment techniques discussed in Chapter 2. Here, you guarantee that both the thread and all the objects ever reachable from the thread cannot be reached via other threads, thus ensuring full *inward* communication closure.

On the other hand, full *outward* communication closure is not attainable: at some level, every service must share resources with others. So you cannot structurally preclude liveness problems resulting from resource contention.

Although the impact of this issue can vary across platforms, there is generally no way to prevent unrelated processes and threads from indefinitely tying up a CPU, memory, network connection, battery power, or any other resource needed for a given Java thread to make progress. As one consequence, without special platform-dependent assurances that go beyond the Java specification, you cannot rely on time-based constructs such as `sleep` to provide hard-real-time guarantees. An awakened thread might not run as soon as it is runnable.

6.5.2 Citizenship

While you may not be able to do much about resource-contention problems stemming from independent threads and processes, you can take steps to lessen the resource demands of any given service relative to others in an application. These steps can in turn help reduce contention problems more globally.

6.5.2.1 *Overhead*

The first question to ask is whether a service should be run in a thread to begin with. The service should be intrinsically time-consuming enough (perhaps looping forever or encountering indeterminate delays) that thread construction overhead is not a major concern. Otherwise, even when calls to the method should logically be asynchronous, it may be better just to call it normally, piggybacking on the caller thread.

In other words, logical asynchrony does not always have to translate into actual asynchrony. Logical asynchrony implies that a client is not directly affected by (or doesn't care about) when an activity begins or when it ends. In some cases, it might as well begin right when the client invokes it, blocking the client from doing anything else while it takes place, and then end sometime later, at which point the client continues on. If this is acceptable, the interaction can be converted to use standard Java method invocations.

There are, of course, many situations in which the added value of asynchrony is worth the overhead. There are even situations in which thread construction is the only reasonable way out of a synchronization problem, so is worth it despite the overhead. For example, as illustrated in Chapter 8, threads can be used to initiate activities that could result in deadlock if they were run in the same thread as the client. New threads start out without any locks, and so may be able to invoke synchronized methods that would deadlock if invoked from a thread already possessing certain locks but ready to relinquish them after constructing the thread.

6.5.2.2   *Scheduling*

Threads should get only enough CPU time and related resources to fulfill their broader roles in an application. Unfortunately, except in some fully controlled closed systems, no thread or its programmer can know for sure how much is "enough". Thus, all approaches to scheduling and resource control in open systems are necessarily heuristic.

The Java run-time scheduler uses priority-based heuristics. Each integer-valued priority is associated with a different scheduling queue. The priority assigned to a given task should reflect the relative urgency of performing it rather than others in its known or expected contexts. For example, when a thread is created to perform some possibly long computation, it is a good idea to give it a relatively low priority so that other threads that deal with users will run instead whenever both are in runnable states. If you don't do this, the rest of the program (especially the user interface) will be at best sluggish, and at worst totally unresponsive.

Priority scheduling works well only if the scheduler occasionally gets a chance to choose some task to run. In Java, scheduling is performed automatically whenever the run state of any task changes. One of the runnable threads with the highest priority is generally chosen to run. However, the Java Language Specification does not guarantee that threads tied for the highest priority are run *fairly*. Java run-time systems may or may not use time slicing to preempt running tasks so that others with equal priority get a chance to run. Similarly, they may or may not guarantee any particular fairness policy (such as first-come-first-served) for choices among tasks with tied priority.

As one consequence, if multiple threads are tied for the highest priority, and one of them is engaged in an autonomous loop that never involves any calls that change its run state, then it may take over the CPU forever when run on some platforms.

When necessary or desirable, preemption can be forced in a relatively simple way. If you reserve the highest available priority for this purpose, you can create a thread that does nothing except cause the scheduler to execute at a given period, forcing time-slicing. To implement this, define a class with a synchronized `run` method of the form:

```
for (;;) {
   try { wait(reschedulingPeriod); }
   catch (InterruptedException ex) {}
}
```

While useful, such tactics do not absolutely guarantee progress of all other threads. The time-slicing thread itself may not get a chance to run if there are other unrelated threads with higher priorities than you are allowed to obtain. This is a special case of the impossibility of controlling independent threads and processes. So, unless you have special knowledge about the run-time environment of a set of threads, priorities cannot be used for fine-grained scheduling control.

Also, preemption does not guarantee fair choice among tasks with tied priorities. Concurrent algorithms or applications that require fairness among a set of tasks can be implemented via special-purpose scheduling techniques presented in Chapter 8.

Individual threads can and should yield control whenever they know that no progress can be made unless some other thread causes some state in some object to change. This is among the reasons for using `wait`, `notifyAll`, and `notify`. If these cannot be used in a class, methods should at least invoke `yield` when there is no chance that they can continue unless actions in other threads intervene. However, even this must be done carefully. To guarantee that a `yield` is effective in reducing CPU demands, the yielding thread must be run at a *strictly* lower priority than those threads that will allow it to proceed. Otherwise the others will not necessarily get a chance to run before it does.

Occasional `yields` or even `sleeps` in low-priority background or computationally intensive tasks may improve responsiveness of other tasks. An alternative, more fine-grained means of controlling the execution of a background task is to have it issue a message back to its client (or any other object) after each iteration of a loop or segment of a time-consuming activity, and then `suspend` until the client issues a `resume`. While more deterministic, this construction is also fragile

211

when it relies on other unrelated objects to assist in scheduling. Additionally, once resumed, the activity is still subject to native Java scheduling rules, and thus may not continue execution right away. However, explicit suspension is one means to absolutely guarantee that a thread temporarily yields control. It forms the basis for implementing special-purpose schedulers described in Chapter 8.

6.6   Further Readings

Many thread-based programming techniques have analogs in strictly parallel programming languages with constructs that initiate separate execution threads on different processors. See the texts on parallel programming listed in Chapter 1.

Futures and related structured concurrent messaging constructs are natively supported in several concurrent OO languages. For example, the versions used in ABCL are described in:

Yonezawa, Aki, and Mario Tokoro. *Object-Oriented Concurrent Programming*, MIT Press, 1988.

Process Groups have been used in many contexts in distributed systems, most notably in Isis. Process Group frameworks differ from those based on Group Proxies described in this chapter by virtue of dealing with distributed process-level objects rather than threads. For more detailed discussions and additional control policies and algorithms, see:

Birman, Kenneth and Robbert von Renesse. *Reliable Distributed Computing with the Isis Toolkit*, IEEE Press, 1994.

Similar techniques are used at finer levels of granularity in Concurrent Aggregates. See the chapter by Andrew Chien in the collection edited by Agha, Wegner, and Yonezawa listed in Chapter 1.

Several of the techniques illustrated with picture-rendering examples in this chapter are also employed in `java.awt.MediaTracker` and related utility classes. These classes can be used to help deal with many common image processing tasks, avoiding the need to create your own special-purpose classes.

Detection of the termination of a group of threads can require more complex protocols when applied in less structured contexts than discussed in this chapter. General-purpose termination detection algorithms are discussed in several of the sources on concurrent and distributed programming listed in Chapter 1.

Fine-grained priority-based scheduling plays a central role in most real-time systems. Details may be found in the sources on real-time programming listed in Chapter 1.

CHAPTER 7

Flow

FLOW patterns extend two-party thread-based designs to collections of objects that are all engaged in some common functionality. Flow patterns help organize large and even small designs in ways that avoid intricate synchronization problems associated with arbitrary interactions among objects participating in different threads. Standardizing flow is the most attractive and commonly applicable strategy for making good on the promises of open systems, where just about any component can be used anywhere, as long as it obeys an appropriate protocol.

7.1 Applications

Flow patterns apply in any kind of system or subsystem supporting one or more series of connected steps or stages, each with a distinct beginning and/or end, and in which each stage plays the role of a *producer* and/or *consumer*. Broad categories include:

Control systems. External sensor inputs ultimately cause control systems to generate particular effector outputs. Applications such as avionics control systems contain dozens of kinds of inputs and outputs. For a plainer example, consider a skeletal thermostatic heater control. (This chapter uses simplified object diagrams in which ovals represent objects and lines represent communication among objects.)

Assembly systems. Newly created objects undergo a series of changes and/or become integrated with other new objects before finally being used for some purpose; for example, an assembly line for Cartons:

Dataflow systems. Each stage transforms or otherwise processes data. For example, in pipelined multimedia systems, audio and/or video data is processed across multiple stages. In *publish-subscribe* systems, possibly many data sources send information to possibly many consumers. In Unix pipes-and-filters shell programs, stages send character data, as in a simple spell checker:

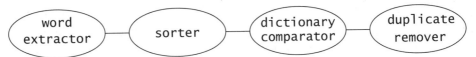

Workflow systems. Each stage represents an action that needs to be performed according to some set of business policies or other requirements; for example a simple payment system:

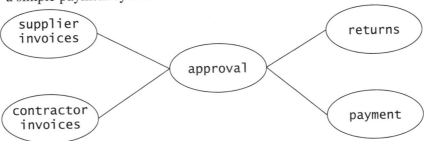

Event systems. Stages pass around and ultimately execute code associated with objects representing messages, user inputs, or simulated physical phenomena. The beginnings of many event systems take the form:

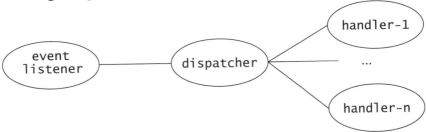

7.1.1 Components

Most differences across these kinds of systems have little impact on the design issues addressed in this chapter. Control systems pass information from stage to stage, assembly systems pass objects to be transformed or used, dataflow systems pass transformable values, workflow systems pass responsibility for actions on objects, and event systems pass representations of messages.

In other respects, basic structure and dynamics take the same general forms. All of these kinds of systems are intrinsically layered, relying on representational, transformational, and control components.

7.1.1.1 *Representational Components.*

Representational components are families of values or objects representing the things the flow is all about. In the introductory examples, temperatures, cardboard sheets, words, invoices, and events serve as the basic kinds of values and objects passed across connected stages.

Often, these components are interesting objects in their own right that can perform services, communicate with other objects, and so on. But when viewed as the raw material for activity flow, they are usually treated as mere passive representations, providing data and/or information rather than behavior.

While they play similar roles in the overall design of a flow system, different categories of representation types affect the details of the rest of the system:

- Information types representing the state of the world (for example pure values like temperatures) differ from most others in that it is often acceptable to reuse old or current best-estimate values if necessary, so that stages need not wait for new values to be made available. In essence, producers have an inexhaustible supply of such values.

- Event indicators normally can be used at most once, although they may be passed around many times before being used.

- Mutable resource types (such as cartons) normally need to be transferred in ways that guarantee exclusive control from one stage to the next, ensuring that each object is being operated upon by at most one stage at any given time. On the other hand, immutable objects can normally be shared across stages.

- Artificial data types can be used for control purposes. For example, a special *null* token may be used as a terminator. Similarly, a special *keepalive* can be sent to inform one stage that another still exists. Alternatively, a distinct set of *sideband* control methods can be employed across stages.

Representation types can change across phases of a flow. For example, a compiler can be described as a flow-based system in which lexical stages input characters and output tokens, parser stages input tokens and output parse-tree nodes, type-checking stages input parse-tree nodes and output semantic-representation nodes, and so on.

7.1.1.2   *Transformational Components (Stages).*

To serve as a stage, a component must be able to accept and/or issue messages that contain and/or serve as instructions about what to do with representational components. Broad categories of stages include:

- Immutable transformational components, sometimes called *filters* and *converters*. For example, a stage may accept two numbers and output their sum.

- Mutable components that internally maintain logical state. For example, in control systems, most stages maintain a model reflecting their (partial) knowledge of the state of the world. A heater switch stage might internally maintain a representation of whether an external physical heating device is on or off. These stages can often be designed and constructed as state machines.

- Components such as buffers that maintain elements only to control their flow through the system.

- Endpoints that deal with external processes, users or objects. For example, an event listener may collect incoming events, and an output stream may be used to store elements in files.

7.1.1.3   *Coordination Components.*

Coordinators link together transformational components to fulfill the goals of a particular flow. They may also monitor and dynamically enable and disable stages during the course of activities.

Unlike systems designed to accommodate other policy layering mechanisms, control components in flow systems arrange for stages to operate *cooperatively*, without otherwise imposing centralized dynamic synchronization control.

At the highest levels, control can be treated as a form of *scripting* in the usual sense of the word — semi-automated programming of the code that glues together instances of existing object types. This is the kind of programming associated with languages like JavaScript, Visual Basic, Unix shells, and FlowMark (a workflow tool). Development of a scripting tool, or integration with an existing one, is an optional step in building systems based around flows. This architecture is analogous to that of GUI builders consisting of a base set of widgets, packers and layout managers, code to instantiate a particular GUI, and a visual scripter that helps set it all up. Alternatively, it may be possible to script flows through direct manip-ulation tools by which, for example, components instantly communicate once dragged-and-dropped to connect with others.

7.2 Flow Policies

Flow design in multithreaded programs is a much more varied and central task than in purely sequential programs. Most design issues stem from considerations of how responsibility and control are managed among the stages.

There are two basic forms of unidirectional flow, *push* and *pull*, plus several variants, including those that accommodate buffering. Briefly, in push-based flow (also called *forward* flow, *data-driven* flow, and just *dataflow*), the direction of control flow matches the direction of information flow, originating ultimately from sources and terminating ultimately at sinks. In pull-based flow (also called *demand-driven* flow, *procedural* flow, and *polling*), control stems from ultimate sinks, so information flows only when requested by consumers.

These flow patterns are larger scale versions of policies listed in Chapter 2 for managing resource ownership. In fact, they serve much the same purpose as (and in practice often overlap with) resource management techniques. They avoid the need for dynamic synchronization policies by laying out structural rules about how different objects may communicate. As a result, choices among these control styles can have large effects on the interfaces and implementations of participating classes.

Flow policies restrict design choices to increase the likelihood that code is both safe and live by construction. Standardizing on a single principal flow policy imposes constraints on the *directionality* and *locality* of control that can preclude problems.

Adoption of a single unidirectional flow policy replaces component-specific liveness constraints with a single architectural rule. For example, if you establish a flow policy in which all instances of stage type A always send messages to those of stage type B but never vice versa, then you do not have to worry about potential deadlock situations in which both simultaneously send messages to each other. However, like other structural solutions to safety and liveness issues, flow policies are essentially unenforceable by compilers: success requires that programmers (perhaps assisted by tools) adhere to the conventions.

Even with these restrictions, single flow policies accommodate plenty of diversity, as catalogued in this section. Many of these forms are illustrated in the extended example at the end of this chapter.

7.2.1 Pull-based Flow

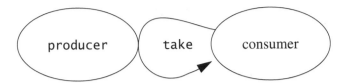

In sequential programs, flows are normally restricted to procedural or functional form. For example, imagine writing cascaded calls corresponding to some of the initial examples:

```
usr.use(fldr.fold(cttr.cut(pntr.paint(new Cardboard()))));

removeDups(compareTo(dict,sort(extractWds(read(myFile)))));
```

Or in a more object-oriented style for the heating system example:

```
class TempSensor { // code fragments

  float currentValue() {                    // source
    // return currently sensed Value
  }

}

class Comparator { // ...
  private TempSensor tempSensor_;
  private float desired_;

  boolean currentLessThanDesired() {    // pull from sensor
    return (tempSensor_.currentValue() < desired_);
  }

}

class Heater { // ...
  private Comparator comparator_;

  void set() {                              // pull from comparator
    if (comparator_.currentLessThanDesired())
    // cause hardware switch to be on
  }

}
```

An activity in a multithreaded program can take this form too, in which case it is often called a pull-based design: the ultimate consumer (*sink*) of the set of activities pulls results from its predecessors, which pull from their predecessors, and so on. Pull-based designs are most applicable in demand-driven contexts, where the flow is initiated by one or more sinks (perhaps containing continuous loops) that lead to a series of request-reply interactions from each stage to its predecessors, and where stages never need to deal with unexpected events from their predecessors.

7.2.1.1 *Structure*

Each stage in a pure pull-based flow possesses:

- Methods of the form `Element take()` that delivers requested objects and/or information. The `take` method may have arguments indicating the kind of result the consumer is interested in taking. It may rely on some kind of matching algorithm to obtain approximate matches, or even support full Strategy objects (see *Design Patterns*) sent by the consumer and used by the producer to select an item of interest. When `take` is allowed to return a logically null result indicating the lack of a ready element, it is often called `poll`. When the operation should not deplete the element from the producer, it is often called `read`. It is of course possible to define stages that support more than one of these methods. Other common names for take-style operations include `ask`, `in`, and `get`.[1]

- Links (references) to predecessor objects that (except in the case of sources) allow the object to pull elements necessary to implement its `take` methods. These links need not be direct. For example, the stages may have a reference to a single mediator or registry that maintains [producer, consumer] pairs for all stages. No matter how links are represented, each stage obtains elements *only* from its immediate predecessors, although it may also exchange control-based information with coordinator or monitor objects. This constraint is a version of the *law of Demeter*, an OO programming guideline for maintaining locality and modularity.

- In fully multithreaded versions, mechanics for each `take` request to be established as a thread, perhaps using a completion callback.

[1.] Common operation names may seem too trivial to bother listing. But using consistent, commonly accepted names for operations obeying common protocols is one of the easiest and most effective ways to convey policy choices to others who use or extend classes.

7.2.2 Push-based Flow

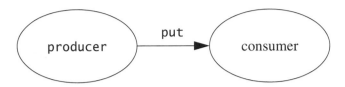

In asynchronous designs, a more fundamental control strategy is to arrange that the ultimate source of an activity initiate the flow to its successors via (conceptually) oneway triggering messages. Push-based designs are most appropriate in event-driven contexts, where the flow is initiated by an external event to the source or by a continuous production loop in the source itself.

For example, each class in a push-based heating system would play the same role as its pull-based counterpart, but would have a completely different interface and protocol:

```
class TempSensor { // fragments
  private Comparator comparator_;

  void detectChange() {
    comparator_.compareTo(currentTemp_); // push to comparator
  }

}

class Comparator { // ...
  private Heater heater_;

  void compareTo(float t) {
    if (t < desired_) heater_.turnOn(); // push to heater
  }

}

class Heater {// ...

  void turnOn() {                          // sink
    // set switch
  }

}
```

7.2.2.1   *Structure*

Each stage in a pure push-based flow possesses:

- Methods of the form `void put(Element r)` that cause it to use or transform r. While normally defined to be used in oneway-style messages, this method can also be defined to return status information or exceptions indicating the consumer's acceptance of the message contents. When the operation is not intended to deplete the element in the producer, it is often called `write`. Other common names for put-style operations include `give`, `accept`, `out`, and `tell`.

- Links to successor objects to which (except in the case of sinks) the stage sends resulting objects and/or information.

- In fully multithreaded versions, mechanics to generate a new thread to carry out each `put`.

7.2.3 Mixtures

Some flow designs intrinsically involve elements of more than one of these styles. In fact some middleware distributed object frameworks, for example OMG's COSS Event Channel services, attempt to support arbitrary mixtures of push and pull flow simultaneously. But at least in smaller-scale concurrent settings, it is simpler, more controllable, more efficient and more practical to gear flows toward one of these standard forms, mixing in elements of other forms only when unavoidable.

However, one mixed strategy, *exchange,* is simple enough to be readily amenable for use in frameworks primarily geared towards unidirectional flow. (A second common mixed strategy, Observer notification protocols, is discussed in Chapter 8.)

7.2.3.1   *Exchanges*

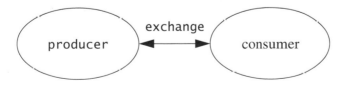

Pure push-based and pull-based designs equate control with element transfer. For example, in push-based designs, producers actually send elements while notifying consumers that elements exist. Exchange-based flows break this tie between element transfer and control while still preserving the goals of establishing simple, regular communication policies. Exchange-based flows are based around protocols in which:

- Every stage always maintains a single element (or as a minor extension, a fixed-sized pool of them).

- The only way to pass an element is to exchange it for another. Instead of having multiple `put` and `take` methods, stages may communicate via an operation of the form `Element exchange(Element)` that transfers one element in each direction.

- Directionality of control is established by other conventions. You cannot always tell by inspecting interfaces whether a given stage serves as a producer, a consumer, or both.

7.2.4 Connectivity

In addition to their interfaces and directionality, stages can be classified according to their connectivity and transfer relations to predecessors and successors. For example, *sources* have zero predecessors, *sinks* have zero successors, and *linear* components have at most one predecessor and one successor. Others include:

- *Splitters* (also known as *Forks*) have multiple successors:

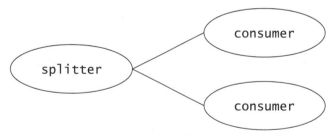

- *Multicasters* send cloned copies of the same value or object down to multiple consumers. (This represents an *AND* relation among consumers.)

- *Routers* inspect elements and/or other control information in choosing a consumer to forward each element. (This represents an *OR* relation among consumers.)

• *Mergers* have multiple predecessors:

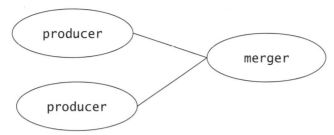

  ❖ *Collectors* (also known as *Multiplexers*) accept inputs on multiple chan-
    nels and interleave them to a single consumer. (This represents an *OR*
    relation among producers.)

  ❖ *Combiners* require an input from each of several predecessors and then
    combine them into a single output. For example, a *Differencer* outputs
    elements representing differences between its inputs. (This represents an
    AND relation among producers.)

• *Conduits* have both multiple predecessors and multiple successors.:

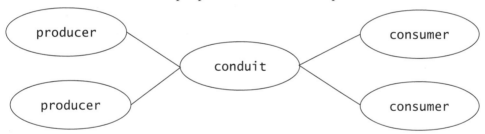

7.2.5 Buffers

Additional forms of control emerge when pairs or sets of stages work off a shared
buffer of some sort. There are three basic forms of buffering, covering all the possibilities:

Put-only Buffer Stages (also known as *relay* buffers) connect push-based stages to
    other push-based stages.

Take-only Buffer Stages (also known as *pre-fetch* buffers) connect pull-based
    stages to other pull-based stages.

Put/Take Buffer Stages (also known, in particular forms, as *blackboards, buses,
    tuple-spaces, channels, producer-consumer buffers*, and, usually, just *buffers*)
    connect push-based stages to pull-based stages.

7.2.5.1 *Applications*

In addition to holding elements, buffers can be convenient and effective tools for handling chores that would otherwise require separate stages. These include:

Managing persistence. For example a buffer can shadow elements on disk as they are received.

Maintaining history. This allows late-joining stages to catch up to the same state as others. For example, in publish-subscribe networks, newly constructed stages need to obtain all the recent postings. This introduces further policy decisions: how much history does the buffer need to maintain?

Chunking elements. For example, a buffer (or a series of them) may be partitioned into sliding *windows,* where all elements in the window are passed as a group to consumers. When any kind of acknowledgment protocol is associated with passing elements, chunking can help cut down message traffic.

Assembly. Buffers can serve as workspaces for aggregate encoding or decoding of elements. For example, a buffer can be used to assemble network packets out of received elements. Series of packet assembly buffers may themselves be staged as flows.

Loosening dependencies. Without buffering, a consumer may be limited to receiving the kind of element that its producer happens to provide at the moment. Buffers can hold instances of several kinds of elements, permitting more flexibility. For example, the Linda programming framework contains mechanisms that can search through a buffer (tuple space) to return any or all elements that match specified wild-cards.

Managing connections. Buffers can serve as general-purpose conduits connecting an unbounded number of other stages.

Dispatching. Buffers can schedule downstream stages to deal with different kinds of items held in the buffer.

Decoupling. A buffer can serve as a manual optimization of a thread. Buffers store only element information, not the entire control state of an activity. However, buffered elements can contain enough thread-like information to allow concurrent designs to be simulated in purely sequential languages. This comes at the expense of explicitly representing all messages (for example, as events) so they can be passed around and buffered. As buffering mechanisms are extended to accommodate more and more concurrent design techniques, they eventually become special-purpose thread packages. Several non-thread-based event frameworks take this form, supporting nearly all aspects of threads except the concurrency.

7.2.5.2 *Put-only Buffer Stages*

Buffers with push-based interfaces act as relays, holding elements received from predecessors while waiting for them to be accepted by their successors. The mechanics might be based around a continuous loop of the form:

```
public class RelayBuffer implements Runnable { // fragments
  protected Stage consumer_;
  protected Buffer buffer_ = new Buffer(...);

  public RelayBuffer(Stage consumer) { // ...
    consumer_ = consumer;
    new Thread(this).start();
  }

  // called only from producer
  public synchronized void put(Element x) {
    buffer_.put(x);
  }

  public void run() {
    for (;;) {
      consumer_.put(buffer_.take());
    }
  }

}
```

Examples of put-only buffers include output buffers used for moving issued data or messages into files or over networks. In these cases, internal threads are not typically necessary; instead, the buffer aggregates items until enough have been received to push on to the next stage.

7.2.5.3   *Take-only Buffer Stages*

Buffers with pull-based interfaces can pre-fetch elements from their predecessors so they will be immediately available to successors. The mechanics are almost entirely symmetrical to those of put-only buffers. For example, here is a code sketch of the canonical form:

```
public class PreFetchBuffer implements Runnable { // fragments
  protected Stage producer_;
  protected Buffer buffer_ = new Buffer(...);

  public PreFetchBuffer(Stage producer) { // ...
    producer_ = producer;
    new Thread(this).start();
  }

  // called only from consumer
  public synchronized Element take() {
    return buffer_.take();
  }

  public void run() {
    for (;;) {
      buffer_.put(producer_.take());
    }
  }
}
```

Examples of pre-fetch buffers include data input buffers which pull blocks of data from files in order to minimize the overhead of one-byte-at-a-time transfer. As with outgoing transport relay buffers, most input buffers do not require their own threads. Instead, they replenish their contents on demand.

Caches are take-only buffers useful in designs based around non-one-shot elements. A cache holds previously fetched elements so that they can be obtained again quickly on subsequent use. In some contexts, pre-fetch buffers have the potential for fetching elements that are never used (or, in the case of caches, never used again), which requires application-specific flushing or aging policies in order to periodically clean out useless elements.

7.2.5.4 *Put/Take Buffer Stages*

Put/Take buffer stages provide the basis for the most classic versions of producer-consumer designs, seen for example in the Event Loop design presented in Chapter 5. For example, a producer-consumer version of the heating system looks like:

```
class TempSensor {  // fragments
  private Buffer temperatureBuffer_;
  void detectChange() {
    temperatureBuffer_.put(currentTemp()); // push to buffer
  }
}

class Comparator { // ...
  private Buffer temperatureBuffer_;
  private Buffer heaterBuffer_;
  void compare() {
    t = temperatureBuffer_.take();        // pull from one buffer
    if (t < desired_)
      heaterBuffer_.put(true);            // push to other
  }
}

class Heater { // ...
  private Buffer heaterBuffer_;
  void set() {
    v = heaterBuffer_.take();             // pull from buffer
    if (v) turnOn(); else turnOff();
  }
}
```

This style of buffering combines aspects of push-based and pull-based flow:

- Buffers support both puts and takes, optionally combined into a single exchange operation. Additionally, buffers can support a read operation that returns an element without removing it.

- Stages maintain connections to buffers to which they may perform puts, takes, or both. At one extreme, there may be a buffer for every pair of communicating objects. At the other extreme, a single buffer may be shared by all objects, in which case some kind of element tagging may be needed.

A suitably defined *resource variable* class (see Chapter 2) can be used as a one-slot put/take buffer connecting a push stage to a pull stage with minimal buffering. An even more extreme form, a zero-slot buffer, can be used to directly couple stages so that each producer must wait for its consumer to take the item. This separates the act of connecting push-based to pull-based stages from that of buffering. There are several ways to implement direct put/take connections, depending on the desired style of synchronization and the kinds of elements; for example:

```java
public class PutTakeConnector {
  boolean putting_ = false; // to disable concurrent puts
  Object item_ = null; // require that actual items be non-null

  public synchronized void put(Object e) {
    if (e == null) return; // nulls are not items
    while (putting_)        // wait for another put to complete
      try { wait(); } catch (InterruptedException ex) {}
    putting_ = true;        // record execution state
    item_ = e;              // transfer item
    notifyAll();            // allow take
    while (item_ != null)   // wait for take
      try { wait(); } catch (InterruptedException ex) {}
    putting_ = false;
    notifyAll();            // enable another put
  }

  public synchronized Object take() {
    while (item_ == null)   // wait for put
      try { wait(); } catch (InterruptedException ex) {}
    Object e = item_;       // transfer item
    item_ = null;
    notifyAll();            // release current put
    return e;
  }
}
```

7.3 Resource Management

In any flow architecture, it is a good idea to standardize object responsibilities for performing any required thread construction and/or buffering. For example, for any stage in a push-based design, you have the (overlapping) options of:

- Having the stage invoke each put in a waiter thread. (This maintains the overall conventions of producer-centered control in push-based flows.)

- Having the stage accept a put by creating a background thread that initiates the associated internal actions.

- Having the stage use an outgoing relay buffer to hold elements until the consumer can process them.

- Having the stage use an incoming relay buffer to hold elements received from its producer.

However, it is hardly ever necessary or desirable to associate a thread or buffer with *each* stage in a flow. For example, a purely *linear* flow is one in which each stage has at most one predecessor and successor. Because linear flows are intrinsically sequential, only one thread need be associated with the entire flow, at least for pure push and pull forms. It suffices in a pull-based linear design to establish a thread only for the ultimate sink stage, and in a push-based design only for the ultimate source stage. Creating additional threads at other stages does not hurt, but can waste resources and complicate flow management.

In nonlinear flows, determining exactly where new threads are required or even useful takes a bit of analysis. A conservative approach is to start out using the default strategy of establishing threads at each stage, and then eliminating those that turn out not to be strictly necessary. However, this is much too awkward to carry out at the implementation level. Instead, thread construction conventions can be based on the structural forms of stages, as illustrated in the following sample case.

Consider a push-based assembly line where a Combiner needs one RedPart and one GreenPart in order to assemble them. If there is only a single thread producing both kinds of Parts, then if the Combiner blocks (via `wait`) when it has only one kind while waiting for the other, then the entire activity will stall. However, this can happen only if the Combiner is fed by two stages operating within the same thread. This can in turn happen only in designs of the form:

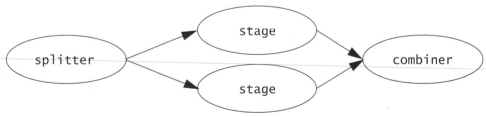

To prevent stalls at the combine point, any design of this form should construct at least one additional thread at the *split* point. As a matter of design policy, you might require that all Splitters in a push-driven system create new threads. This is a very natural convention — Splitters are typically employed in the first place as means to increase opportunities for concurrency.

It is normally possible for *one* of the Splitter outputs just to use the current thread. (This is done, for example, in the Unix `fork` system call which splits processes). But as a convention, it may be worth it to perform all Splitter outputs in new threads, in part just to make it simpler to reason about and interconnect stages.

An alternative solution here is to buffer Combiners so that they can store unusable parts until matches occur. The buffer must either be unbounded or have at least as many slots as the maximum number of unusable elements that can be produced.

7.3.1 Limiting Flow

Even when not strictly required as a means to preserve liveness, buffers, multiple threads, or both are often used in attempts to maximize concurrency by decoupling stages. However, this is not always effective or even a good idea:

Unbounded buffers. If a buffer is unbounded (uses an extensible data structure such as a linked list or resizable array), then if producers are on average faster than consumers, there is a possibility that the buffer will eventually grow to exhaust all available memory, causing system failure.

Unbounded threads. Having too many threads can exhaust system resources more quickly than having too many buffers or buffered elements.

Bounded buffers. A buffer of bounded capacity will tend to be in either of two states: it will almost always be empty if the producer is on average slower than the consumer, and it will almost always be full if the producer is on average faster than the consumer. In both of these boundary states, buffering serves no useful role in decoupling stages: items get transferred only on a one-by-one basis; the producer and consumer remain coupled. On the other hand, bounding precludes resource-based system failure as long as the total numbers and/or capacities of buffers themselves are also limited.

Bounded thread pools. Instead of relying on direct thread construction, you can use a Thread Factory managing a fixed pool, stalling new constructions whenever too many threads are in use. However, these tend to be harder to use and control than bounded buffers since there are fewer opportunities to look at elements to see if there are alternative courses of action.

Across any of these options, flow designs with push-based stages, buffering and/or multiple threads may require safeguards to avoid situations where unneeded and/or unusable items are pushed onto consumers, piled into buffers, or held by stalled threads.

In fine-grained parallel and real-time programming, rate-limiting is sometimes accomplished by "clocking" the flow using hardware or low-level software techniques that cause elements to proceed through stages in a lock-step fashion.

This is seen, for example, in *data-parallel* algorithms in which each node performs the same actions but on different data, and the data are moved around once per logical clock tick. In coarser-grained concurrent applications, rate-limiting must be accomplished by neither buffering nor allowing multiple threads at critical junctures, while still maintaining liveness.

In light of such considerations, buffering is most applicable when one or more of the following hold. Analogous concerns apply under suitable translation to multiple thread creation.

- The producer is on average no faster than the consumer, but one or both are bursty, causing occasional pileups that the buffer can smooth out.

- Due to other system requirements, there is a known maximum number of items that can or should ever be placed in the buffer. This would hold, for example, if the producer generates items in lots of ten that must be processed completely before it should produce the next lot.

- You cannot predict relative rates, but need to avoid the potential for resource exhaustion while still allowing limited decoupling. With a bounded buffer, producers will stall if they get too far ahead of consumers.

- An exception policy can be associated with `put`, so that an attempted `put` into a full buffer raises an exception sent back to the producer, which takes some kind of evasive action.

- You can implement *rate-adjustment* policies. For example, the producer may possess a callback method invoked by the buffer when it is almost full, asking the producer to slow down. Such *back-pressure* methods are common in packet-based networking systems. When applied to synchronization across multiple flows (as in multimedia systems), nearly perfect information about expected flow rates is needed to control buffering.

- You can implement a *send-back* protocol in which the buffer sends the item back to the producer if it cannot handle it. (This is a variant of an exchange protocol.)

- You can implement a *drop* policy, in which items are somehow discarded when the buffer becomes full. This may entail either replacing unprocessed old items with new ones or failing to insert new ones. This policy is hardly ever really desirable, but is sometimes the only valid engineering option. It is sometimes employed in audio and video applications, where loss of a few snippets of sound or picture every now and then can be tolerated.

- Buffering is just plain required; for example, if the flow crosses machines via network mechanisms with intrinsic buffering. In this case, you are forced to

establish drop, windowing, send-back, rate-adjustment, and/or exception policies or to cope with pre-existing ones.

The opposite kinds of problems can be encountered in polling pull-based
designs in which consumers spin idly waiting for new inputs to appear. Polling
problems can be addressed by imposing and tuning delays (for example via
sleep), using pre-fetch buffers, and/or adding more work for consumers to perform during times when they would otherwise be spinning.

7.3.1.1 *Buffer Exchanges*

In buffered designs, exchange protocols can be used to limit the total number of
buffers in use at any given time. In the two-object case, this amounts to a form of
double buffering. This policy is frequently used in graphics applications that perform screen updates. Extended forms can be used in more general flow contexts.
For example, a stage that packs up data that is to be transported across a network
can take the form:

```
public class Transporter { // fragments
  Buffer buffer_;

  public synchronized Buffer exchange(Buffer b) {
    Buffer old = buffer_;
    buffer_ = b;
    processBuffer();
    return old;
  }

  protected void processBuffer() { /* ... */ }
}
```

The exchange method here accepts a buffer full of data to transport and
passes back another buffer that the client can then fill up with more data.

Buffer exchange protocols can also be used in source stages that perform
external data input operations such as reading from files or sockets. In addition to
establishing a means for controlling resources, this also rate-limits the flow. If an
input operation must wait for a buffer exchange before reading a chunk of data, it
cannot flood the rest of an application with data that it is not ready to use.

A centralized pool can be used to avoid equipping each stage with a buffer
that it does not always need. When a stage needs a buffer in order to perform its
role, it can acquire one from the pool. When it is done participating in the flow
(perhaps only for a while), it can give the buffer back to the pool.

7.4 Assembly Line

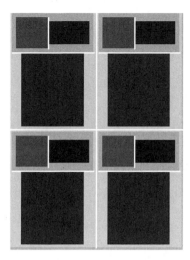

The remainder of this chapter illustrates the design and implementation of push-based flow systems via an example assembly line applet that builds series of "paintings" in a style vaguely reminiscent of the artists Piet Mondrian and Mark Rothko. Only the principal classes are given here. Some include unimplemented method declarations. The full code may be found in the on-line supplement, which also includes other application-level examples of flow-based systems.

7.4.1 Representations

To start out, we need some base representation types. In this system, all elements can be defined as subclasses of abstract class Box, where every Box has a color and a size, can display itself when asked, and can be made to deeply clone (duplicate) itself. The color mechanics are default-implemented. Others are left abstract, to be defined differently in different subclasses:

```
public abstract class Box {
  protected Color color_ = Color.white;

  public synchronized Color color() {
    return color_;
  }

  public synchronized void color(Color c) {
    color_ = c;
  }

  public abstract Dimension size(); // uses java.awt.Dimension

  public abstract Box duplicate(); // clone

  public abstract void show(Graphics g, Point origin);// display

}
```

The overall theme of this example is to start off with sources that produce simple basic boxes, and then push them through stages that paint, join, flip, and embed them to form the paintings. BasicBoxes are the raw material:

```
public class BasicBox extends Box {
  protected Dimension size_;

  public BasicBox(int xdim, int ydim) {
    super();
    size_ = new Dimension(xdim, ydim);
  }

  public synchronized Dimension size() {
    return size_;
  }

  public void show(Graphics g, Point origin) {
    g.setColor(color_);
    g.fillRect(origin.x, origin.y, size_.width, size_.height;
  }

  public synchronized Box duplicate() {
    Box p =  new BasicBox(size_.width, size_.height);
    p.color(color_);
    return p;
  }
}
```

Two fancier kinds of boxes can be made by joining side-by-side two existing boxes and adding a line-based border surrounding them. Joined boxes can also flip themselves. All this can be done either horizontally or vertically. The two resulting classes can be made subclasses of `JoinedPair` to allow sharing of some common code:

```
public abstract class JoinedPair extends Box {
  protected Box fst_; // one of the boxes
  protected Box snd_; // the other one

  protected JoinedPair(Box fst, Box snd) {
    super();
    fst_ = fst;
    snd_ = snd;
  }

  public synchronized void flip() { // swap fst/snd
    Box tmp = fst_; fst_ = snd_; snd_ = tmp;
  }

  //  other internal helper methods

}

public class HorizontallyJoinedPair extends JoinedPair {

  public HorizontallyJoinedPair(Box l, Box r) {
    super(l, r);
  }

  public synchronized Box duplicate() {
    HorizontallyJoinedPair p =
      new HorizontallyJoinedPair(fst_.duplicate(),
                                 snd_.duplicate());
    p.color(color_);
    return p;
  }

  // ... other implementations of abstract Box methods
}

public class VerticallyJoinedPair extends JoinedPair {
  // similar
}
```

The final kind of fancy box wraps one Box within a border:

```
public class WrappedBox extends Box {
  protected Dimension wrapperSize_;
  protected Box inner_;

  public WrappedBox(Box inner, Dimension wrapperSize) {
    super();
    inner_ = inner;
    wrapperSize_ = wrapperSize;
  }

  // ... other implementations of abstract Box methods
}
```

7.4.2   Stages

Representations are now set up to support the following kinds of stages:

BasicBoxSource. Create a new BasicBox.

Painter. Change the color of any kind of Box.

Flipper. Flip (up-down or left-right) a JoinedPair.

HorizontalJoiner. Combine two Boxes left-right, creating a new composite.

VerticalJoiner. Combine two Boxes up-down, creating a new composite.

Wrapper. Wrap a Box inside a border, creating a new composite.

Cloner. Make a copy of a Box; pass the original to one successor and the clone to
    another.

Alternator. Pass alternate inputs through to alternate successors.

Screener. Pass some kinds of Boxes to one stage and others to another.

Collector. Direct the results of two independent assembly lines to a single
    successor.

Two of these stages (Painters and Flippers) change the states of their
sources using methods supported by the represented objects themselves, and then
pass them on to other stages. Others accept zero (BasicBoxSource), one (Wrapper) or two (Joiners) incoming objects to create new kinds of boxes. Cloners,
Alternators, and Screeners are kinds of Splitters. Collectors and related
stages come into play as utilities to help with some of the plumbing.

7.4.2.1 *Interfaces*

Looking ahead to how we might want to string these stages together, it is worthwhile to standardize interfaces. We'd like to be able to connect any stage to any other stage for which it could make sense, so we would like bland, noncommittal names for the principal methods.

Since we are doing push-based flow, these interfaces mainly describe put-style methods. In fact, we could just call them all `put`, except that this doesn't work very well for two-input stages. For example, a `VerticalJoiner` needs two put methods, one supplying the top `Box` and one the bottom `Box`. We could avoid this by designing `Joiners` to take alternate inputs as the tops and bottoms, but this would make them harder to control. Instead, we'll use the somewhat ugly but easily extensible names `putA`, `putB`, and so on:

```
public interface PushSource {
  public void start();
}
```

```
public interface PushStage {
  public void putA(Box p);
}
```

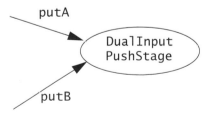

```
public interface DualInputPushStage extends PushStage {
  public void putB(Box p);
}
```

We can make the "B" channels of DualInputPushStages completely transparent to other stages by defining a simple Adapter class that accepts a putA but relays it to the intended recipient's putB. In this way, most stages can be built to invoke putA without knowing or caring that it is being fed into some successor's B channel:

```
public class DualInputAdapter implements PushStage {
  protected DualInputPushStage stage_;

  public DualInputAdapter(DualInputPushStage stage) {
    stage_ = stage;
  }

  public void putA(Box p) {
    stage_.putB(p);
  }

}
```

And, while we are focused on interfaces and Adapters, here is a simple Runnable Adapter that helps perform any putA in a new Thread:

```
public class PutARunner implements Runnable {
  protected PushStage target_;
  protected Box arg_;

  public PutARunner(PushStage target, Box arg) {
    target_ = target;
    arg_ = arg;
  }

  public void run() {
    target_.putA(arg_);
  }

}
```

7.4.2.2 *Sinks*

Sinks have no successors. The simplest kind of sink doesn't even process its input, and so serves as a way to throw away elements. In the spirit of Unix pipes and filters, we can call it:

```
public class DevNull implements PushStage {
  public void putA(Box p) { }
}
```

More interesting sinks require more interesting code. For example, in the applet used to produce the image shown at the beginning of this section, the `Applet` subclass itself was defined to `implement PushStage`. It served as the ultimate sink by displaying the assembled objects.

7.4.2.3 *Connections*

Interfaces standardize on the method names for stages but do nothing about the linkages to successors, which will be maintained using some kind of instance variables in each stage object. Except for sinks such as `DevNull`, each stage has at least one successor. There are several implementation options, including:

- Have each object maintain a collection object holding all of its successors.

- Use a master connection registry that each stage knows about and interacts with to find out its successor(s).

- Create the minimal representation: define a base class for stages that have exactly one successor and one for those with exactly two successors.

The third option is simplest and works fine here. (In fact, it is always a valid option. Stages with three or more outputs can be built by cascading those for only two. Of course, you wouldn't want to do this if most stages had large and/or variable numbers of successors.) This leads to base classes supporting either one or two links and having one or two corresponding attachment methods, named using a similar ugly suffix convention (`attach1`, `attach2`):

```
public class SingleOutputPushStage {
  protected PushStage next1_ = null;

  public void attach1(PushStage s) {
    next1_ = s;
  }

}
```

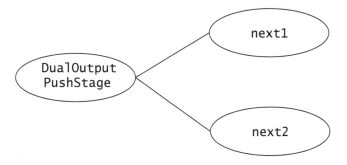

```
public class DualOutputPushStage extends SingleOutputPushStage {
  protected PushStage next2_ = null;

  public void attach2(PushStage s) {
    next2_ = s;
  }

}
```

Now we can build all sorts of classes that extend either of these base classes, simultaneously implementing any of the standard interfaces.

7.4.2.4 *Linear Stages*

The simplest transformational stages are linear, single-input/single-output stages.
Painters, Wrappers, and Flippers are just:

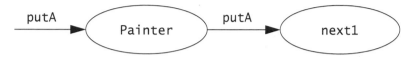

```
public class Painter extends SingleOutputPushStage
                       implements PushStage {
  protected Color color_; // the color to paint things

  public Painter(Color c) {
    super();
    color_ = c;
  }

  public synchronized void putA(Box p) {
    p.color(color_);
    next1_.putA(p);
  }

}
```

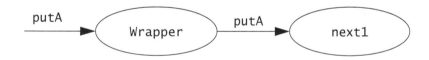

```
public class Wrapper extends SingleOutputPushStage
                       implements PushStage {
  protected int thickness_;

  public Wrapper(int thickness) {
    super();
    thickness_ = thickness;
  }

  public synchronized void putA(Box p) {
    Dimension d = new Dimension(thickness_, thickness_);
    next1_.putA(new WrappedBox(p, d));
  }

}
```

241

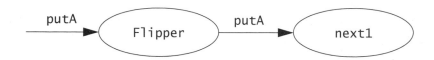

```
public class Flipper extends SingleOutputPushStage
                    implements PushStage {
  public synchronized void putA(Box p) {
    if (p instanceof JoinedPair)
      ((JoinedPair) p).flip();
    next1_.putA(p);
  }

}
```

Painter and Wrapper stages apply to any kind of Box. But Flippers only make sense for JoinedPairs: if a Flipper receives something other than a JoinedPair, it just passes it through. In a more "strongly typed" version, we might instead choose to drop boxes other than JoinedPairs by sending them to DevNull.

7.4.2.5 *Dual Input Stages*

The most basic kind of dual input stage is a simple Collector that accepts messages on either channel and relays them on to a single successor:

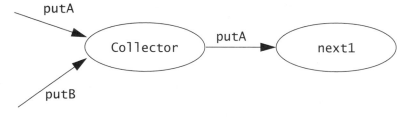

```
public class Collector extends SingleOutputPushStage
                       implements DualInputPushStage {

  public synchronized void putA(Box p) {
    next1_.putA(p);
  }

  public synchronized void putB(Box p) {
    next1_.putA(p);
  }

}
```

   We have two kinds of Combiners, horizontal and vertical `Joiners`. Like the representation classes, the stage classes have enough in common to build a common superclass. Joiner stages block further inputs until they are able to combine one item each from `putA` and `putB`. This can be implemented via the usual guard mechanics:

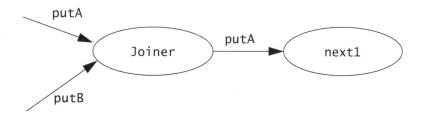

```
public abstract class Joiner extends SingleOutputPushStage
                               implements DualInputPushStage {
  protected Box a_ = null;   // incoming box from putA
  protected Box b_ = null;   // incoming box from putB

  protected abstract Box join(); // differs in subclasses

  protected void output() {// pass on a completed pair
    if (a_ != null && b_ != null) {
      next1_.putA(join()); // send combined box
      a_ = b_ = null;
      notifyAll(); // allow new puts
    }
  }

  public synchronized void putA(Box p) {
    // block until held a_ part is successfully joined with a b_
    while (a_ != null)
      try { wait(); } catch (InterruptedException e) { return; }
    a_ = p;
    output();
  }

  public synchronized void putB(Box p) { // symmetrical to putA
    while (b_ != null)
      try { wait(); } catch (InterruptedException e) { return; }
    b_ = p;
    output();
  }

}
```

```
public class HorizontalJoiner extends Joiner {

  protected synchronized Box join() {
    return new HorizontallyJoinedPair(a_, b_);
  }

}

public class VerticalJoiner extends Joiner {

  protected synchronized Box join() {
    return new VerticallyJoinedPair(a_, b_);
  }

}
```

7.4.2.6 *Dual Output Stages*

Our multiple-output stages should generate threads to drive at least one of their outputs (it doesn't matter which). This maintains liveness in cases where elements are ultimately passed to Combiner stages (here, the Joiners).

Alternators output alternate inputs on alternate channels:

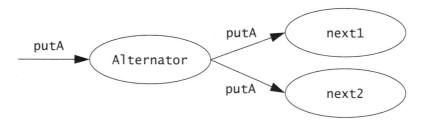

```
public class Alternator extends DualOutputPushStage
                        implements PushStage {
  protected boolean outTo2_ = false; // control alternation

  public synchronized void putA(Box p) {
    if (!outTo2_)
      next1_.putA(p);
    else
      new Thread(new PutARunner(next2_, p)).start();

    outTo2_ = !outTo2_; // change state for next time
  }

}
```

Cloners multicast the same element to both successors:

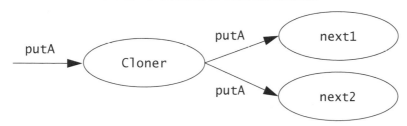

```
public class Cloner extends DualOutputPushStage
                    implements PushStage {

  public synchronized void putA(Box p) {
    Box p2 = p.duplicate();
    new Thread(new PutARunner(next1_, p)).start();
    next2_.putA(p2);
  }

}
```

A Screener is a stage that directs all inputs obeying some predicate to one channel, and all others to the other:

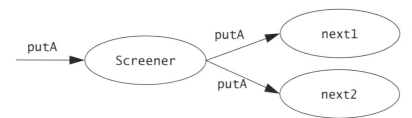

We can build a generic Screener by encapsulating the BoxPredicate to check in an interface and implementing it, for example, with a class that makes sure that a Box fits within a given (symmetric, in this case) bound. The Screener itself accepts a BoxPredicate and uses it to direct outputs:

```
public interface BoxPredicate {
  public boolean test(Box p);
}
```

```
public class MaxSizePredicate implements BoxPredicate {
  private int max_; // max size to let through

  public MaxSizePredicate(int max) {
    max_ = max;
  }

  public boolean test(Box p) {
    return p.size().height <= max_ && p.size().width <= max_;
  }

}

public class Screener extends DualOutputPushStage
                      implements PushStage {
  BoxPredicate pred_;

  public Screener(BoxPredicate pred) {
    super();
    pred_ = pred;
  }

  public synchronized void putA(Box p) {
    if (pred_.test(p))
      new Thread(new PutARunner(next1_, p)).start();
    else
      next2_.putA(p);
  }

}
```

7.4.2.7   *Sources*

Here is a sample source, one that produces `BasicBoxes` of random sizes. For convenience, it is also equipped with an autonomous loop repeatedly invoking `start`, interspersed with random production delays:

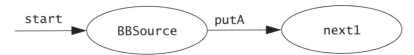

```
public class BasicBoxSource extends SingleOutputPushStage
                            implements PushSource, Runnable {
  protected Dimension size_; // maximum sizes
  protected int productionTime_; // simulated delay

  public BasicBoxSource(Dimension size, int productionTime) {
    size_ = size;
    productionTime_ = productionTime;
  }

  protected synchronized Box produce() {
    return new BasicBox((int)(Math.random() * size_.width) + 1,
                        (int)(Math.random() * size_.height) + 1);
  }

  public synchronized void start() {
    next1_.putA(produce());
  }

  public void run() {
    for (;;) {
      start();
      try {
        Thread.sleep((int)(Math.random() * 2*productionTime_));
      }
      catch (InterruptedException ex) { return; }
    }
  }

}
```

7.4.3 Coordination

Without a scripting tool based on these classes, we have to program assembly lines by manually creating instances of desired stages and linking them together. This is easy in principle, but tedious and error-prone in practice because of the lack of visual guidance about what stages are connected to what. Here's a fragment of the flow used in the applet that produced the image displayed at the beginning of this section:

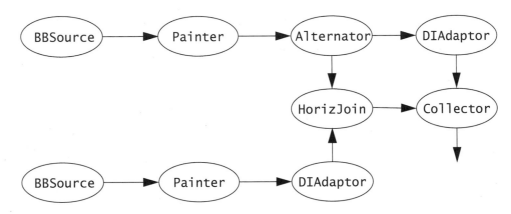

The code setting this up may be found in the on-line supplement. It mainly consists of many lines of the form:

```
Stage aStage = new Stage();
aStage.attach(anotherStage);
```

7.5 Further Readings

Flow patterns often serve as the computational versions of use cases, scenarios, scripts, and related concepts from high-level object-oriented analysis. Most of the books on OO design and on design patterns listed in Chapter 1 describe issues relevant to the analysis, design and implementation of flow-based systems.

Packet networking, telecommunications, and multimedia systems often require fairly elaborate flow-based designs. For discussion of domain-specific issues, see the texts on concurrent and distributed systems listed in Chapter 1.

Linear logic may someday provide tools that can be used to formally analyze the kinds of flow-based structures described in this chapter. See, for example, the papers by Andreoli and colleagues in the collection edited by Agha, Wegner, and Yonezawa listed in Chapter 1.

Linda is an example of an entire programming framework based on a particular flow model built upon buffers serving as tuple spaces. See:

Carriero, Nicholas, and David Gelernter. *How to Write Parallel Programs*, MIT Press, 1990.

A more extensive account of the *Resource Exchange* pattern may be found in Sane and Campbell's paper in the 1995 volume of *Pattern Languages of Program Design* listed in Chapter 1.

Flow architectures are only one aspect of task coordination. For a wide-ranging survey, see:

Malone, Thomas, and Kevin Crowston. "The Interdisciplinary Study of Coordination". *ACM Computing Surveys*, March 1994.

CHAPTER 8

Coordinated Interaction

THE flow patterns presented in Chapter 7 achieve simplicity and generality by restricting the directionality and locality of interactions among objects. But unidirectional flow patterns cannot be used when synchronized bidirectional and/or nested interaction among participants is intrinsic to a design. This chapter surveys three approaches to the design of less constrained cooperative components and frameworks:

Transaction-based techniques provide general-purpose but sometimes heavyweight solutions to problems requiring the coordination of independent objects and activities.

Notification-based techniques provide more specific, more efficient, but sometimes more complex and delicate solutions to problems requiring the coordination of coupled objects and activities.

Scheduling techniques employ meta-level representations to oversee and control the execution of sets of related activities.

Each of these approaches leads to extensive and well-studied sets of techniques for structuring and managing interactions among multiple objects. This chapter does not attempt to cover any of them in their entirety. Instead, it presents basic design principles, design patterns, and Java implementation techniques that can serve as foundations for further extensions.

8.1 Transactions

In the context of concurrent OO programming, a *transaction* is an operation performed by an arbitrary client that invokes an arbitrary set of methods on an arbitrary set of *participant* objects, all without interference from other threads.

Transaction techniques extend delegation-based synchronization and control to multiple delegates (participants). Each participant may be unaware of the atomicity constraints being placed on its actions, and cannot necessarily rely on structural exclusion techniques that would make dynamic synchronization unnecessary.

This section describes transaction-based techniques applicable in general-purpose concurrent programming contexts. It begins with simple block synchronization and proceeds with descriptions of classic optimistic and pessimistic approaches. While these stem from strategies used in database systems, the designs presented here deal only with internal concurrency, and not explicitly with persistence or distribution. Even ignoring these issues, setting up classes to guarantee atomicity of arbitrary code sequences is not always an easy task.

8.1.1 Synchronizing Multiple Objects

Java block synchronization constructions can be extended to deal with multiparticipant transactions.

Explicitly transactional classes are probably the most common contexts for transactional methods. But they are also seen in "ordinary" classes in which a method takes another object as an argument and steps both the other object and itself through a code sequence that must be atomic. For example the swapContents method in the Cell example from Chapter 3 is of this form. It is repeated here using an ATOMICALLY pretend-keyword enclosing the code that should be performed without interference from other threads:

```
pseudoclass Cell { // pseudocode version
  private int value_;
  // ...
  public void swapContents(Cell other) {
    ATOMICALLY {
      int newValue = other.value_;
      other.value_ = value_;
      value_ = newValue;
    }
  }

}
```

Here is an implementation using nested block synchronization:

```
public void swapContents(Cell other) {
  synchronized(this) {
    synchronized(other) {
      int newValue = value;
      other.value_ = value_;
      value_ = newValue;
    }
  }
}
```

In the language of transactions, this is called *two-phase* locking. In the first phase *all* locks are acquired at once, and then after the actions are performed, all are released.

This version has exactly the same potential for deadlock as the original version. If `Cells` x and y both start executing `swapContents` for each other at about the same time, then x could be holding the `synchronized(this)` lock while waiting for the `synchronized(other)` lock at the same time that y is in the opposite situation, leading to deadlock.

8.1.1.1 *Resource Ordering*

There are no universal, magical solutions to deadlock prevention in transactional methods. However, the technique of *resource ordering* removes the potential for deadlock in this particular kind of construction. It is so easy to apply in Java that it should be used routinely in all methods involving multiple block synchronization.

The idea behind resource ordering is to associate a numerical (or any other strictly orderable data type) tag with each object that can ever be held in a nested `synchronized` block. If synchronization is always performed in least-first order with respect to object tags, then situations can never arise in which one thread has the synchronization lock for x while waiting for y and another has the lock for y while waiting for x. Instead, they will both obtain the locks in the same order, thus avoiding this form of deadlock. More generally, resource ordering can be used whenever there is a need to arbitrarily break symmetry or force precedence in a concurrent design.

The reason resource ordering is easy to apply in Java is that each `Object` already comes with a numerical tag, its `hashCode`. While hash code values are not guaranteed to be unique, the probability of a clash is extremely small, and is in fact zero in current Java implementations unless you override the `hashCode` method in a way that defeats this property.

Lock-ordering problems are by no means restricted to methods using nested block synchronization. The issue arises in any code sequence where a synchronized method holding the lock on one object in turn calls a synchronized method on another object. However, there is rarely any opportunity to apply resource ordering in cascaded calls: one object cannot know for sure which other objects will be involved in downstream calls and whether they require synchronization. This is one reason that deadlock can be such a hard problem in open designs.

8.1.1.2 *Aliasing*

One further check can be applied in methods using multiple block synchronization to handle cases in which two (or more) of the references are actually bound to the same object. For example, in swapContents, you can check whether a Cell is being asked to swap with itself. This kind of check is strictly optional. Java synchronization lock access is per-thread, not per object. Additional attempts to synchronize on already-held objects will still work. However, routine alias-checking is a useful way to forestall downstream functionality, efficiency, and synchronization based complications.

8.1.1.3 *Example*

Applying both resource ordering and alias detection, we can write a better version of swapContents as:

```
public void swapContents(Cell other) {
  if (other == this) return; // alias check
  Cell first = this;         // resource ordering
  Cell second = other;
  if (this.hashCode() > other.hashCode()) {
    first = other;
    second = this;
  }
  synchronized(first) {
    synchronized(second) {
      int newValue = value;
      other.value_ = value_;
      value_ = newValue;
    }
  }
}
```

If Cells were used in a flow-based design of the sort described in Chapter 7, we would surely establish a policy and protocol that eliminates the possibility of deadlock. For example, we might require that Cells only swap with left-hand neighbors. Resource ordering achieves a similar effect here by dynamically forcing an ordering in the event of conflict.

8.1.1.4 *Limitations*

Client-side block synchronization by itself cannot be guaranteed to result in atomic actions and transactions for arbitrary kinds of participant objects. Two intertwined problems can be encountered, as illustrated in the next two examples.

8.1.1.5 *Subclassing*

A common reason for considéring delegation-style block synchronization is to lock a check-and-act sequence around another object, first checking if the object is in some state and then, if so, performing an action without allowing the object to change state in the meantime. However, this technique might not strictly guarantee the desired effects.

To illustrate, consider a stripped-down bank account class written in balking form, and usages such as a method to get money from an account:

```java
public class InsufficientFunds extends Exception {}

public class BankAccount {
  protected long balance_ = 0;

  public synchronized long balance() {
    return balance_;
  }

  public synchronized void deposit(long amount)
   throws InsufficientFunds {
    if (balance_ < -amount)
      throw new InsufficientFunds();
    else
      balance_ += amount;
  }

  public void withdraw(long amount) throws InsufficientFunds {
    deposit(-amount);
  }

}
```

```
class User {
  long cashOnHand_;

  synchronized void getMoneyV1(BankAccount acct, long amount) {
    try {
      acct.withdraw(amount);
      cashOnHand_ += amount;
    }
    catch (InsufficientFunds ex) { evasiveAction(); }
  }

  void evasiveAction() { /* deal with failure */ }

}
```

The getMoney code looks a bit inefficient because of the exception mechanics. It would be nicer to call withdraw conditionally, avoiding the potential for exceptions via a check-and-act design. However, all attempts to do so lead to potential problems. For example, consider adding a conditional:

```
synchronized void getMoneyV2(BankAccount acct, long amount) {
  if (acct.balance() >= amount) {              // questionable
    try {
      acct.withdraw(amount);
      cashOnHand_ += amount;
    }
    catch (InsufficientFunds shouldNotHappen) { } // wrong
  }
}
```

Even if the conditional holds true, an attempted withdrawal can fail and raise an exception if some other thread performs withdraw between the condition and action. At best then, this version might lessen the probability of an exception, so the catch clause must still be implemented.

To counter this, you might try adding block synchronization. Because the BankAccount class is fully synchronized, the synchronized(acct) code here locks the acct object so that the entire code block is atomic and cannot be interfered with by other threads:

```
synchronized void getMoneyV3(BankAccount acct, long amount) {
  synchronized (acct) {                          // questionable
    if (acct.balance() >= amount) {
      try {
        acct.withdraw(amount);
        cashOnHand_ += amount;
      }
      catch (InsufficientFunds shouldNotHappen) { } // wrong
    }
  }
}
```

But this tactic can also fail. While it may work acceptably with class `BankAc-
count` itself, the `getMoney` operation is parameterized to accept an instance of
class BankAccount *or any of its subclasses*.

In the absence of documented conventions and constraints on the permitted
forms of `BankAccount` subclasses, the client cannot know anything about the
exception or synchronization conditions that might be employed in all of the infinite possible subclasses of `BankAccount`. In particular, unless `BankAccount` is
declared as a `final` class, or there is any kind of policy requirement placed upon
all such classes, the client does not know for sure that the precondition check is
actually sufficient to prevent exceptions in all possible subclasses.

8.1.1.6 *Nesting*

A serious problem with client-side synchronization of all kinds is that users of a
class cannot always know of all of the internal assumptions and dependencies of
the classes they are trying to control, and in particular whether these objects
require additional synchronization on other independent helpers in order to perform series of operations safely.

In particular, block synchronization techniques can fail when applied to
objects with nested structure unless all of their references are fixed and unique.
For example, suppose you have a design of the form:

```
class Helper { // ...
  void aMethod() { /* ... */ }
}

public class Host {
  protected Helper helper_;

  public Host(Helper h) {
    helper_ = h;
  }

  public void delegatedMethod() {
    helper_.aMethod();
  }

}
```

No amount of synchronization control on a `Host` will automatically control its `Helper` unless it is somehow known that the `Helper` is exclusively managed by the `Host`. When defensible, exclusion measures are among the best ways to ensure composability, although at the price of inflexibility. In other cases, you may be able to propagate control by creating special-purpose coordinated subclasses of participants that manage helper objects accessed via `protected` references.

8.1.2   Structured Transactions

When the need for layered control runs up against the problems induced by locking conflicts, nesting, and subclassing, you must rely on designs in which each class, at each layer, supports a standardized transaction protocol that propagates control down through successive layers.

Each method in each class in a structured transaction framework possesses a control argument in addition to its normal arguments:

```
ReturnType aMethod(Transaction t, ArgType normalArgs)
```

Here, `Transaction` is any type that supplies the necessary control information. This transaction information must be propagated throughout all methods invoked in the course of a particular transaction, including nested calls to helper objects.

The simplest and by far most common kind of transaction argument is a *transaction key* that uniquely identifies each transaction. Each method in each participating object is then responsible for using this key to manage and isolate actions in accord with a given transaction policy.

Keys are used as transaction arguments in all examples in this section. However, a transaction argument may instead refer, for example, to a special control or coordinator object that possesses methods that help participants perform their roles in transactions.

Participating objects must also support a standardized interface to coordinate their actions with others participating in the same transactions. For example, most schemes require a method that introduces a new transaction key. This method is called before any other method that uses that key as a control argument.

The resulting class designs employ a much more extreme form of delegation than that seen in Chapter 5. In transaction frameworks, each participant object gives up its local autonomy in deciding how to perform concurrency control. Participants instead rely on other objects to tell them how and when to perform actions and/or to commit to their effects.

One of the principal disadvantages of transactional techniques is that conformance to a transaction protocol impacts the method signatures and implementations of every participant class. This often spreads in turn through most classes in an entire application or framework. Worse, it is often troublesome at best to make a set of classes using one set of standardized transaction interfaces to work with those using another. And because "transactionality" tends to infiltrate the details of ground-level code, these problems resist smoothing over via Adapters and the like.

Thus, even though objects supporting standardized transaction protocols are highly usable and reusable, the heaviness of transaction frameworks usually restricts their use to contexts in which you really need to set up objects so as to guarantee atomicity of arbitrary code sequences without using simpler dynamic or structural exclusion strategies.

There are two broad categories of transaction policies, optimistic and pessimistic (conservative). Under optimistic policies, each participant object attempts the action associated with its part of a transaction, but does not commit to the action's effects until the success of all actions by all participants is assured. Under pessimistic policies, each participant object employs a form of locking that guarantees that each transaction is not interfered with by others. However, unlike the analogous check-and-act single-object designs (Chapter 4), pessimistic transactions almost always include optimistic-style mechanics that allow transactions to be rolled back in case of deadlocks or other failures.

Choices among these approaches rest on the same kinds of considerations as described in Chapter 4, for example trading off efficiency and the probability of failure against the cost and complexity of recovery under each scheme.

8.1.3 Optimistic Transactions

Participants in optimistic transactions attempt to perform actions, but re-establish initial states upon failures stemming from interference. The main applicability constraint is that all participants in the transaction must be instances of classes supporting rollbacks that revert their state to initial conditions upon failure.

As an example, consider writing a `transfer` operation for the `BankAccount` class. We'd like this code to be executed without any possibility of interference from other threads while at the same time maximizing, or at the very least permitting, concurrency:

```
pseudoclass AccountUser { // pseudocode version
  TransactionLogger log_; // any kind of logging facility
  // ...

  // Attempt transfer; return true if successful
  public boolean transfer(long amount,
                          BankAccount source,
                          BankAccount destination) {
    ATOMICALLY {
      if (source.balance() >= amount) {
        log_.logTransfer(amount, source, destination);
        source.withdraw(amount);
        destination.deposit(amount);
        return true;
      }
      else
        return false;
    }
  }

}
```

There are two principal steps in setting up optimistic transactions for solving this kind of problem: writing special classes for each participant object that supports transactional usage according to a standard interface, and then writing the corresponding transaction code.

8.1.3.1 *Participants*

Participant objects can support rollbacks via strategies similar to those used in the single-object optimistic designs described in Chapter 4. However, in order to support multiple-object version-based transactions, analogs of operations that are strictly internal in the single-object case must be made externally accessible in a standardized manner.

Transaction control information in optimistic designs can be represented via unique transaction keys that serve as the analogs of internal version indicators used in single-object optimistic designs. Each method in each participating object accepts a key argument indicating the transaction to which the associated actions should be applied.

Just about any kind of data type suffices to represent keys. The simplest representation choice in Java is to use references to arbitrary `java.lang.Objects`. Since references to distinct `new Objects` are guaranteed to be unique, you don't need to build any special facilities to otherwise guarantee uniqueness.

For concreteness, `Object` keys are used in all following examples. However, key representations need not be so simple to obtain or create. It is of course possible to employ encryption schemes to produce unforgeable keys that aid in security.

A representative choice for a control interface is:

```
public class KeyException extends Exception {}

public interface Transactor {

  // enter a new transaction
  public void join(Object key) throws KeyException;

  // return true if this transaction can be committed
  public boolean canCommit(Object key);

  // update state to reflect current transaction
  public void commit(Object key) throws KeyException;

  // roll back state (No exception; ignore if inapplicable)
  public void abort(Object key);

}
```

For simplicity of illustration, a single exception type is associated with these operations, as well as all others in this series of examples. Participant objects are allowed to raise exceptions when they encounter actual or potential conflicts and when they are requested to participate in transactions that they do not know about. In practice, you'd want to subclass these exception types and use them to provide additional information to clients in cases of failure.

The transactional classes themselves can implement extensions of the `Transactor` interface. For example:

```
public interface TransBankAccount extends Transactor {

  public long balance(Object key) throws KeyException;

  public void deposit(Object key, long amount)
    throws InsufficientFunds, KeyException;

  public void withdraw(Object key, long amount)
    throws InsufficientFunds, KeyException;

}
```

Under such an interface, the inner workings of each method of each participant are similar to those in seen in single-object designs. But rather than keeping old versions valid until updates are complete, updates are performed when requested, at least so far as clients supplying the same key are concerned. The old version is kept around to roll back to if necessary.

For example, one set of solutions takes the form:

join. Make a copy of the current version of state as the working version to be associated with key. Since join is allowed to fail, the object may refuse to join if it is already participating in another transaction. (This allows even relatively simple objects to participate in transactions, although only one at a time.) Otherwise, multiple shadow versions of the internal state must be associated with multiple keys. Ensure that all independent helper objects internally referenced through instance variables and used by any update methods also implement Transactor. Upon join, propagate to all such delegates.

abort. Propagate to all delegates. Then throw away the working version of state associated with key and perform any other necessary recovery actions.

commit. Propagate to all delegates. Then swap in the working version as the permanent version.

canCommit. First check all nested objects, returning false if any of them do. Otherwise return true unless some sort of local failure or inconsistency has been encountered, for example because some other incompatible commit on a different key has intervened. It is generally wrong to return true for a canCommit on one key after already returning true for another unless they are known to be compatible. You can invest an arbitrary amount of effort in determining whether two otherwise independent commits are compatible (for example, by using conflict sets — see Chapter 5).

Other methods. Add key as an argument to all other normal methods and ensure that the action code operates on the version of state associated with key.

8.1.3.2 *Example*

When applied to the `BankAccount` class, taking the simplest possible option at each step leads to a version that is not fit for serious use. Among other scale-downs, it maintains only a single shadow copy of state, so can be used only for non-overlapping transactions. But it suffices to illustrate the general structure of optimistic classes and also, implicitly, how much more code would be required to build a more useful version.

```java
public class OptimBankAccount implements TransBankAccount {
  protected long balance_ = 0;
  protected long workingBalance_ = 0; // single shadow copy
  protected Object currentKey_ = null; // single transaction key

  public synchronized long balance(Object key)
   throws KeyException {
    if (key != currentKey_)
      throw new KeyException();
    return workingBalance_;
  }

  public synchronized void deposit(Object key, long amount)
   throws InsufficientFunds, KeyException {
    if (key != currentKey_)
      throw new KeyException();
    if (workingBalance_ < -amount)
      throw new InsufficientFunds();
    workingBalance_ += amount;
  }

  public synchronized void withdraw(Object key, long amount)
   throws InsufficientFunds, KeyException {
    deposit(key, -amount);
  }

  public synchronized void join(Object key) throws KeyException {
    if (currentKey_ != null)
      throw new KeyException();
    currentKey_ = key;
    workingBalance_ = balance_;
  }

  public synchronized boolean canCommit(Object key) {
    return (key == currentKey_);
  }

  public synchronized void abort(Object key) {
    currentKey_ = null;
  }
```

```
public synchronized void commit(Object key)
 throws KeyException {
  if (key != currentKey_)
    throw new KeyException();
  balance_ = workingBalance_;
  currentKey_ = null;
 }

}
```

Classes obeying the `Transactor` interface can also employ arbitrary degrees of shared nesting among participants. For example, you could construct a Proxy account that just forwards messages to another unrelated and otherwise uncontrolled account. Classes with nested structure can take the form:

```
public class ProxyAccount implements TransBankAccount {
  private TransBankAccount delegate_;

  public void join(Object key) throws KeyException {
    delegate_.join(key);
  }


  public long balance(Object key) throws KeyException {
    return delegate_.balance(key);
  }

  // and so on...

}
```

8.1.3.3 *Transactions*

Transactions that employ participants obeying the `Transactor` interface take a standard form, performing the following steps:

- Invoke `join` on all participants using a new transaction key.

- Try the entire action, aborting all participants on any failure and also rolling back any other auxiliary actions.

- Upon completion, collect votes using `canCommit` and then `commit` or `abort`.

The same failure alternatives apply here as for other optimistic techniques: inaction, throwing exceptions, or retrying from scratch.

In most applications, it simplifies matters if the classes initiating transactions also support the `Transactor` interface. They may additionally support a subinterface `TransactionCoordinator`, which extends `Transactor` by adding method `newTransaction` to issue a new `key`. They may also support other methods that set up logging and related bookkeeping matters.

8.1.3.4 *Example*

A version of the example `transfer` operation can be coded as an independent method, without the need for a `TransactionCoordinator` class. In the version below, failure can occur for any of three reasons:

Semantic failure. There may not be sufficient funds in the accounts, in which case the method returns `false`. In this example, there is not even a pre-check that the source holds a sufficient balance. Even if it reported true, the `withdraw` attempt may fail anyway. Similarly, since the `amount` is allowed to be negative, it is possible for `destination.deposit` to fail even if the `source.withdraw` succeeds. (For a negative amount, a deposit acts like a withdraw and vice versa.)

Interference. If either account cannot join or cannot commit to this transaction due to interference by another concurrent transaction, an exception is thrown indicating that the action is retryable.

Transaction error. Unrecoverable operation failure can occur if objects fail to commit even after they say they can. There is nothing that can be done about this internal error, so the exception is propagated back to clients.

The recovery action for each of these cases happens to be identical in this example (and is factored into a helper method). The `abort` clauses perform the state rollbacks. But the log must be canceled independently. This could be avoided if it were acceptable to log transfers only upon success, in which case the call could be moved down beyond all failure points.

```
public class FailedTransferException extends Exception {}

public class RetryableTransferException extends Exception {}

public class AccountUser {
  TransactionLogger log_;

  public AccountUser(TransactionLogger log) {
    log_ = log;
  }
```

```
public boolean transfer(long amount,
                        TransBankAccount source,
                        TransBankAccount destination)
  throws FailedTransferException, RetryableTransferException {

 if (source == destination) return true; // avoid aliasing

 Object key = new Object();             // new transaction id

 log_.logTransfer(amount, source, destination); // record

 try {
   source.join(key);
   destination.join(key);

   source.withdraw(key, amount);
   destination.deposit(key, amount);

   // try to commit
   if (source.canCommit(key) && destination.canCommit(key)) {
     try {
       source.commit(key);
       destination.commit(key);
       return true;
     }
     catch(KeyException k) { // commitment failure
       rollback(key, amount, source, destination);
       throw new FailedTransferException();
     }
   }
   else { // can retry later if cannot now commit
     rollback(key, amount, source, destination);
     throw new RetryableTransferException();
   }
 }

 // deal with semantic failures:
 catch (InsufficientFunds ex) {
   rollback(key, amount, source, destination);
   return false;
 }

 // all other transaction failures retryable
 catch (KeyException k) {
   rollback(key, amount, source, destination);
   throw new RetryableTransferException();
 }
}
```

```
  // helper method called on any failure
  void rollback(Object key, long amount,
                TransBankAccount src, TransBankAccount dst) {
    log_.cancelLogEntry(amount, src, dst);
    src.abort(key);
    dst.abort(key);
  }

}
```

8.1.4 Locks

In pessimistic transactions, the transaction argument used in each method controls
locking. Each participant arranges to synchronize its methods in accord with a
lock associated with the given transaction. This rules out the kinds of interference
that can occur in optimistic transactions, at the expense of synchronization overhead.

Special-purpose lock classes provide a foundation for pessimistic transaction
frameworks, as well as for other applications that need to overcome the limitations
of native Java locking mechanisms:

- The "methods" on native Java locks are invisible — you can only control their
  use via the synchronized keyword.

- It is not possible to time-out waiting for a native Java lock.

- Native Java locks cannot be subclassed or otherwise specialized. For example,
  you cannot define subclasses requiring authentication of users.

- Native locks are intimately tied to Java Thread mechanics.

- Because you cannot reference native Java locks, you cannot track them to
  implement deadlock detection algorithms (see Further Readings) or perform
  special recovery measures upon deadlock.

8.1.4.1 *Interfaces*

Because there is so much room for variation in both policy and implementation,
lock classes should be defined in terms of a standard interface, for example:

```
public interface Lock {

  // associate key with lock
  public void acquire(Object key) throws KeyException;

  // return true if key is associated with lock
  public boolean hasKey(Object key);

  // access protected code
  public void enter(Object key) throws KeyException;

  // get rid of key (no exception; ignore if not applicable)
  public void release(Object key);

}
```

A common variant merges `acquire` and `enter`. This may apply when entry can occur only in the context of associating a new one-shot key. An `exit` method can also be defined to bracket protected code so that `release` is never called prematurely. Another common although less secure variant is to support a method that returns the key currently associated with the lock.

8.1.4.2 *Implementations*

Different classes can implement a common `Lock` interface to reflect particular transaction policies. For example, here is an implementation that uses time-outs as a heuristic approach to deadlock detection. Waits for new keys and uses of existing keys time-out and raise exceptions after a predetermined period. Clients catching these exceptions are then responsible for taking evasive action, normally under the assumption that the time-outs were caused by deadlocks and so should be aborted and perhaps retried later:

```
public class SimpleTimeOutLock implements Lock {
  public static final long timeOut = 1000; // time-out period

  // Simple key generator
  public static Object newKey() { return new Object(); }

  protected Object key_ = null; // current key

  public boolean hasKey(Object key) {
    return key == key_;
  }
```

```
  // associate lock with new key
  public synchronized void acquire(Object key)
   throws KeyException {

    // block until released or time-out
    // (OK here to re-acquire same key.)
    while (key_ != null && key_ != key) {
      try { wait(timeOut); }
      catch (InterruptedException ex) {
        throw new KeyException();// fail on interrupt
      }
      if (key_ != null && key_ != key)
        throw new KeyException();// fail on time-out
    }

    key_ = key;
    notifyAll(); // notify threads waiting to enter on this key
  }

  // wait until key matches current key
  public synchronized void enter(Object key)
   throws KeyException {
    while (key != key_) {
      try { wait(timeOut); }
      catch (InterruptedException ex) {
        throw new KeyException();
      }
      if (key_ != key)
        throw new KeyException();
    }
  }

  // clear key so can accept another
  public synchronized void release(Object key) {
    if (key_ == key) {
      key_ = null;
      notifyAll(); // notify threads waiting to acquire
    }
  }

}
```

8.1.5 Pessimistic Transactions

Pessimistic transaction protocols generalize policies and mechanisms used in single-object check-and-act designs:

- Actions are triggered via waits on the lock objects associated with transaction keys rather than using synchronized methods, blocks or guards.

- Participants support some capability for rollback so that transactions can be aborted in the case of deadlock or other failures. This is not strictly required, but without rollback support, many of the advantages for using transaction frameworks are defeated.

- Transaction control is applied to all nested calls to helper objects, all of which conform to the same transaction interface.

Interfaces for pessimistic transactions can take the same form as those for optimistic transactions. For example, pessimistic classes can conform to the `Transactor` interface by implementing methods with the help of a `Lock` object as follows:

`join`. `Acquire` the key and make a backup copy of current state to roll back to if necessary. Propagate the key to all delegates. Alternatively, when semantics allow, nested locking can be done only as needed in the course of other methods by establishing *subtransaction*s with their own `keys`.

`commit`. Propagate to all delegates. Then `release` the key.

`abort`. Propagate to all delegates. Then revert to the backup copy of current state, perform any other necessary recovery actions, and `release` the key.

`canCommit`. First check all delegates, returning `false` if any of them do. Otherwise return `true` unless some sort of local failure has been encountered.

Other methods. Use `enter` to block until the current key matches the argument, then perform base functionality (under internal synchronization if necessary to preserve safety in the presence of multithreaded transactions).

8.1.5.1 *Example*

Here is a pessimistic version of the bank account class. An associated `transfer` operation could take precisely the same form as the optimistic version. The only possible client-visible differences lie in the fact that retryable failures here result from presumed deadlock, while in the optimistic version, they result from conflicts among concurrently executing transactions. However, these differences typically do not influence decisions about whether or not to retry.

```
public class PessimBankAccount implements TransBankAccount {
  protected long balance_ = 0;
  protected Lock lock_ = new SimpleTimeOutLock(); // fixed
  protected long backupBalance_ = 0; // for rollback on abort

  public long balance(Object key) throws KeyException {
    lock_.enter(key);
    synchronized(this) {
      return balance_;
    }
  }

  public void deposit(Object key, long amount)
   throws InsufficientFunds, KeyException {
    lock_.enter(key);
    synchronized(this) {
      if (balance_ < -amount)
        throw new InsufficientFunds();
      else
        balance_ += amount;
    }
  }

  public void withdraw(Object key, long amount)
   throws InsufficientFunds, KeyException {
    deposit(key, -amount);
  }

  public void join(Object key) throws KeyException {
    lock_.acquire(key);
    synchronized(this) {
      backupBalance_ = balance_;
    }
  }

  public void abort(Object key) {
    lock_.release(key);
    synchronized(this) {
      balance_ = backupBalance_;
    }
  }

  public boolean canCommit(Object key)  {
    return lock_.hasKey(key);
  }

  public void commit(Object key) throws KeyException {
    lock_.release(key);
  }
}
```

8.2 Notifications

Transaction frameworks are well suited for problems requiring control of objects that serve requests originating from external sources, but are not always applicable to problems requiring coordination of direct peer-to-peer interactions.

Notification techniques form the basis for many efficient and effective cooperative concurrent designs in which objects notify each other about conditions and events. These same techniques are also among the main causes of the high coupling, complexity and context-dependence of some concurrent designs. This section surveys the territory. It starts off with a discussion of concurrent versions of the Observer pattern, the most common notification-based design pattern used in sequential OO programming. It continues with presentations of both specializations and generalizations of the basic elements of the Observer pattern to address design problems of increasing complexity.

8.2.1 Observer

In the Observer pattern, Subjects (sometimes called *Observables*) maintain some kind of representation of the state of something they are modeling, along with operations to reveal and change this state. Observers somehow display (or otherwise use) the state represented by Subjects. When a Subject's state is changed, it merely informs one or more Observers that it has changed. Observers are responsible for probing the Subjects to determine the nature of the changes via callbacks checking whether, for example, Subject representations need to be re-displayed on a screen.

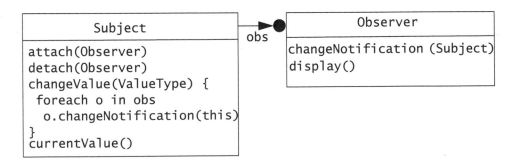

Viewed from a control-flow perspective, the Observer protocol has a very simple push component in which the source stage (Subject) informs its consumers (Observers) that some action needs to be performed. Each Observer then pulls (although normally without depleting) particular information from the source to find out the specific action to be taken. This leads to a two-phase protocol in which the first phase is push-based, and the second pull-based:

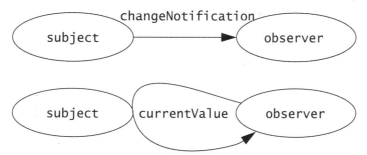

A variant of the Observer pattern is supported in the `java.util.Observable` and `java.util.Observer` classes. But for illustration, here is a simpler (sequentially oriented) version in which the state value maintained by the Subject is just represented as a `double`, each Observer maintains a reference to only a single Subject, and the list of observers is maintained using a `java.util.Vector`:

```
public class Subject {
  protected double val_;                    // modeled state
  protected Vector obs_ = new Vector();     // observers

  public Subject(double initstate) {
    val_ = initstate;
  }

  public synchronized void attach(Observer o) {
    obs_.addElement(o);
  }

  public synchronized void detach(Observer o) {
    obs_.removeElement(o);
  }

  public synchronized double currentValue() { return val_; }

  public synchronized void changeValue(double v) {
    val_ = v;
    // generate notifications to each observer
    for (Enumeration e = obs_.elements(); e.hasMoreElements();){
      Observer o = (Observer)(e.nextElement());
      o.changeNotification(this);
    }
  }
}
```

```
public class Observer {
  protected double cachedState_; // last known state of subject
  protected Subject subj_;        // only one in this version

  public Observer(Subject s) {
    subj_ = s;
    cachedState_ = s.currentValue();
    display();
  }

  public synchronized void changeNotification(Subject s) {
    if (s != subj_) return; // only one subject supported
    double oldState = cachedState_;
    cachedState_ = subj_.currentValue();      // probe
    if (oldState != cachedState_) display(); // redisplay
  }

  protected synchronized void display() { // default version
    System.out.println(cachedState_);
  }
}
```

The sequential version of this pattern is conceptually unsatisfying. When a Subject changes state, it rarely cares exactly when or how its changes are processed and displayed by Observers. The Subject's only responsibility is to perform the notifications.

At the implementation level, things are even worse. Because of the bidirectional flow, it is possible for this version to encounter a deadlock situation when used in multithreaded applications. This could occur if in one thread a Subject issues a change notification, while at the same time in another thread the Observer is trying to check that Subject's current value.

To illustrate the potential for concurrency, a slightly more abstract version of the Observer protocol is shown in the interaction diagram. The lack of any dependency on (or even mention of) a return message for changeNotification means that a Subject may continue along asynchronously after sending this message. This could be implemented by issuing the notification in a new thread.

Multithreading also removes the potential for deadlock. A new thread constructed to carry out changeNotification does not possess the synchronization lock on the Subject. The thread that invokes changeNotification can return immediately without holding onto either lock, allowing each thread (eventually) to continue. To implement this without changing the original Observer class, a multithreaded subclass of Subject could be defined to use a Waiter:

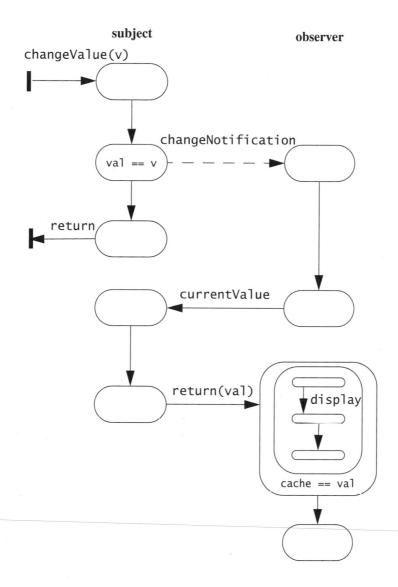

```
public class MTSubject extends Subject {
  public MTSubject(double initstate) { super(initstate); }

  public synchronized void changeValue(double newstate) {
    val_ = newstate;
    // generate a notification thread for each observer
    for (Enumeration e = obs_.elements(); e.hasMoreElements();){
      Observer o = (Observer)(e.nextElement());
      new Thread(new Notifier(this, o)).start();
    }
  }

}

class Notifier implements Runnable {// the waiter class
  private Subject  sub_;
  private Observer obs_;

  Notifier(Subject s, Observer o) {
    sub_ = s;
    obs_ = o;
  }

  public void run() {
    obs_.changeNotification(sub_);
  }

}
```

8.2.2 Delegated Notifications

Consider the mapping from the Observer protocol to the basic wait/notifyAll protocol described in Chapter 4:

- The Subject aspects/roles of an object maintain some state (normally as instance variables).

- The Observer aspects/roles of an object are methods that take some action upon certain state transitions (as defined in guarded methods).

- Subjects may have multiple Observers (waiting threads).

- When a subject changes state, it sends a change notification to all Observers via notifyAll.

- When an Observer receives a notification, it probes for details to find out whether that state change requires any action, and if so performs it, otherwise rewaits.

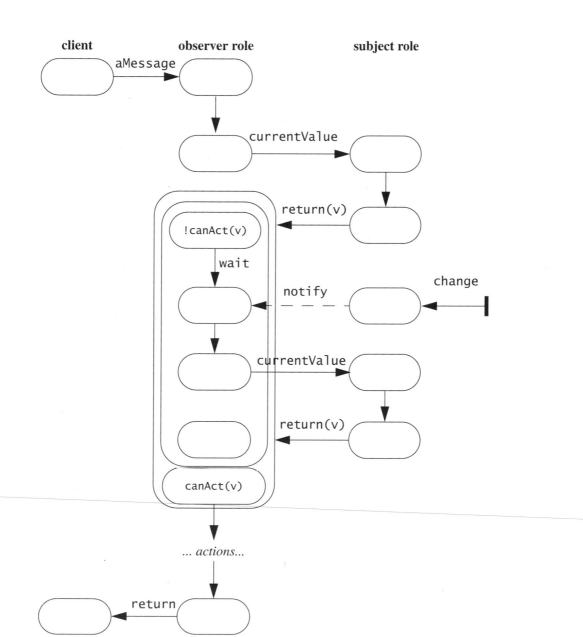

When all of these roles are localized within a single object, then the built-in `notify` and `notifyAll` mechanisms suffice to control behavior. In this case, the accompanying interaction diagram is just an expansion of the inner workings of the `inRightState` nodes illustrating guarded constructions in Chapter 4. (Note the rearrangement of columns from the previous diagram.) But when some or all of one object's action control depends on other objects, you can extend these mechanisms in accord with an Observer scheme, often simplifying those aspects that need not apply (for example, normally you'd restrict Subjects to have at most one Observer).

8.2.2.1   *Dependent Notifications*

The simplest applications of Observer-based techniques avoid synchronization problems by adding enough structural constraints to evade the need for coordination. Strict *dependent notification* designs arise when you partition state representations for a class, say `Host`, using one or more objects of class, say `Helper`, and when:

- The helper objects play no other role than to maintain state for a host. Helper methods are called only from the host. In the simplest cases, each helper is exclusively managed by one host.

- State changes in the helpers never need to be synchronized with actions of the host. That is, helpers need only inform hosts of changes and do not otherwise coordinate resulting actions.

When these conditions are not met, solutions may require the heavier techniques described later in this chapter. But the design space for problems falling under these constraints is wide open. Each `Helper` class can be structured as a Subject, and the `Host` class can serve as an Observer. In particular, to build dependent notification classes:

- Ensure that there are sufficient accessor methods in the `Helpers` for `Hosts` to assess their logical state.

- For each `Helper`, provide a way to attach a `Host` as an Observer, for example using a single instance variable that references a `Host`, initialized in a constructor.

- Upon each state change, have each `Helper` issue a notification. Possible implementations include:

    ◆ Invoke `host.notifyAll`.

- ◆ Invoke a method in the `Host`, say `changeNotification(Helper a)`, that transmits the identity of the helper that actually changed. The `Host` can then record the identity and internally perform `notifyAll`.

- ◆ Invoke an extended form, such as `changeNotification(Helper a, ValueType newValue)`, that transmits the new value so the `Host` does not have to probe for it.

- In each `Host`, maintain references to each `Helper` needed for assessing logical state in guard conditions.

- Write guard conditions and, when applicable, change notification methods accordingly.

8.2.2.2 *Example*

One application of this pattern is to create little helpers that serve as *condition variables* for a host class, signaling it when a logical condition changes. For example, a `NotifyingLong` class can be used to issue a `notifyAll` to any observer object whenever it changes value:

```
public class NotifyingLong {
  private long value_;
  private Object observer_;

  public NotifyingLong(Object o, long v) {
    observer_ = o;
    value_ = v;
  }

  public synchronized long value() { return value_; }

  public void setValue(long v) {
    synchronized(this) {
      value_ = v;
    }
    synchronized(observer_) {
      observer_.notifyAll();
    }
  }
}
```

The `NotifyingLong` class can be used, for example, to create yet another version of `BoundedCounter`. Here, changes in the `NotifyingLong` are used to unblock guarded waits in the boundary states. The resulting class differs from the

Adapter version in Chapter 5 only in that the helper object provides the change notifications on behalf of the host.

```
public class BoundedCounterVNL implements BoundedCounter {
  private NotifyingLong c_ = new NotifyingLong(this, MIN);

  public synchronized long value() {
    return c_.value();
  }

  public synchronized void inc()  {
    while (c_.value() >= MAX)
      try { wait(); } catch(InterruptedException ex) {};
    c_.setValue(c_.value()+1);
  }

  public synchronized void dec()  {
    while (c_.value() <= MIN)
      try { wait(); } catch(InterruptedException ex) {};
    c_.setValue(c_.value()-1);
  }

}
```

The relative simplicity of the `BoundedCounterVNL` class stems from the constrained relationship between the host and helper classes. Less constrained designs can run up against four problems requiring more complex solutions: deadlocked notifications, missed signals, slipped conditions, and lockout.

8.2.2.3 *Deadlocked Notifications.*

The `NotifyingLong.setValue` method illustrates a small but general idiom. When signaling other objects, it is a good idea to release as much synchronization as possible. In `setValue`, only the update is performed under synchronization on the `NotifyingLong` itself. Synchronization is released before the notification. This is a routine way to forestall unnecessary deadlock problems and to maximize chances that awakened threads can continue soon. Neither of these issues are really concerns in this design; the construction is used just as a matter of programming practice.

In Java, `notifyAll` must be used in code synchronized on its target, not necessarily its sender. When objects notify themselves, the sender is the same as the target, so synchronization is inevitable. However, when both the Subject and Observer roles are housed in the same object and guarding is implemented using `wait`, the Observer protocol does not deadlock. In Java, `wait` releases the synchronization lock for the target, so that a change-style method can still execute.

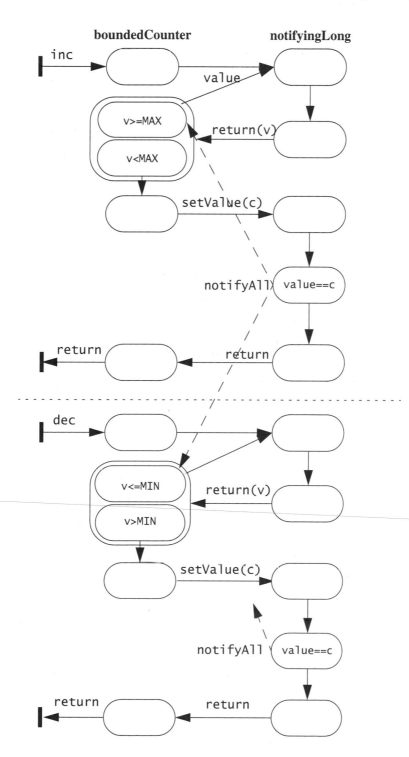

When it is not strictly needed, synchronization on `this` can be dropped before the notification. This tactic can even prevent deadlock in some versions of the full Observer protocol. However, locally releasing synchronization inside a method is not effective in releasing the lock on `this` when the method is called (perhaps indirectly) from another method that already possesses the lock. And these problems cannot always, or even often, be solved by adding threads. For example, if actions in the Subject must be coordinated with those in the Observer, then any new thread would need to acquire the same set of locks that causes deadlock problems in the single-threaded version.

8.2.2.4   *Missed Signals*

Consider the code in `BoundedCounterVNL.inc`:
```
while (c_.value() >= MAX)
  try { wait(); } catch(InterruptedException ex) {};
```
In the general case, this construction is quite risky. If the `NotifyingLong` object is independent of the counter, then it could change state and perform a notification after the test but before the wait. This would lead to a liveness failure: the counter could be stuck forever waiting for a notification that was issued before it even started waiting. This cannot happen here because the `NotifyingLong` is strictly contained — all messages to it originate from synchronized code in the counter.

8.2.2.5   *Slipped Conditions*

The guarded wait in `inc` is followed by:
```
c_.setValue(c_.value()+1);
```
The `inc` method assumes that this code can be executed safely after passing the guard. This always holds here, again because of strict containment. But it would not necessarily hold if the `NotifyingLong` could also receive messages from other objects. In these cases, the guard condition could slip (cease to hold) between the check and the action.

8.2.2.6   *Lockout*

All the waiting in this design is performed by the host object, not the helper. If the `waits` were moved into the `NotifyingLong` class, it would be possible for a thread to `wait` while holding onto the synchronization lock for the counter. This is an instance of the nested monitor problem (see Chapter 4). Synchronized waiting would lock out any threads that could ever release it from a wait.

8.2.3 Synchronized Joint Actions

Joint action frameworks provide a more general setting to attack more general kinds of notification designs. From a high-level design perspective, joint actions are guarded methods that involve conditions and actions among multiple participant objects. They can be described in an abstract form reflecting the intention that some action involving two (or more) objects must be performed when some predicate concerning their *joint* current states holds:

```
void jointAction(A a, B b) {
  WHEN (inRightState(a, b))
    performAction(a, b);
}
```

Joint action problems taking this general, unconstrained form are encountered in distributed protocol development, triggers in active databases, and concurrent constraint programming. Even applications of the Observer pattern and other ordinary-looking design patterns require this kind of treatment when otherwise independent actions in otherwise independent objects must be coordinated.

Unless you have a special-purpose solution, the first order of business in dealing with joint action problems is translating vague intentions and/or declarative specifications into something you can actually program. Most considerations are similar to those encountered in the design of transaction frameworks. The main differences here stem from the fact that actions are triggered and controlled by the participants themselves, rather than external or layered agents:

Allocating responsibility. Which object has responsibility for executing the action? One of the participants? All of them? A separate coordinator?

Detecting conditions. How can you tell when the participants are in the right states? Do you ask them by invoking accessors? Do they tell you whenever they are in the right state? Do they tell you whenever they *might* be in the right state?

Programming actions. How are actions in multiple objects arranged? Do they need to be atomic? What if one or more of them fails?

Linking conditions to actions. How do you make sure that the actions occur only under the right conditions? Are false alarms acceptable? Do you need to prevent one or more participants from changing state between testing the condition and performing the action? Do the actions need to be performed when the participants enter the appropriate states, or just whenever the conditions are noticed to hold? Do you need to prevent multiple objects from attempting to perform the action at the same time?

283

No small set of solutions address all of these issues across all contexts. But the most widely applicable general approach is to create designs that combine the notification and callback techniques seen in Observer protocols with special synchronization policies. Participants tell each other when they are (or may be) in appropriate states for a joint action, while at the same time preventing themselves from changing state again until the action is performed.

Synchronized notification designs provide efficient solutions to joint action problems. However, they can be fragile and non-extensible, and can lead to high coupling of participants. They are potentially applicable when you can build special subclasses or versions of each of the participant classes to add particular notifications and actions, and when you can prevent or recover from deadlocks that are otherwise intrinsic to many joint action designs.

The main goal is to define notifications and actions within synchronized code that nests correctly across embedded calls, in a style otherwise reminiscent of *double-dispatching* and the Visitor pattern (see the *Design Patterns* book). Very often, good solutions rely on exploiting special properties of participants and their interactions. The combination of direct coupling and the need to exploit any available constraints to avoid deadlock accounts for the high context dependence of many joint action designs. This in turn can lead to classes with so much special-purpose code that they must be marked as `final`.

8.2.3.1 *Structure*

For concreteness, the following descriptions are specific to the two-party case (for classes A and B), but can be (awkwardly) generalized to more than two. The basic scheme is a symmetrical, synchronized version of Observer in which state changes in either participant can lead to notifications to the other, and in which these notifications can lead to coordinated actions in either or both participants.

Designs can take either of two characteristic forms. *Flat* versions couple participant objects directly:

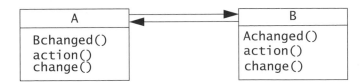

Explicitly *coordinated* versions route some or all messages and notifications through a third object that may also play some role in the associated actions. Coordination through third parties is rarely an absolute necessity, but can add flexibility and can be used to initialize objects and connections:

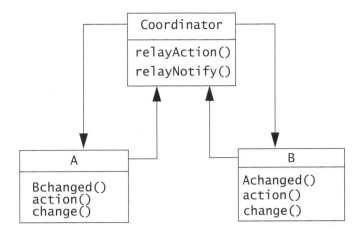

8.2.3.2   *Classes and Methods*

The following generic steps for building classes and methods can often be simplified and/or combined by exploiting available situation-dependent constraints. For example, several substeps disappear when notifications and/or actions are always based in only one of the participants. Similarly, if the changed conditions involve simple latches (see Chapter 4), then there is typically no need for synchronization to bridge notifications and actions.

- Define versions (often subclasses of) of A and B that maintain references to each other, along with any other values and references needed to check their parts in triggering conditions and/or perform the associated actions. Alternatively, link participants indirectly with the help of a coordinator class.

- Write one or more methods that perform the main actions. This can be done by choosing one of the classes to house the main action method, which in turn calls secondary helper methods in the other. Alternatively, the main action can be defined in the coordinator class, in turn calling helper methods in A and B. Or you could just write compatible versions of the main actions in both classes.

- In both classes, write synchronized methods that are designed to be called when the *other* object changes state. For example, in class A, write method BChanged, and in class B, write AChanged. In each, write code to check if the host object is also in the correct state. If the resulting actions involve both participants, they must be performed *without* losing either synchronization lock.

- In both classes, arrange that the other's Changed method is called upon any change that may trigger the action, as in any notification-based design. When necessary, ensure that the state-change code that leads to the notification is appropriately synchronized, guaranteeing that the entire check-and-act sequence is performed before breaking the locks held on both of the participants at the onset of the change.

- Ensure that connections and states are initialized before instances of A and B are allowed to receive messages that result in interactions. This can be done most easily via a coordinator class.

8.2.3.3 *Deadlock*

When all notifications and actions are symmetrical across participants, the above steps normally result in designs that have the potential for deadlock. A sequence starting with an action issuing AChanged can deadlock against one issuing BChanged. While there is no universal solution, *conflict-resolution strategies* for addressing deadlock problems include the following. Some of these remedies require extensive reworking and iterative refinement of a design.

Forcing directionality. For example requiring that all changes occur via one of the participants. This is usually possible only if you are allowed to change the interfaces of the participants.

Precedence. For example using resource ordering to avoid conflicting sequences.

Generating new threads. As seen in the multithreaded version of Observer, this may allow the participant that generates the thread to release all locks. This applies only if it is safe to break the lock connecting changes and actions.

Back-offs. For example, ignoring an update obligation if one is already in progress. As illustrated in the following example, update contention can sometimes be simply detected and safely ignored. In other cases, detection may require the use of special lock classes supporting time-outs, and semantics may require that a participant retry the update upon failure.

Token passing. For example, enabling action only by a participant that holds a certain resource, controlled via ownership transfer protocols (Chapter 2).

Weakening semantics. Loosening synchronization guarantees when they turn out not to impact broader functionality.

Refactoring. Reassigning responsibility for actions to avoid the need for interaction.

Explicit scheduling. Representing and managing objects representing tasks, as described later in this chapter.

8.2.3.4 *Example*

Consider a service that automatically transfers money from a savings account to a checking account whenever the checking balance falls below a threshold, but only if the savings account is not overdrawn. This operation can be expressed as a pidgin-Java joint action:

```
void autoTransfer(BankAccount checking,
                  BankAccount savings,
                  long threshold,
                  long maxTransfer) {
  WHEN (checking.balance() < threshold &&
        savings.balance() >= 0) {
    long amount = savings.balance();
    if (amount > maxTransfer) amount = maxTransfer;
    savings.withdraw(amount);
    checking.deposit(amount);
  }
}
```

We'll base a solution on the simple, original version of class `BankAccount`:

```
public class BankAccount { // repeated
  protected long balance_ = 0;

  public synchronized long balance() {
    return balance_;
  }

  public synchronized void deposit(long amount)
   throws InsufficientFunds {
    if (balance_ < -amount)
      throw new InsufficientFunds();
    else
      balance_ += amount;
  }

  public void withdraw(long amount) throws InsufficientFunds {
    deposit(-amount);
  }
}
```

Here are some observations that lead to a solution:

- There is no compelling reason to add an explicit coordinator class. The required interactions can be defined in special subclasses of `BankAccount`.

- The action can be performed if the checking balance decreases or the savings balance increases. The only operation that causes either to change is `deposit` (since `withdraw` is here just defined to call `deposit`), so versions of this method in each class initiate all transfers.

- Only a checking account needs to know about the `threshold`, and only a savings account needs to know about the `maxTransfer` amount. (Other reasonable factorings would lead to slightly different implementations.)

- On the savings side, the checking and action code can be rolled together by defining the single method `transferOut` to return zero if there is nothing to transfer, and otherwise deduct and return the amount.

- On the checking side, a single method `tryTransfer` can be used to handle both checking-initiated and savings-initiated changes.

Without further care, the result would be deadlock-prone. This problem is intrinsic to symmetrical joint actions in which changes in either object could lead to an action. Here, both a savings account and a checking account can start their deposit sequences at the same time. We need a way to break the cycle that could lead to both being blocked while trying to invoke each other's methods. (Deadlock could not occur if we required only that the action take place when checking balances decreased. This would in turn lead to a simpler solution all around.)

For illustration, potential deadlock is addressed here in a common (although of course not universally applicable) fashion, via a *back-off* protocol. The `tryTransfer` method uses a special boolean class that supports a `testAndSet` method that atomically both sets its value to `true` and reports its previous value.

```
public class TSBoolean {
  private boolean value_ = false;

  // set to true; return old value
  public synchronized boolean testAndSet() {
    boolean oldValue = value_;
    value_ = true;
    return oldValue;
  }

  public synchronized void clear() {
    value_ = false;
  }

}
```

An instance of this class is used to control entry into the `synchronized` part of the main checking-side method `tryTransfer`, which is the potential deadlock point in this design. If another transfer is attempted by a savings account while one is executing (always, in this case, one that is initiated by the checking account), then it is just ignored without deadlocking. This is acceptable here since the executing `tryTransfer` and `transferOut` operations are based on the most recently updated savings balance anyway. The resulting protocol commencing with a withdrawal on a checking account is shown in the interaction diagram.

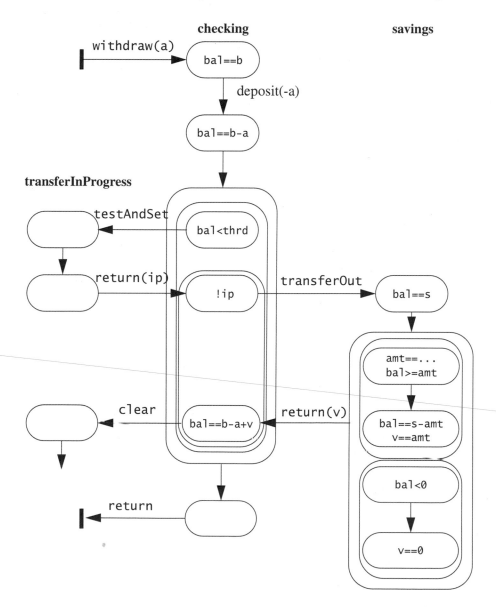

All this leads to the following very special subclasses of BankAccount, tuned to work only in their given context. Both classes rely upon an initialization process to establish interconnections before being used.

The decision about whether to mark the classes as final is a close call. However, there is just enough room for minor variation in the methods and protocols not to preclude knowledgeable subclass authors from, say, modifying the transfer conditions in shouldTry or the amount to transfer in transferOut.

```java
public class ATCheckingAccount extends BankAccount {
  protected ATSavingsAccount savings_; // fixed after init
  protected long threshold_;
  protected TSBoolean transferInProgress_ = new TSBoolean()

  public ATCheckingAccount(long threshold) {
    threshold_ = threshold;
  }

  // call only upon initialization
  void setSavings(ATSavingsAccount s) {
    savings_ = s;
  }

  protected boolean shouldTry() {
    return balance_ < threshold_;
  }

  void tryTransfer() { // called internally or from savings
    if (!transferInProgress_.testAndSet()) { // if not busy ...
      synchronized(this) {
        if (shouldTry())
          balance_ += savings_.transferOut();
      }
      transferInProgress_.clear(); // allow other entries
    }
  }

  public synchronized void deposit(long amount)
   throws InsufficientFunds {
    if (balance_ < -amount)
      throw new InsufficientFunds();
    else {
      balance_ += amount;
      tryTransfer();
    }
  }

}
```

```
public class ATSavingsAccount extends BankAccount {
  protected ATCheckingAccount checking_; // fixed after init
  protected long maxTransfer_;

  public ATSavingsAccount(long maxTransfer) {
    maxTransfer_ = maxTransfer;
  }

  // call only upon initialization
  void initChecking(ATCheckingAccount c) {
    checking_ = c;
  }

  synchronized long transferOut() { // called only from checking
    long amount = balance_;
    if (amount > maxTransfer_) amount = maxTransfer_;
    if (amount < 0) amount = 0;
    balance_ -= amount;
    return amount;
  }

  public synchronized void deposit(long amount)
   throws InsufficientFunds {
    if (balance_ < -amount)
      throw new InsufficientFunds();
    else {
      balance_ += amount;
      checking_.tryTransfer();
    }
  }
}
```

8.2.4 Delegated Actions

Synchronized notification techniques can be used to address a potential source of inefficiency in standard guarded methods. In many guard-based designs, different threads in a wait queue can be waiting for different logical conditions. A notify-All intended to alert threads about one condition also wakes up threads waiting for completely unrelated conditions. Useless signals can be minimized by delegating operations with different wait conditions to different helper objects.

Splitting up classes with state-dependent actions relies on the ideas seen in Chapter 3 for splitting objects with respect to synchronization locks, as well as some ideas from the States as Objects pattern (see *Design Patterns*). However, development runs up against several complicating factors. The design space is restricted to a fairly narrow range of constructions due to constraints that include:

- Assuming that the helpers must access common state, you cannot fully isolate each helper along with its own self-contained representation. (If you can, the design problem simplifies accordingly.) Independent access to common representations across helpers requires appropriate synchronization.

- Each of the helpers that might affect guard conditions for another must provide it with effective notifications while still avoiding missed signals, slipped conditions, and deadlocked cross-notification sequences.

- Synchronization of helper methods involving wait-queue mechanics must avoid nested monitor problems (Chapter 4).

8.2.4.1 *Generic Solutions*

One way to approach these constraints is to first tear the `Host` class into its smallest possible pieces: one class for the shared state representation and one each per kind of helper. You can then deal with the resulting coordinated joint action design problem. Finally, you can organize the pieces into useful classes:

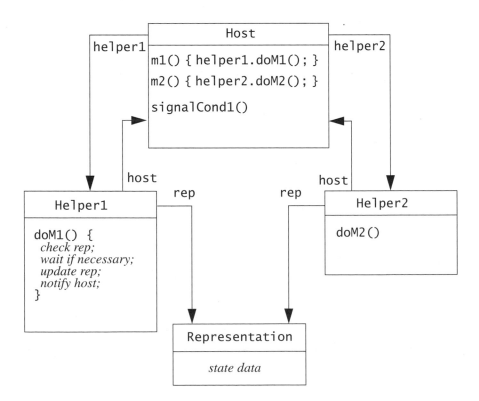

- Define a class, say `Representation`, to hold instance variables that are used across more than one method. Shared representations should be minimized to avoid as many synchronization requirements as possible. The class may be just a bare, unprotected data-representation class since arbitrary kinds of accesses and updates will need to be performed within special synchronized blocks. Alternatively, define all possible operations to be performed as methods.

- Define a `Helper` class for each set of functionality that shares the same wait conditions. Each `Helper` class requires instance variables referencing the host and the representation (this reference may be indirect via the host).

- Define the `Host` class as a pass-through: Each public `Host` method should be an unsynchronized forwarding method. Also define unsynchronized methods designed to be called by helpers whenever they change states in ways that may affect other helpers. Relay the associated `notify` or `notifyAll` calls. (Alternatively, these notifications can be sent directly among helpers.) The host should also initialize all helper objects in its constructor.

- Each helper method must avoid liveness failures while still preserving safety. In particular:

  - If the condition checks involve the shared representation, they must be performed while both the representation and helper are locked.

  - The representation lock must be released before entering the wait queue, but the lock on the helper must be retained to avoid the potential for missed signals.

  - Notification relays must be initiated without synchronization to avoid potential deadlocks.

A typical helper method can take the form:

```
void doM() {
  boolean canAct = false;       // the wait condition
  while (!canAct) {             // wait loop
    synchronized(this) {        // check->wait must lock this
      synchronized(rep) {       // check->act must lock rep
        canAct = inRightState(rep);
        if (canAct) update(rep);
      }                         // break rep lock before wait
      if (!canAct) wait();
    }                           // break lock before signal
  }
  host.signalChange();
}
```

8.2.4.2 *Example*

BoundedBuffers can be implemented using any of the techniques exemplified in this book with BoundedCounters. However, all the solutions presented so far have a potential inefficiency stemming from the need for two logical wait conditions: a put must wait if the buffer is full, and a take must wait if it is empty. The usual notification techniques wake up all threads waiting on either condition, even though at most one waiting thread will ever be able to proceed after any given put or take. This is not a major concern unless there a lot of threads. But it could lead to measurable efficiency problems in designs with very heavy contention among threads.

We'll base a delegated solution on the same basic representation and algorithm as the original version in Chapter 4. Since the context here is gaining efficiency, we'll exploit special characteristics of this data structure and algorithm to obtain better performance.

We need to split up helper objects to do put and take. Delegation designs normally require a helper class per method. But here, we can get away with only one helper class (with two instances) by exploiting an observation about ownership transfers. As noted in Chapter 2, the single operation exchange can be used to perform both put-style and take-style transfers. For example, exchange(null) accomplishes a take. The buffer-based version of exchange substitutes the old value with the argument at the current array slot and then circularly advances to the next array position.

The helper class Exchanger needs instance variables referencing the host and the array serving as the shared representation. We also need a slot counter variable to tell when an exchange operation must stall because there are no more items. For the helper doing put, the counter starts off at capacity and for take, it starts off at zero. An exchange operation can proceed only if the number of slots is greater than zero.

Each successful exchange operation decrements the count. Waits on zero counts can be broken only by the helper performing the complementary operation, which must provide a notification. This is implemented by issuing a removedSlotNotification. The host class is responsible for forwarding this information to the other exchanger via an addedSlotNotification.

Another special consideration in this particular design leads to another economy. Even though the data array must be shared across the two helpers, it does not need synchronization protection so long as put and take are the *only* operations supported. This can be ensured by declaring the host class final. We can make do without a synchronization lock because, in this algorithm, any given put *must* be operating on a different array slot than the one being accessed by any executing take.

As a further performance enhancement, notifications here use `notify`, since the conditions for its use are met: (1) Each waiting task in each helper is waiting on the same logical condition (non-emptiness for `take`, and non-fullness for `put`). (2) Each notification enables at most a single thread to continue — each `put` enables one `take`, and each `take` enables one `put`. To squeeze another bit of efficiency out of this, we keep track of whether there are any waiting threads, and issue `notify` only if there so. (Conditionals are a bit faster than `notify`.)

Given all this, the host class itself just serves to set up the connections and direct traffic:

```java
public final class BoundedBufferVH implements BoundedBuffer {
  private Object[] array_;
  private Exchanger putter_;
  private Exchanger taker_;

  public BoundedBufferVH(int capacity)
   throws IllegalArgumentException {
    if (capacity <= 0)
      throw new IllegalArgumentException();
    array_ = new Object[capacity];
    putter_ = new Exchanger(this, array_, capacity);
    taker_ = new Exchanger(this, array_, 0);
  }

  public int count() {
    return taker_.slots();
  }

  public int capacity() {
    return array_.length;
  }

  public void put(Object x) {
    putter_.exchange(x);
  }

  public Object take() {
    return taker_.exchange(null);
  }

  void removedSlotNotification(Exchanger h) { // relay
    if (h == putter_)
      taker_.addedSlotNotification();
    else if (h == taker_)
      putter_.addedSlotNotification();
  }

}
```

```
class Exchanger {
  protected BoundedBufferVH host_;   // the coordinator
  protected Object[]  array_;        // shared representation
  protected int ptr_ = 0;            // circular index
  protected int slots_;              // number of usable slots
  protected int waiting_ = 0;        // number of waiting threads

  Exchanger(BoundedBufferVH h, Object[] a, int slots) {
    host_ = h;
    array_ = a;
    slots_ = slots;
  }

  int slots() {          // accessor needed by host
    return slots_;
  }

  synchronized void addedSlotNotification() {
    ++slots_;
    if (waiting_ > 0) // unblock a single waiting thread
      notify();
  }

  Object exchange(Object x) { // replace old with x; advance
    Object old = null; // return value

    synchronized(this) {
      while (slots_ <= 0) { // wait for slot
        ++waiting_;
        try { wait(); } catch(InterruptedException ex) {};
        --waiting_;
      }

      --slots_;                  // use slot
      old = array_[ptr_];
      array_[ptr_] = x;
      ptr_ = (ptr_ + 1) % array_.length; // advance position
    }

    host_.removedSlotNotification(this); // notify of change
    return old;
  }

}
```

8.2.4.3 *Collapsing Classes*

Synchronization splitting of all kinds can be accomplished in two ways in Java. In the case of lock-splitting (Chapter 3), you can either create new helper classes and forward operations from the host, or you can just keep the methods in the host but invoke them under synchronization of `Objects` that conceptually represent the different helpers. The same principle holds when splitting state-dependent actions: rather than delegating actions to helpers, you can keep the methods in the host class, adding `Objects` that conceptually represent the helpers.

`Objects` used solely for synchronization serve as locks. Those used for waiting and notification serve as monitors — places to put threads that need to wait and be notified.

Combining helpers into a host class makes the host class more complex but also potentially more efficient due to short-circuited method calls and the like. Performing such simplifications along the way, we can define a more concise, slightly more efficient, and surely more frightening version of `BoundedBuffer`:

```java
public final class BoundedBufferVC implements BoundedBuffer {
  private Object[]  array_;       // the elements

  private int putPtr_ = 0;        // circular indices
  private int takePtr_ = 0;

  private int emptySlots_;        // slot counts
  private int usedSlots_ = 0;

  private int waitingPuts_ = 0;   // counts of waiting threads
  private int waitingTakes_ = 0;

  private Object putMonitor_ = new Object(); // waiting threads
  private Object takeMonitor_ = new Object();

  public BoundedBufferVC(int capacity)
   throws IllegalArgumentException {
    if (capacity <= 0)
      throw new IllegalArgumentException();
    array_ = new Object[capacity];
    emptySlots_ = capacity;
  }

  public int count() {
    return usedSlots_;
  }

  public int capacity() {
    return array_.length;
  }
```

```
public void put(Object x) {
  synchronized(putMonitor_) { // specialized exchange code
    while (emptySlots_ <= 0) {
      ++waitingPuts_;
      try { putMonitor_.wait(); }
      catch(InterruptedException ex) {};
      --waitingPuts_;
    }

    --emptySlots_;
    array_[putPtr_] = x;
    putPtr_ = (putPtr_ + 1) % array_.length;
  }

  synchronized(takeMonitor_) { // directly notify
    ++usedSlots_;
    if (waitingTakes_ > 0)
      takeMonitor_.notify();
  }
}

public Object take() { // symmetric to put
  Object old = null; // return value

  synchronized(takeMonitor_) {
    while (usedSlots_ <= 0) {
      ++waitingTakes_;
      try { takeMonitor_.wait(); }
      catch(InterruptedException ex) {};
      --waitingTakes_;
    }

    --usedSlots_;
    old = array_[takePtr_];
    array_[takePtr_] = null;
    takePtr_ = (takePtr_ + 1) % array_.length;
  }

  synchronized(putMonitor_) {
    ++emptySlots_;
    if (waitingPuts_ > 0)
      putMonitor_.notify();
  }
  return old;
}
}
```

The design and implementation measures leading to classes such as `Bounded-BufferVC` are rarely necessary, and need be undertaken only when justified by actual performance concerns. It is impossible to provide fixed rules about when such tuning and optimization will be productive for general-purpose components such as buffers. But as a rough guide, here is a sample empirical comparison of this class versus the much simpler `BoundedBufferVST` class from Chapter 4:

In one set of tests (run on a SparcStation using Sun JDK 1.02) with 64 threads producing elements and 64 threads consuming them, the simpler `Bounded-BufferVST` class provided about 10% *better* throughput than the optimized `BoundedBufferVC` class when the buffer capacity was greater than 16 elements. Thus, even under moderate levels of contention, the slightly higher fixed overhead of the `BoundedBufferVC` class overshadows its other advantages. However, when the buffer capacity was set to only 4 elements, throughput using the simpler `BoundedBufferVST` decreased by about factor of three (that is, sample tests ran three times more slowly), while throughput using the optimized version remained approximately constant. Thus, the `BoundedBufferVC` class is surely worth using in situations that may encounter extremely high contention among threads.

8.2.5 Specific Notifications

General-purpose approaches to delegation can be complex and hard to get exactly right. When you suspect that a design problem can ultimately be solved through the use of collapsed helper classes (as in `BoundedBufferVC`), you can approach it from this direction at the outset.

The specific notification pattern devised by Tom Cargill takes precisely this tactic. Here, instead of treating the little helper `Objects` seen in collapsed designs as the culmination of efforts, you treat them as tools that may be useful when implementing any design problem amenable to solution via split wait queues.

The basic idea is to put tasks to sleep via `wait`s in monitors — ordinary Java `Objects` used solely for their wait queues. One `Object` is used for each task or set of tasks that must be individually notified. In some cases, this requires one monitor per thread; in others a group of threads that should all be awakened at once can use the same monitor. These `Object` monitors serve similar purposes as the *condition queues* that are natively supported in some monitor-based concurrent programming languages. The main difference is that without native support, these helper monitors must be dealt with more carefully to avoid nesting problems.

Specific notifications may apply whenever you need threads to `wait` and the notification policy does not dynamically depend on the properties of the threads. Once a thread is put in its wait queue, it is impossible to access it in any way other than to wake it up. Among the common applications that fall under these constraints are:

- Supporting fair scheduling through the use of a first-in-first-out queue.

- Dividing incoming tasks into different queues depending on the method they are waiting to perform.

8.2.5.1   *Design Steps*

Create or modify a class, say `Host`, as follows:

- For each thread or set of threads that need specific notification, declare an `Object` serving as a monitor. These monitors may be arranged in arrays or other collections, and/or dynamically created during execution.

- In each method in which tasks are to be suspended, use `monitor.wait()` with the appropriate monitor object. This code must avoid nested monitor problems by ensuring that the `wait` is performed within code regions that are *not* synchronized on the host object. A standard form is:

```
boolean needToWait; // to remember value after synch exit
synchronized(monitor) {
  synchronized (this) {
    needToWait = ...;
  }
  if (needToWait) try { monitor.wait(); } ...
}
```

- In each method in which tasks are to be resumed, use `monitor.notify()` with the appropriate monitor object(s).

8.2.5.2   *Example*

Specific notifications can be used to implement more sophisticated policies in the Readers and Writers pattern. We'll illustrate with a policy differing from the one described in Chapter 5 in that:

- Waiting Readers are preferred if there is currently an active Writer, but a waiting Writer is preferred if there are active Readers.

- Waiting Writers are guaranteed to enter in first-come-first-served order.

The implementation strategy is otherwise identical to that in the RW class from Chapter 5. To help implement the first-come-first-served policy, a queue of monitors (implemented using `java.util.Vector`) holds the waiting Writers so they can be notified one by one in oldest-first order. A single monitor object is used to hold all waiting Readers, since they are always notified as a group. This Reader monitor can be optimized away by using the host object itself as the monitor, but is explicitly shown here for clarity.

```
public abstract class RWVSN { // Readers and Writers
  protected int activeReaders_ = 0;      // counts
  protected int activeWriters_ = 0;
  protected int waitingReaders_ = 0;
  // the size of the waiting writers vector serves as its count

  // one monitor holds all waiting readers
  protected Object waitingReaderMonitor_ = new Object();

  // vector of monitors each holding one waiting writer
  protected Vector waitingWriterMonitors_ = new Vector();

  protected abstract void read_(); // implement in subclasses
  protected abstract void write_();

  public void read() { // setup for before/after methods
    beforeRead();
    read_();
    afterRead();
  }

  public void write() {
    beforeWrite();
    write_();
    afterWrite();
  }

  protected boolean allowReader() { // call under proper synch
    return activeWriters_ == 0 &&
           waitingWriterMonitors_.size() == 0;
  }

  protected boolean allowWriter() {
    return waitingWriterMonitors_.size() == 0 &&
           activeReaders_ == 0 &&
           activeWriters_ == 0;
  }

  protected synchronized void notifyReaders() { // waken readers
    synchronized(waitingReaderMonitor_) {
      waitingReaderMonitor_.notifyAll();
    }
    activeReaders_ = waitingReaders_; // all writers now active
    waitingReaders_ = 0;
  }
```

```
protected synchronized void notifyWriter() { // waken 1 writer
  if (waitingWriterMonitors_.size() > 0) {
    Object oldest = waitingWriterMonitors_.firstElement();
    waitingWriterMonitors_.removeElementAt(0);
    synchronized(oldest) { oldest.notify(); }
    ++activeWriters_;
  }
}

protected void beforeRead() {
  synchronized(waitingReaderMonitor_) {
    synchronized(this) { // test condition under synch
      if (allowReader()) {
        ++activeReaders_;
        return;
      }
      else
        ++waitingReaders_;
    }
    try { waitingReaderMonitor_.wait(); }
    catch (InterruptedException ex) {}
  }
}

protected synchronized void afterRead()  {
  if (--activeReaders_ == 0)
    notifyWriter();
}

protected void beforeWrite() {
  Object monitor = new Object();
  synchronized (monitor) {
    synchronized(this) {
      if (allowWriter()) {
        ++activeWriters_;
        return;
      }
      waitingWriterMonitors_.addElement(monitor); // append
    }
    try { monitor.wait(); } catch (InterruptedException ex) {}
  }
}
```

```
protected synchronized void afterWrite() {
  --activeWriters_;
  if (waitingReaders_ > 0) // prefer waiting readers
    notifyReaders();
  else
    notifyWriter();
}

}
```

8.3 Scheduling

Classes that impose policy control and/or coordinate delegated actions using the designs presented so far in this chapter do so by wrapping concurrency control around code that implements ground-level functionality. These designs meet their limitations when faced with problems in which ground-level actions cannot be made to coexist with concurrency control. Creating explicit representations of the ground-level messages and actions overcomes these limitations and allows you to impose control via special-purpose, localized scheduling systems.

Scheduling is a well-studied aspect of computing. This section confines itself to the general forms of designs that enable you to use scheduling techniques and algorithms that you can either devise yourself or investigate in standard sources on operating systems, real-time systems, and other concurrent systems.

You can usually rely on the built-in Java queuing and scheduling mechanisms for suspending, waking up and running threads. However, there are times when it pays to build your own special-purpose mechanisms for particular groups of threads. Reasons for doing this (which in practice often overlap) include:

- You need to represent waiting tasks for some other bookkeeping purpose anyway.

- You need to be able to independently start, suspend, resume, and stop any of a set of threads that all access a common resource.

- You are using an algorithm that can be implemented more efficiently if you arrange scheduling explicitly.

- You are using algorithms that rely on *deterministic* policies. The Java language specification allows considerable implementation freedom (see Chapter 6). If you need stronger guarantees, you can implement them yourself so long as you can make them coexist with default policies.

As a famous example, consider a class controlling read and write access for a disk containing many cylinders but only one read/write head. The interface for the service just contains `read` and `write` methods. (In practice, it would surely use file block indicators instead of raw cylinder numbers and would deal with and/or throw various I/O exceptions.)

```
public interface Disk {
  public byte[] read(int cylinderNumber);
  public void write(int cylinderNumber, byte[] buffer);
}
```

Rather than servicing access requests in the order that they arrive, it is much faster on average to sweep the head across the cylinders, accessing cylinders in ascending order and then resetting the head position back to the beginning after each sweep. (Depending in part on the type of disk, it may be even better to arrange requests in both ascending and descending sweeps.) This concurrency control policy would be tricky to implement without some kind of auxiliary data structure. The enabling condition for a request to execute is:

> Wait until the current request cylinder number is the least greater cylinder number relative to that of the current disk head of all of those currently waiting, or is the least numbered cylinder if the head cylinder number is greater than that of all requests.

This condition is too awkward, inefficient, and possibly even deadlock-prone to check within a standard guard construction. But it can be implemented fairly easily with the help of an ordered queue. Tasks can be suspended and added to queues in cylinder-based order, then removed and woken up when their turns arrive. (This "elevator algorithm" is easiest to arrange by using a two-part queue, one for the current sweep and one for the next sweep.)

8.3.1 Building Schedulers

Overriding built-in Java run-time support typically involves four kinds of classes:

- Tasks are the threads (or the principal objects run in threads) being managed.

- Proxy Encoders generate Task objects.

- Queues hold waiting tasks.

- Schedulers manage suspension and resumption.

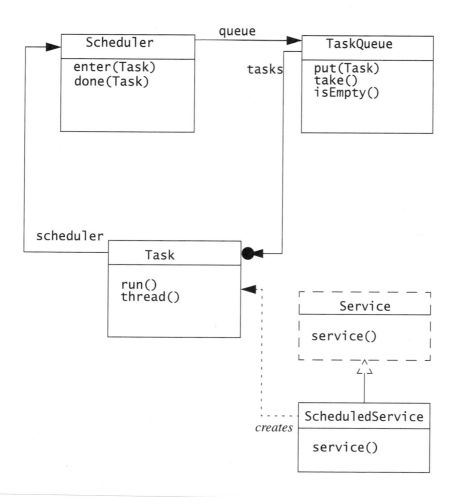

8.3.1.1 *Tasks*

Task classes contain the code that performs the main action of a task (for example accessing a disk), as well as accessors for attributes needed by the scheduler (including an accessor, say `thread`, revealing its `Thread`). Since control is managed by the scheduler, Task methods should not themselves be synchronized. For convenience, the principal method can be called `run` and the Task class can implement `Runnable`. (In this manner, Task classes serve as a form of message type in the sense of Chapter 5.) In any case, the method should take the form:

```
scheduler.enter(this);
performTheAction();
scheduler.done(this);
```

8.3.1.2 *Proxy Encoder*

The main class(es) that place new tasks into the scheduler serve as proxies linking the outside world of Java invocations to the inside world of Tasks. Each externally accessible method should include steps to:

- Generate a new Task object to represent the request.

- Run the Task.

- Upon completion, relay back any results maintained by the Task object.

8.3.1.3 *Queue*

One or more application-specific classes can serve as queues holding elements of class Task. Normally, the queue maintains all of the ordering policy for the scheduler. But there is room for variation in splitting up responsibilities among the queue and scheduler. There is also a huge territory of possible queuing disciplines, policies, and implementations. Sources on operating systems and real-time, simulation, and concurrent systems listed in Chapter 1 describe different scheduling policies. But as a quick guide, ordering may rely on any of the following:

- Intrinsic attributes of the tasks (class and instance variable values).

- Representations of task priority, cost, price, or urgency.

- The number of tasks waiting for some condition.

- The time at which each task is added to a queue.

- The nature of conditions (for example, availability of a particular resource) being waited for by any task.

- Fairness — guarantees that each waiting task will eventually run.

- The tasks that are currently running.

- The expected duration or time to completion of each task.

- The desired completion time of each task.

- Termination dependencies among tasks.

- The number of tasks that have completed.

- The current time.

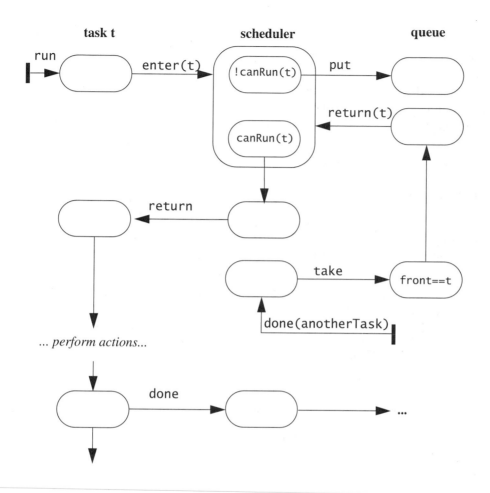

8.3.1.4 *Scheduler*

The Scheduler maintains the queue and contains methods that enter and remove tasks from the scheduling system, minimally:

void enter(Task x), called by a Task to suspend and enqueue the task if necessary, ultimately returning when the task is deemed ready to run.

void done(Task x), called by a Task to indicate that it is finished with the action that is being scheduled, so that the scheduler can start running another task.

Among other variants and extensions, you can also define a yield method that resuspends and reschedules a partially completed task.

The heart of the scheduling system lies in the before/after-style `enter` and done methods. The accompanying interaction diagram provides a high-level view of a common protocol. (It cannot be implemented directly since the return from `take` is not sent to its caller.) There are number of strategies for structuring these operations, depending for example on whether more than one task is allowed to run simultaneously and whether tasks can ever be requeued.

In the common case of one-at-a-time, one-shot tasks and a queue that handles all prioritization, these operations take a common form. In these situations, the scheduler knows exactly when each task should run or wait, so control can be based on `suspend` and `resume` of the `Thread`s, or more flexibly, on `wait` and `notifyAll` (or `notify`) of the `Task`s. Here is a sample implementation:

```
public class SchedulerVSR { // generic one-at-a-time version
  protected TaskQueue queue_;      // fixed, unique
  protected Task running_ = null; // currently running task

  public void enter(Task t) {
    synchronized (t) {          // lock t in order to use wait below
      for (;;) {
        synchronized(this) {
          if (running_ == null || t == running_)
            running_ = t;
            return;
          }
          else
            queue_.put(t);   // will be dequeued by done method
        }
        try { t.wait(); } catch (InterruptedException ex) {}
      }
    }
  }

  public void done(Task t) {
    synchronized(this) {
      if (t != running_)
        return; // minor safeguard
      else if (queue_.isEmpty()) {
        running_ = null;
        return;
      }
      else
        running_ = queue_.take();
    }
    synchronized(running_) { running_.notifyAll();}
  }
}
```

8.3.1.5 *Example*

In the disk scheduler problem, requests can be represented as `DiskTask` objects generated by a Proxy Encoder that serves as the publicly accessible implementation of the `Disk` interface. The scheduler is not shown since it can just take the same form as the generic version:

```
public class DiskScheduler { /* ... */ }

public abstract class DiskTask implements Runnable {
  protected int cyl_;                     // fixed; cylinder to access
  protected DiskScheduler scheduler_;   // the scheduler
  protected Thread me_;                   // thread running this task
  protected byte[] buff_;                 // buffer to read/write

  public DiskTask(int cyl, byte[] b, DiskScheduler s) {
    cyl_ = cyl;
    buff_ = b;
    scheduler_ = s;
    me_ = Thread.currentThread();
  }

  public int cylinder() { // for use in ordering
    return cyl_;
  }

  public Thread thread() {
    return me_;
  }

  protected abstract void access(); // specialize in subclasses

  public void run() {
    scheduler_.enter(this);
    access();
    scheduler_.done(this);
  }

}

public class DiskReadTask extends DiskTask { // ...
  protected void access() { /* ... read ... */ }
}

public class DiskWriteTask extends DiskTask { // ...
  protected void access() { /* ... write ... */ }
}
```

```
public class DiskTaskQueue { // sample implementation
  protected Vector currentScan_ = new Vector();
  protected Vector nextScan_ = new Vector();
  protected int currentCyl_ = 0;

  public synchronized boolean isEmpty() {
    return currentScan_.size() == 0 && nextScan_.size() == 0;
  }

  public synchronized void put(DiskTask t) {
    if (t.cylinder() >= currentCyl_)
      add(t, currentScan_);
    else
      add(t, nextScan_);
  }

  public synchronized DiskTask take() { // return null if empty
    if (currentScan_.size() == 0) { // if one queue empty, swap
      Vector tmp = currentScan_;
      currentScan_ = nextScan_;
      nextScan_ = tmp;
    }

    if (currentScan_.size() == 0) // other queue is empty too
      return null;

    DiskTask t = (DiskTask)(currentScan_.firstElement());
    currentScan_.removeElementAt(0);
    currentCyl_ = t.cylinder();
    return t;
  }

  // utility to add in order to either queue
  protected void add(DiskTask t, Vector v) {
    for (int i = 0; i < v.size(); ++i) {
      DiskTask d = (DiskTask)(v.elementAt(i));
      if (t.cylinder() < d.cylinder()) {
        v.insertElementAt(t, i);
        return;
      }
    }
    v.addElement(t); // append if greater than all others
  }

}
```

```
public class ScheduledDisk implements Disk {
  public static final int diskBufferSize = 1024; // for example

  // Use the same scheduler for all requests
  protected static DiskScheduler scheduler = new DiskScheduler();

  public byte[] read(int cyl) {
    byte[] buff = new byte[diskBufferSize];
    DiskTask job = new DiskReadTask(cyl, buff, scheduler);
    job.run();
    return buff;
  }

  public void write(int cyl, byte[] buffer) {
    DiskTask job = new DiskWriteTask(cyl, buffer);
    job.run();
  }
}
```

8.4 Further Readings

Dozens of strategies have been proposed for performing transactions, especially in the context of databases, in which the term is usually used in the broader sense of any atomic, consistent, isolated and durable action. Transactional forms dealing with persistence and distribution issues are discussed in the texts on databases listed in Chapter 1.

The Ada *rendezvous* construct natively supports a specialized form of synchronized joint action. Accounts of implementation strategies for supporting Ada rendezvous can be found in the collection edited by Gehani listed in Chapter 1.

Buffering and queuing are among the most thoroughly studied problems in concurrent algorithm design. The sources on concurrent programming listed in Chapter 1 present a number of solutions not discussed in this book.

Attempts to control the intrinsic complexity of cooperative design problems underlie a large fraction of special-purpose algorithms described in the technical literature on concurrency. Texts and technical papers on concurrency often discuss notification-based solutions to textbook examples, for example the famous Dining Philosopher problem. Even if you never employ them directly, reading about different special-purpose notification design patterns for textbook problems can give you ideas about how to attack real problems.

Most texts on operating systems, real-time systems, and other specialized concurrent systems listed in Chapter 1 not only present in-depth accounts of different scheduling algorithms, but also present analytic and/or empirical characterizations of their behavior (for example, average throughput under various loads and kinds of tasks).

Joint actions serve as a unifying framework for characterizing multipartici- pant actions in DisCo (Jarvinen, Kurki-Suonio, and colleagues) and are further pursued in a slightly different context by Francez and Forman in IP. For additional discussion and extensions, see the works by these authors listed in Chapter 1.

Francez and Forman (among others) also discuss the range of senses of *fair- ness* that may apply to joint action designs. For example, designs for some prob- lems exist that avoid conspiracies among some participants to starve out others.

Coordination frameworks provide the basis for implementing the internal mechanisms supporting distributed protocols. For some forward-looking presenta- tions and analyses of protocols among distributed objects, see:

Rosenschein, Jeffrey, and Gilad Zlotkin. *Rules of Encounter: Designing Conventions for Automated Negotiation among Computers*, MIT Press, 1994.

Fagin, Ronald, Joseph Halpern, Yoram Moses, and Moshe Vardi. *Reasoning about Knowledge*, MIT Press, 1995.

Index

Note: Entries of the form DP(nnn) are references to Gamma, Erich, Richard Helm, Ralph Johnson, and John Vlissides. *Design Patterns: Elements of Reusable Object-Oriented Software*. Addison-Wesley, 1995.

A

abort operation
   in optimistic transactions; 262
   in pessimistic transactions; 270
abstract
   data type
      closed; 37
      copying; 39
      instance variable value dependencies; 67
      representing values; 37
   state; 84
`accept` (code); 147
`Acceptor` (code); 147
`Acceptor(s)`; 146-156
   object model relations; 160
access
   See also visibility
   disk, scheduling; 304, 309
   instance variables, restricting; 64
accessors; 63
   inspective, Readers as; 131
   unsynchronized; 63, 65
`Account` (code); 141
`AccountHolder` (code); 143
`AccountRecorder` (code); 143
`AccountUser` (code); 260, 265
accurate value
   stable value contrasted with; 66
acknowledgements
   of message receipt; 179
acquaintance; 46
   "Design Patterns" discussion; DP(22)
acquiring exclusive resources; 48

`action method,` *See* `Acceptors`
actions
   See also state(s), -dependent actions
   delegated; 291
   synchronization requirements; 293
   joint; 283
   multiple, state-dependent action policy; 83
   preconditions for; 108
   state-dependent, (chapter); 79
   encapsulation of in `Runnable` classes; 165
   unconditional; 80
activation, thread
   client-controlled; 172
   using Proxies; 174
   `Runnable` class relationship; 172
   server-controlled; 172
active
   execution state; 40
   messages, *See* command objects
   objects; 2
   models; 158, 159
   state variables, *See* execution, state variables
actors, *See* active, models
ad-hoc networking; 155
Ada
   concurrency constructs; 89
   rendezvous; 311
`AdaptedPerformer` (code); 134
Adaptee, *See* Adapters
Adapter(s); 134-145
   See also containment; delegation; Proxy;
       Composite
   class composition with; 134-145
   "Design Patterns" discussion; DP(139)
   exclusive resources use; 48
   with legacy code; 136
   meta-object style compared with; 147
   Read-Only; 139-142
   Runnable; 176
   Synchronized; 136

I

time-outs
    in guarded methods; 110
    as heuristic for deadlock detection; 268
    with joins; 192, 200
    for locks; 268
time-slicing; 211
TLQNode (code); 77
token ring networks, *See* exclusive resources
tokens, *See* exclusive resources
top-down class design strategy
    See also guarded methods
    safety emphasis in; 60
trace diagrams
    notation; 16
tracking
    state; 97
    state variables; 101
transactions; 252-271
    control parameters; 258
    coordinator; 265
    database; 31, 311
        bibliographic references; 31
    impact on method signatures; 259
    key; 258, 261, 268
    nested; 263
    optimistic; 259, 260, 263
    pessimistic; 259, 270
    relation to delegation; 259
    structured; 258
    term definition; 252
Transactor (code); 261
transBankAccount (code); 262
transfer (code); 260, 266
transfer, *See* exclusive resources; flow
TransferDaemon (code); 185
transformation(al)
    flow system components; 216
transient states; 39
Transporter (code); 232
try-and-see policies
    See balking; provisional action; recovery;
        retry; rollback
TSBoolean (code); 288
tunability; 62
    as reusability criteria; 62
tuple-spaces, *See* buffers
TwoLockQueue (code); 76
type safety
    multithreaded safety compared with; 36

U

unconditional action
    as state-dependent action policy; 80
unique annotation; 46
Unity
    bibliographic reference; 32, 120
Unix shells
    flow system control compared to; 216
unsynched-host/synched-helper strategy; 72
UpdatableAccount (code); 141
UpdatableAccountObject (code); 142
update(s)
    database; 113
    methods; 63
    in optimistic transactions; 262
    of state-variables; 101
    static variables; 42
URLs
    online supplement; 7
URLReader (code); 169
utility; 62
    as reusability criteria; 62

V

V semaphore operation
    Java equivalent; 97
value(s)
    abstract data types; 37
    accurate; 66
    copying; 39
    dependencies; 67
    instance variables; 63
    shadow copies; 113
    stable; 66
variables
    execution state; 124
    immutable; 37
    instance, *See* instance variable(s)
    latches; 102
    meta; 87
    mutable; 63
    resource; 53, 227
    role; 86
    representing logical state with; 86
    shared; 44
    state
        active; 87
        execution; 87
        tracking; 101
    static
        See static variables